THE COLORS OF LIFE

THE COLORS
OF LIFE

Janusz Subczynski

KELLER PUBLISHING
Marco Island, Florida

ISBN-13: 978-1-934002-00-1
ISBN-10: 1-934002-00-3

Composed in Warnock Pro at
Hobblebush Books, Brookline, NH
Printed in the United States of America

Published by
KELLER PUBLISHING
590 Fieldstone Dr.
Marco Island, FL 34145

www.KellerPublishing.com

*Dedicated to the
memory of my father*

Contents

Illustrations

Preface

THIS BOOK IS a collection of memories, experiences, and reflections from the years I have lived on American soil. The experiences of my past in Poland can be found in the book, *In the Shadow of Satan*. I think that its title is well justified in that it captures the essence of my personal drama. I grew up, developed, and was educated in the shadow of two satanic systems—Nazism (Hitlerism) and communism.

My destiny rolled along rather strange tracks. I extracted myself from the oppression of the Soviet occupier and found myself on American soil. I received my license to practice medicine and passed a required examination to become a Diplomate of the American Board of Neurological Surgery.

Polish affairs, however, never stopped being important to me. Here, in my adopted new homeland, I fought in every way I could for a free Poland, dividing my time between the difficult responsibilities of a neurosurgeon and the obligations of an active Pole. My activism and that of those with whom I worked closely on the socio-political level was not, up until now, ever documented in any lasting editorial account. I hope that this book, *The Colors of Life*, will play at least a small role in illuminating this aspect of the role of Polish immigration into the United States.

A long and difficult life impels one to reflect at the end. Such reflections became the substance of the last few chapters of this book. They do not presume any philosophical or eschatological synthesis. They are simply the expression of all the questions that people have been asking themselves from the dawn of time and that reveal themselves before each person at life's end.

—*Janusz Subczynski*

THE COLORS OF LIFE

1

Washington's Land

I FINISHED THE STORY of the stages of my life spent in Poland in the first volume, *In the Shadow of Satan*, at the moment in which I landed at Heathrow airport in London. The first person I saw there was a mechanic standing near the airplane. Seeing my curious face in the window, he smiled and waved his hand in a characteristic gesture—left to right, different from a wave in Poland. This gesture proved to me that I was in another world, that I had pulled myself out of the grip of the Soviet occupier. But what did the future hold for me? I was alone without anyone's support, or even, it seemed, the possibility of help. And most importantly, I could not ever return to Poland, especially after the proposition made to me just before my departure by two agents from the GRU (Soviet counter intelligence) in Warsaw to perform intelligence work.

I also didn't have much hope that I would ever be able to get my parents out from behind the Iron Curtain. So, would I ever see them again by my side?

The danger of the final days there, the uncertainty of the undercover agents' acquiescence to my departure, and finally, just fatigue began to numb my feelings. From that huge airport, surrounded by strangers and foreign languages, I was to fly to New York, the goal of my exodus. Work awaited me there.

No one in particular was waiting for me. My arrival didn't interest anyone other than the agent checking my passport and visa or the customs officer who suspiciously looked over my camera, which I had purchased during my last stay in the United States.

Finally, I walked out of the airport with my suitcase. It was late afternoon, and the sun was still shining over this foreign land. I got a cab and told the cabbie to take me to the Wales Hotel. It was the same hotel on Lexington Avenue where I had spent my last week before returning to Poland. It was old and dark, built sometime around the turn of the century. The rooms were cheap. They had kitchenettes, so you could cook something for yourself. Those who lived there were mostly old retirees, vegetating in similar rooms.

I got a room that faced the street. The constant hum of cars penetrated the closed window. I went into the bathroom and turned on the light to wash up. That caused a stir among a mass of gigantic cockroaches, obviously upset by my entry and now by the bright light. I wasn't bothered by their presence having already stayed with these same permanent tenants in this old and somewhat dilapidated hotel.

I went out on the street to get something to eat. I bought some produce, went back to my room, ate, drank some hot tea, and threw myself onto the bed. Images of the last few days stood before my eyes—my parents behind the wire mesh fence at Okecie airport, the undercover agents involved in blackmail, and in the background, the faces of my colleagues. All of these images quickly ran together in a surreal mush.

The sun was already high in the sky when I awoke. My one contact on American land was Professor Tarlov. I called him. He was astonished that I was in New York. Astonished and worried. He was a kind man, known in New York as a distinguished neurosurgeon, though not known for his organizational skills or initiative. In spite of his promise, he still had not prepared anything for my arrival. I was dumbfounded! After a moment, however, sensing my

4

anxiety, he said that he would arrange a neurosurgery residency for me at Metropolitan Hospital. I would have a terrible salary, and he would look around in the meantime to get patients for me for stereotactic surgeries at Flower and Fifth Avenue Hospital.

I waited a few days. The meager funds that I had collected for my stay in America were depleting at a frightening pace. And just as they were coming to an end, Professor Tarlov informed me that I would be the chief neurosurgery resident at Metropolitan Hospital and could immediately begin working there. The hospital did not, however, have an available room for me.

I went there immediately after the professor's phone call. Metropolitan Hospital was located in a huge, modern building with large windows on the East River which is really just the eastern branch of the Hudson River. On one side, it bordered a nice neighborhood of eastern Manhattan, and on the other, a sea of colorful people, mostly black and Latino. After walking along several side streets to the east, you stepped into a somewhat different world, another civilization. The apartment buildings were dirty and falling apart, and children of many colors and both sexes played in the middle of the street. By the walls, teenagers would look at a white man suspiciously and threateningly.

A large square in front of the hospital divided it from some new apartment buildings that were occupied by a different sort of people; they were neat and white. The contrast was striking.

To the left of the hospital building were the lead-colored waters of the East River. There you could see barges, their sides covered in tires. Seagulls floated through the air, now and then diving suddenly into the water for an obvious purpose.

I was told by the hospital administration that I would get my own room but that it would take a week before they could empty it for me. Besides the private rooms, Metropolitan Hospital also had several rooms for on-call residents. These large and light rooms had bunk beds and a small table by the window. Because my money was quickly running out, I decided to stay in one of those call-room bunk beds while waiting for my private room. During the day, it was fairly quiet there. Despite the constant slamming of the door and loud conversations, I could stretch out on the bed. And what's more, I had free meals at the hospital cafeteria.

The nights, however, were awful. You couldn't sleep even an hour without being brutally awakened by harsh light, conversations, and the ring of the telephone—the nurses calling now and then for the on-call residents. After a week of such living, I was getting dizzy from lack of sleep. I was in such a stupor that I could almost fall asleep standing up at any given moment.

But then, a miracle happened. I was called into the administrative office and got the key to my own room. It was large and clean, with a comfortable bed and a huge curtained window with a view of the hospital yard. The happy scene was completed by a small desk near the window, a closet for my things, and a phone.

I finally stopped obsessively calculating the exchange of dollars into zloty, knowing that a return trip to Poland was not a possibility and that exchange in zloty would never again be necessary for me. There was only forward movement from now on. The awareness of this was also a powerful stimulus—you have crossed over the Rubicon, so now don't look back!

I got to work. The humid heat of Manhattan and the suffocating air permeated by a multitude of smells didn't make the concentration that was essential to my work any easier. The room didn't have air-conditioning. Sweat covered my skin. I went to the first decent store I saw and bought a small air-conditioner. I installed it myself. The relief was enormous. Its hum was soothing. Finally, I could rest after work.

After a few days, I bought a piece of carpeting at the flea market that I put in the middle of the room along with a large Grundig radio. I still have it to this day—the antique plays music more clearly than many of the newer models. During breaks from work, I could listen to good music and news and live with the illusion that I was not so awfully alone.

The neurosurgery ward of Metropolitan Hospital was not active enough for its resident to take a specialty exam. In other words, working on this ward meant that I was losing valuable time. The only advantage was the countless number of stereotactic surgeries that I did for Tarlov at the Flower and Fifth Avenue Hospital. He paid me for them—an important addition to my budget. It allowed me to start saving. I had my sights set on bringing my parents from Poland. I was still formally in a foreign country, not a citizen of the United States. My strategy was based on arranging a "trip" for them to a Western country. I sent an informational brochure to them about such trips. My mother categorically forbade me from sending more of such information. I didn't understand why she treated it so definitively. I thought to myself that perhaps I would ruin their own plans. It was well known that the post offices were opening all the mail from the United States.

Metropolitan Hospital was an municipal hospital, accepting anyone, even homeless people and drug addicts off the street— people with no means from which to live and who were also uninsured. Located close to Harlem, a mostly black and Latino neighborhood, it was made up of a conglomerate of patients from different races, backgrounds, and life stages. It was closely tied to the university center at Flower and Fifth, which had been created mainly so that students with a Jewish upbringing had a chance at finishing medical school. During the years preceding my arrival to the United States, there had been a lot of discrimination against accepting anyone for higher education who was not a WASP— White, Anglo-Saxon, Protestant.

The Jewish people first established Mount Sinai Hospital as a primary base; it was a terrific medical center. A second base was created at Albert Einstein University. Flower and Fifth existed as yet another addition and fulfillment of the educational network for Jewish people pursuing medicine.

Metropolitan Hospital was an excellent center for specialty education because of the wealth of its clinical "material." There were the appropriate wards for gynecology and obstetrics, surgery, orthopedics, pediatrics, neurology, and neurosurgery. Professors from Flower and Fifth University were the chiefs of individual branches of medicine. They made up, as did many other special-ists, a so-called visiting staff. This didn't exactly mean that they just "visited" the hospital. They didn't have established work hours; instead, they worked in accordance with their own daily schedules. In cases that were emergencies, one of them had to show up immediately if it was his day on-call.

Their work at Metropolitan Hospital was, in a sense, social work, charity work, but prestigious all the same, because the bulk of their income came from private patients who they took care of at Flower and Fifth Hospital or at other hospitals where they had privileges to operate and to treat patients. Their offices were outside the grounds of the hospital.

A second category of doctors hired by Metropolitan Hospital were residents—doctors specializing in various medical disciplines. There were about five residents in each specialty, from the youngest intern to the oldest, chief resident, who performed all the surgeries under the watchful eye of a "visiting" doctor who was there as the specialist that day.

Specialties were approved by administrative bodies of specialty privileges known as boards. Their requirements were the same throughout the United States. Receiving specialty privileges depended upon completing a residency that usually lasted five years followed by a written and oral exam.

This particular neurosurgery program, with Dr. Tarlov as its head, didn't count as a neurosurgical residency program, because it didn't meet the criteria of performing a specified number of brain tumor surgeries annually. Professor Tarlov hoped that my being the chief resident would help to fulfill the requirements of the American Board of Neurological Surgery.

What was my workday like? Besides me, there were also two young residents: Dr. Sidhu, a Sikh (who wore a turban on his head) and also a Hindu, whose name I don't remember now. My responsibilities included morning rounds on patients, preparing patients for surgery, then informing Dr. Tarlov (or whoever was responsible for running the ward and surgeries that week) about the day's events.

Because I had not yet been approved as a specialist by the board, I couldn't operate alone. The reality, however, was slightly different. The attending or visiting specialist would come to the operating room, look at the history and physical and additional tests and recommend that I operate with a younger assistant! They all knew very well that I was a qualified surgeon. So while they were calmly sipping coffee in the physician's lounge, I performed surgeries no worse than they would have.

One day, an older black man was admitted in the emergency room—a very poor man in a serious state with an acute subdural hemorrhage. He needed immediate surgery. I informed the operating room, did the essential additional tests in a flash, and informed the on-call attending about the necessity of immediate surgery. He responded that he couldn't come and suggested calling the next attending. That one rather vulgarly sent me to a third! Without the presence of one of them, I couldn't operate, and the man was near death. Not really thinking, I wrote down the details of my three phone calls in the patient's chart and concluded that the patient would die without immediate surgery—adding that I was powerless, because I didn't have the rights of an independent surgeon! Deeply angered, I went to the administration with this document in hand. I told them that I was powerless in the situation, so I was going to go home.

The administrator, a Greek-American who was thin, with a tousled black hairdo and similar eyes, started to panic. He grabbed the phone in search of the attendings. Before I reached the main doors, two neurosurgeons showed up. So, now I could operate in their presence. I removed the clot, and the patient survived, later leaving the hospital in good health.

Both surgeons were furious. They pleaded with me to rip out the pages of my testimony from the patient's chart. There was nothing else to do—I ripped them out. I knew that from then on, they were no longer my friends.

One of the most frightening places in that huge hospital was the emergency room. It was run by a doctor specializing in trauma medicine. In the waiting room, there was a constant crowd of those waiting for help—a crowd of poor people, speaking all different languages. Inside the ER, in a few rooms, gurneys were separated from one another with a moveable drape.

Is there anyone or anything I didn't see there? Drug addicts were screaming from a lack of drugs. There were those dying from overdoses. When drug dealers figured out that a client didn't have any money to pay for a hit even if he stole, they would give him a higher dose of heroin, a fatal dose, simply to get rid of him! Many such poisoned people came into the hospital in a near-death state.

I saw young girls, mostly Puerto Rican, beautiful with dark skin, black hair and eyes, who were prostitutes in Harlem for heroin. Dealers of this drug hung around schools, giving children candy laced with heroin. After one dose, a child could become addicted to heroin and ready to submit to the most degrading sexual acts so as to get the coveted "hit." I found out about these expert methods of "producing" drug addicts from a heroin dealer who was my patient.

There were also patients in the last stages of tuberculosis, mainly from Harlem and islands in the Caribbean, and some who had advanced syphilis or parasites. I had never seen such awful things as a doctor in Poland as I did in that emergency room. And it went on like that at full throttle day and night.

I was frequently called in to cases requiring neurosurgical intervention. I was the chief resident, so the nurses didn't bother calling the younger physicians; they immediately called me in. I had to learn basic Spanish, because almost one-third of the patients didn't speak any other language. I also got by with German, and even, though seldom, with Russian.

Daily work was rather easy. The problem was being on-call. More than once, I got five or six calls from the emergency room. The chief resident in neurology, a Greek, when called into the ER, suggested calling me first. When I did all the work, even when it had nothing to do with neurosurgical intervention, the Greek suggested admitting the patient to the ward—all the while not even bothering to leave his cot and see the patient.

This obvious tactic made me furious. I didn't want to let myself be taken advantage of endlessly. But what could I do so as to put an end to it? Finally, I found a way. I told the nurses from the emergency room to call me in for patients with any neurological problems and not to call the Greek "gentleman" until they spoke with me. That night, there were seven patients. I worked until one o'clock in the morning, wrote my consults, and then told the nurses to call him every half an hour to each patient. They hated him, because he was arrogant, so they happily took part in my strategy for justice.

At two o'clock in the morning, he got the first phone call. He reacted normally. "Call in Subczynski."

Then, he heard, "Dr. Subczynski already saw him and is calling for a consultation from you."

There was nothing he could say in response to that statement. He got up from his cot and went to see the patient.

When he fell fast asleep again, there was another phone call with the same purpose, and so on until dawn, every half an hour. In the morning, he looked at me with hatred. From that night on, however, my being called in to the ER was limited to neurosurgical cases.

Dr. Sidhu, my support and right-hand man, lived in a tiny apartment with his wife. They were a rather exotic pair. He was a Sikh with a turban, beneath which raven black hair gathered at the top in a knot, dark skin, dark eyes, and a black, curly beard. She appeared in a colorful sari with big almond eyes, dark eyelashes that cast a shadow on dark-skinned cheeks, and full lips that almost always had a smile on them. We became friends almost immediately. They were intelligent and educated. Like me, they were trying to begin a new life in Washington's land. They often invited me over for dinner or just to stop by in the evening. The conversations were always interesting, but the meals were a serious problem for me. Trying to accommodate European tastes, Mrs. Sidhu lessened the amount of seasonings she used so that they wouldn't burn or paralyze my mouth. But nevertheless each morsel burned my palate like a blazing fire. I tried to quell the fire with an incredible amount of water. Hindu cuisine is rather tasty, though some of the spices are quite shocking. They got a package of conserved mango, a Hindu delicacy, from his mother in India.

After swallowing a piece, I had the feeling that hot coal was moving down through my esophagus, becoming milder only when it reached my stomach.

There, in India, near Dr. Sidhu's parents' home, in the mountains, there is a small Buddhist temple, famous for its monks, who could supposedly divine your future. A believer first had to knock on the side doors. A monk would appear and ask the visitor for his last name, first name, and date of birth. Then, he would lead him to a vast courtyard and tell him to wait. After a while, he would come back, tell of the man's past, and acquaint him with what his future would hold.

An American colleague was staying with the Sidhus; he had been invited by them to India. He was to return to the United States in three days, but he wanted to go visit the prophesying temple before leaving. After telling him about his past, the monk suddenly said that he would be staying in India for another three months. It seemed like obvious nonsense, because he had his return ticket in his pocket and work awaited him in the United States.

That same day he fell ill with acute appendicitis. Due to following complications he left India after three months. I listened to this tale and had no reason not to believe my colleague—he was a very ethical person and never lied.

Just before noon, I was called in to a trauma that had happened in front of the hospital.

In a small, private room, I saw a maybe sixteen-year-old young girl. She lay unconscious, and her hair was covered in blood. She had already been intubated, and the respirator rhythmically moved her rib cage up and down. As it turned out, a thug had given her a swift hit to the back of the head and had then run away.

The young black nurse was horrified. "Doctor, do something, she cannot die!"

I told her the plain truth—the young woman had a damaged brain stem, and there was nothing that could be done.

I sat down in the nurses' station to write up the accident report.

After half an hour, I went in to the patient. Her heart was not beating, though the respirator was still going. I told the nurse to turn off the respirator and formally pronounced the time of death. I went to the nurses' station so as to routinely inform the local coroner.

During my conversation with him, the nurse ran in. "Doctor! She's alive! I hear her heart beating! I won't turn off the respirator!"

I interrupted the conversation with the coroner and went to the patient.

"She's dead," I said. "There is no heartbeat!"

"No! I hear a heartbeat," the nurse said stubbornly.

I called in a cardiologist to perform an EKG. The tests confirmed the absence of any heartbeat.

"No, it's not possible, for such a young life to be wasted like this, it's not possible—impossible!" she yelled. Obviously she was not thinking rationally but expecting a miracle. Her whole idea of justice was totally shattered.

I looked at the quiet, still body of the young girl. The shadow of death loomed already on the young features. I had also the feeling of total injustice and nonsense and somehow could sympathize with the young nurse.

I saw many deaths, many tragedies, and of all of them, two burned themselves not only into my memory, but also into my soul.

During my first trip to America (1961–63) while working at St. Barnabas Hospital under the direction of Dr. Cooper,[1] part of my responsibilities included taking care of patients located on the top fifth floor. Patients were placed there who had undergone unsuccessful surgeries—usually after a stroke or hemorrhage. Cooper didn't have a lot of such cases, but it did happen.

In the same ward a well-known actress was quietly dying of cancer in one of the rooms. No one took much interest in her. The only person she had in this stage of her life was a nineteen-year-

1. My two-year Fellowship with Dr. Irving Cooper is detailed in my earlier book, *In the Shadow of Satan.*

old son. A smile appeared on her face when I would go in to see her whenever I was taking care of her. She would tell me about her rich past, though the conversations really tired her out. One morning, I saw her in a very bad state, with her face sharply contorted in pain and suffering. In a quiet voice, she told me that she had a big favor to ask of me.

"I will soon die. Please, sir, don't let my son in here. I want him to remember me as I once was."

I kept my word. Under some pretext, I didn't allow her son in to see her on her deathbed. She died a few days later.

Her death was so full of peace, with such concern for her son and not for herself; this death became a kind of sign for me for the rest of my life. I wish, I so very deeply wish, that in the last moments of my own life, I could be like her, in agreement with God, with the world, and with myself.

The other unforgettable experience of death, this time in Metropolitan Hospital, was a woman about sixty years old, with acute pain caused by the metastases of a tumor. Her ragged features could not be disguised by the heavy makeup. She was continuously complaining that her medical care was poor. For many years she had a lover, a doctor, who would come to visit her. In the beginning, he came with flowers, first everyday, then less and less frequently. Her condition quickly grew worse, and eventually I was the only doctor who was there with her everyday. She was full of bitterness towards everyone and everything. She couldn't come to terms with her unavoidable departure from this world. She blamed the nurses, me, her old lover. In the end, she died not accepting her fate, full of hatred and holding a grudge. To whom? To God? I don't think that she was a religious person. I was and still am convinced that the death of this woman was hell, because hell is the lack of hope and a mutiny against fate.

And that's how the hot New York summer passed. In my spare time, I spent hours walking around the streets of Manhattan. I would stop on the corner of Lexington Avenue and 86th Street, where I ate bratwurst with sauerkraut—supposedly the best in New York. I would look at the endless waves of people, look through the windows of countless antique shops filled with old paintings, silver, and yellowing books.

I happened to run into an old beggar. He called to me from afar:

"Doctor, doctor! It's me! Do you remember me?"

Yes! This was the patient from whom I had removed a subdural hematoma!

To this day, I like Manhattan—multicultural and particular. There are skyscrapers and, in between them, old apartment buildings, hustle and bustle, neon, stores—life in full force, in full motion, though truthfully barely moving.

Long ago, Manhattan was purchased by the Dutch and named New Amsterdam. Not many people know that when this transaction was taking place, a Polish ship, most likely a pirate ship, sailed in along with the Dutch. When the Dutch began bargaining for the island, the captain of the Polish ship decided to "take care of" the daughter of one of the Native American chiefs. The chief caught them in a very compromising situation. He gave the captain an ultimatum: he could either die immediately or marry the daughter! If he chose the latter, he would be given the position of chief of one of the local Native American tribes as part of the dowry. The trapped lover of course chose the latter. And as it was later told around Manhattan, you could often come across a Native American with blue eyes.

I was also drawn to Central Park. Lying out lazily on a bench, I would look out beneath my somewhat closed eyelids at young mothers with carriages, running children, tall policemen's horses, horse carriages driven by gentlemen in stiff top hats, and finally, a countless variety of dogs and puppies.

Everyday life at the hospital was sometimes overwhelming. At midnight or in the early morning, I would have coffee in the hospital cafeteria, usually alone or in the company of a Jesuit, a Catholic chaplain, or a rabbi who served the spiritual needs of the Jewish patients. We were a strange group, these three who gathered around coffee and debated issues. We were linked by the necessity of doing nighttime work—mine having to do with the body, theirs having to do with the spirit. More than once I tried to provoke them into a debate about religion, but they were much too smart to be drawn into such a trap.

2

Rescuing My Parents

I RECEIVED A LETTER from my mother in the fall. She told me that my father had suffered a stroke. He came out of it with partial paralysis on the left side. This news hit me like a thunderclap on a clear day. I was powerless. I couldn't even call them, because they didn't have a phone.

Only after a few more weeks did I receive another letter. My father's condition had greatly improved, the paralysis of his leg had completely gone away, and he only had difficulty making fine movements with his left hand.

Many of the following weeks passed in a similar way. I rested in bed until the phone rang, one of many calls that would come constantly throughout the day and night. And then, suddenly one day, I heard my mother's voice! And her voice was not the only surprise. She was calling from Istanbul! She told me that she had taken a trip with my father on the Mediterranean Sea, on a Romanian ship, without passports, guarded by the secret police. Once there, she found a phone so as to get the news to me. Their goal was to escape at the moment they reached Rome. She was going to call me from there, and from now until then, I had to make some kind of arrangements for them to stay in Rome.

I was completely stunned—and happy. At the same time, I couldn't understand how my father, especially after a stroke, could manage to go on such a long trip. And what's more, how would they manage in Rome?

The next day, I went to the Italian embassy and asked to speak with the consul. A young man with an antipathetic look showed up in the waiting room. In proper English with an Italian accent, he asked me what I wanted. I told him honestly—my parents were hoping to stay in Rome, choosing freedom. What could I do so as to help them with this? How could I arrange that with the Italian authorities? He replied ill-manneredly that he couldn't help me at all with this and that my parents shouldn't do such a thing, for they would be breaking both Polish and Italian laws!

He tried to get rid of me without giving me a concrete answer. I figured out that this person did not directly speak for the Italian authorities. I asked to speak with his superior. He asked me angrily, "Do you understand Italian?"

I replied that I do not. He walked out. After a moment, he came back with an older gray-haired man with a kind smile. The young man started speaking to him in Italian, and even though he spoke very quickly and I didn't understand the language, I knew that he was twisting my words and lying. I yelled out, "That's not true! That's not it at all!"

Then, the young man, completely furious, turned to me and barked, "It's you who's lying! You said you didn't know Italian!"

The older man calmly waited for the end of this outburst. He said in English, "I will take care of this matter alone. You're free to go," he said to the young man.

When he left the consul at that time, or so I assume he was, began apologizing for his behavior. At a certain moment, he added, "Well then, unfortunately, we have a lot of communists in Italy. You happened to run into one of them."

I found out that the Italian authorities couldn't intervene until my parents asked for political asylum. He recommended that I go to Cardinal Speelman's residence. Near the archdiocese, there was a branch of a Catholic organization called Catholic Relief

Services. It took care of political refugees among others. The branch of his organization in Rome was run by a Scottish man named McKiewer.

I went to the cardinal's residence right away. The woman there brimmed with polite kindness. I got the address of the organization's headquarters in Rome and all necessary phone numbers. She suggested that my parents go there immediately after making their decision to escape.

The days started dragging. I knew from what my mother had told me that the route of their trip took them to Egypt, from Alexandria to Cairo, then by ship to Naples, and finally by bus to Rome.

And, finally, I got a phone call! The out-of-breath, excited voice of my mother, saying, "We are at the post office in Rome—we ran away from the group, and we don't know where to go or what to do! We don't have anything with us, not even a suitcase!"

She was calling for free. The Italian officials, with whom she had communicated in French, understood the seriousness of the situation and connected her to me. I gave her the name and address where they should go.

The gears were set in motion. McKiewer suggested that they go to the home of Mr. Zaorski. He was to ensure a night's stay and a meal for them. I told my mother that I was going to wire them 250 dollars.

And again, there was a curtain of silence for several days. I was unbelievably worried, but I couldn't do anything. I didn't even have their phone number, though I really couldn't afford to be making transatlantic phone calls.

After a week went by, a letter arrived. They lived for a week with an Italian Arabic lady, to whom they had been directed by Zaorski. My dollars obviously were helpful in this situation. I learned that they had run away when the bus stopped for a moment in front of the main post office in Rome. They knew that as soon as they got inside the building, the Polish guards wouldn't be able to do anything. So, they jumped off the bus and ran as fast as they could to the post office. Some UB agents were already chasing after them, but the postal guards figured out what was happening and blocked their path!

That's how it was in those days. This was the only way to escape the clutches of the Soviet tyranny.

From the next letter, I found out that my mother had met Mrs. Marie DaVinci completely by coincidence. This Italian woman, from an aristocratic, though now impoverished family, voluntarily helped Polish refugees, who were detained among other places in a well-known Latina camp.

Another happy coincidence was that Mrs. Marie DaVinci knew my aunt, Jadzia Wiszowata, quite well. Mrs. DaVinci's husband, who was of Polonized German, had been an Uhlan cavalry captain in the same tenth regiment in which Lieutenant Wiszowaty served. He died on the front lines during the September attacks. After the Germans entered Poland, she reported as an Italian citizen, asking if she would be permitted to depart for Italy. She got permission because of the strong pact at that time between Rome and Berlin.

She welcomed my parents with all her heart. They found out from her that Zaorski was a double agent, working for the American embassy as well as the authorities of the People's Republic of Poland. He had terribly hurt many, many Polish refugees. He had even been the cause of several desperate suicides!

So, the first thing my parents had to do was to get themselves out of his clutches. Mrs. DaVinci lived in a rather large apartment, so she gave my parents a room. The dollars I sent them were enough for a meager payment for the room, for food for my parents, and also to a great extent, for food for Mrs. DaVinci and her son. She was a strange aristocrat—a cultured woman, fluent in Italian and Polish, and impoverished, while trying all the same to help all those around her as much as she could. Famished Poles could find relief at her apartment; my mother took care of feeding them. Mrs. DaVinci's son was thrilled with the situation that had come about. He claimed that he had never before eaten such delicious meals!

Then began the stage of taking care of the formalities. My parents had to go through the crossfire of Interpol.

Then the Italians were supposed to give them documents as political refugees. The affair became quite well known, even got into the press. A friend of Mrs. DaVinci, Mr. Notari, the head of the secret police in Rome, helped a lot. He was a cultured man, fluent in French, so he could communicate with my mother.

Mr. Notari helped my parents a lot, but nevertheless they still had to go to Trieste, where there was a refugee camp. Thanks to Mr. Notari's influence and my dollars, they were allowed to live outside the camp. They rented a tiny room in an old tavern.

November came, and then December, the time of cold winds from the ocean. My parents had a small iron stove called a "bombola" for heat. My mother started getting sick. Thankfully, their stay in Trieste was drawing to a close. They returned to Rome, having been granted political asylum. Then began the second and very difficult stage—trying to get permission to immigrate into the United States. Zaorski, who was furious that my parents had pulled themselves out of his clutches, did what he could to make things difficult for them at the American embassy to delay their getting visas.

January and February were filled with interrogations at the American embassy, but still no decision had been made.

Mrs. DaVinci introduced my parents to two older ladies who had been ladies-in-waiting for the late King Emmanuel. These ladies had learned about my parents' situation in the press and wanted to meet them. They politely welcomed my parents to their luxurious house filled with statues, paintings and antique furniture. offering cakes and tea. The conversations were in French as they enjoyed the afternoon tea. After a decent interval, my parents stood up, thanking them for their hospitality and prepared to leave. The ladies looked at them with such dismay that my mother asked outright, "You seem troubled. Is anything wrong?"

"Aren't you going to ask us for anything?"

"No," replied my mother. "It was very nice meeting both of you."

One of the women said frankly, "You are the first couple who has not asked us for anything. How nice it is to meet such people!"

During their first weeks in Rome and then in Trieste, I didn't have any certainty that they would be able to get political asylum. Filled with anxiety, I searched out the Polish American Congress in New York. I ended up at a run-down building in the middle of Manhattan. The headquarters of the Congress was located on one of the floors. There was a dirty, large waiting room with a young woman near the desk and some dignitary behind the glass doors. Through those doors, I could hear a loud booming voice. "What does he want?"

The secretary disappeared behind the doors. I heard some commotion. Then I heard, "Well, too bad, let him come in!"

I found myself in a dirty, large room. A painting of the Virgin Mary of Czestochowa that was covered in fly excrement hung on the wall and beneath it a crowned eagle.

"What do you want?" demanded the older man, who had gray hair and a similarly gray, long mustache.

I explained the situation to him briefly, still daunted by that "what do you want" and by the fact that he didn't even get up to greet me, didn't offer his hand. I was quite disillusioned.

"If they escaped from Poland, then they should go back and stay there and rot in jail! That's all they deserve!" this dignitary of the PAC (Polish American Congress) barked.

I quickly regained my nerve. "I hope that God will one day repay you for this good deed!"

I turned around and walked out. That was the first contact I had with the Polish American Congress.

Then I went to the office of Immigration and Naturalization Services (INS). I met an older inspector of the institution. I explained the situation to him, asking for asylum for myself. He looked over my passport.

"At this moment, you are legally on United States territory. We cannot do anything in this situation. You have to stay in the states until your visa expires. Then, you will be breaking U.S. law, and then we will be able to make the appropriate decision."

Another stop on my pilgrimage was a certain Catholic organization, from which I was directed to a charity office that handled helping people in situations like mine. A young Serbian woman there asked me for all my documents, along with my passport, the certification of my diploma in America, and my Polish diplomas and grade books. She was supposed to arrange asylum for me in the United States. Fortunately, I very quickly figured out that her goal was not asylum for me, but to marry me! I went to her office in the morning and calmly asked for my documents back. She started skirting the issue. I asked emphatically. Surprised by my resolute manner, she took my documents out of her desk. I checked to make sure they were all there and then left.

I found a lawyer who had been recommended by someone I knew. We went to the INS together; my visa in the United States was running out. The same inspector met with us. He said in an official tone, "You have broken the law of the United States by staying longer than your visa allowed. You are now under the jurisdiction of the United States. Please, turn in your passport!"

Giving him my passport, I said rather boldly, "Thank God!"

He smiled. Then he said quietly, "I have a feeling that we will do you no harm."

This meant that I would be able to stay in the United States as long as I wanted. Still, I didn't have any rights of citizenship. I was in a tough situation. I could work, but I could not further advance in my profession.

After receiving asylum, I went to the FBI, so as to tell them, showing my loyalty, about the propositions I had been offered by the GRU agents before I left Poland. I felt that this was now my duty. I was directed to the office of Inspector Collins.

I knocked on his door with great apprehension. I saw a maybe forty-year-old man behind the desk. He had a briefcase full of documents in front of him. I found out that they all concerned me! We looked in each other's eyes with mutual respect. I didn't understand his reason for it, but then he said, "So you are the Dr. Subczynski who operated on my father at Dr. Cooper's!" he cried.

I was horrified. With fear, I asked about his father's health.

"He feels terrific!" he replied. "We are very indebted to you."

After this beginning, I felt a lot better. I was in awe of the accuracy of their information about me. He reminded me of many facts from my life that I had already forgotten as irrelevant. He had it all there in the documents. I gained respect for the FBI. If they bring someone in for "observation," they already know almost everything about him. I told Collins about my parents' difficult ordeal. He promised me that he would try to help quicken the process of taking care of formalities at the American Embassy in Rome.

"But they shouldn't be suffering in Rome. McKiewer will give them food and ensure that they have some place to stay."

His knowledge on this particular matter happened to be illusory. I told him that McKiewer hadn't helped my parents at all, and that if it weren't for my dollars, they would be lost. He got angry. He suggested that I go immediately to see Mr. Murphy, the head of Catholic Relief Services in Washington, D.C.

"He'll straighten out Mr. McKiewer, you can be sure of that!"

The next day, I took the train from Grand Central Station to Washington, D.C., and stood before the head of the Catholic Relief Services. He asked me to sit down and tell him about the matter at hand. Learning that McKiewer hadn't offered my parents anything, he became furious. "I'll show that scoundrel, that drunk! Please, don't worry. In two days, the matter will be settled."

He happened to ask what I was planning to do. I told him that as a person with asylum, I didn't have the right to pursue a license in any way so as to advance further in the medical profession. In order to do that, you had to have citizenship or a permanent visa, called a green card.

"Don't worry, my child," he said, speaking from old age and authority. "I know something you don't. You cannot take the licensing exam in any of the states, but you can take it on federal ground, as in Washington, D.C.!"

This was unbelievably valuable information. It would play a crucial role in my life.

After getting home, I got another letter from my mother; it was full of despair. Zaorski was trying to blackmail them. He went to them and threatened that they would never be able to come to the United States.

I wrote back right away telling her that they would soon get visas. My mother wrote back that she couldn't believe that to be true. She also told me about a strange incident—a truck full of huge packages stopped in front of their home (at Mrs. DaVinci's— "For Mr. and Mrs. Subczynski." There was flour, sugar, cookies, and canned goods. It was enough to last for months!)

Mr. Murphy had kept his word.

Everyone was happy—Mrs. DaVinci, my parents, and the dozens of hungry Polish refugees.

And then, again, there were a few weeks of silence. And then a letter "drunk" with happiness from my mother, informing me that they already had their visas in their possession, visas for permanent residence in the United States, and that they could leave at any time! They could only buy one ticket on Alitalia with their savings. Then, a friend of mine, a Jewish woman from Poland, a kind doctor trying to certify her diplomas, told me that there was a travel agency in Manhattan run by a Polish woman who was very upstanding. I also still had an airline ticket for my return trip to Poland that I had purchased with U.S. dollars. I went there, thinking that an exchange might be possible. The owner of the agency was a large, hefty young Polish woman with dyed charcoal black hair and bright makeup who spoke Spanish well to appeal to the Latino clientele. As soon as I got there, I explained the situation. How could I change my ticket to Poland for a ticket for my father in the other direction?

She looked at the ticket. Then I heard, "No problem," and she immediately got to work. My ticket was transferred to Air France from New York to Paris. This time the passenger was to be Stanislaw Subczynski. This ticket was in turn transferred to Lufthansa, and Stanislaw Subczynski was to go from Germany to New York. That was half the maneuver—the ticket on Lufthansa was then transferred to a ticket on Alitalia from Rome to New York.

I was dumbfounded.

"How is that possible?"

"It's simple," she replied. "Your father will fly here on the ticket to New York, and every other airline will be turning to the previous airline for financial reimbursement. It can take up to a year, but ultimately, LOT (Polish airlines) will have to pay them with the money they got from you!"

I thanked her profusely. I sent my ticket to Italy. To this day, I have deep gratitude for that Polish woman who showed me such selfless sympathy.

My parents were supposed to arrive at Kennedy Airport. It just happened that Tarlov had me scheduled for a stereotactic surgery on a private patient at Flower and Fifth Avenue Hospital. It was scheduled at one o'clock in the afternoon, so I had very little time to get to the airport and meet my parents. I operated carefully but very quickly. I finished in an hour. I begged the taxi driver to hurry, and we raced to the airport.

I watched as passengers came out of the airplane, but I didn't see my parents! The last passengers left through the door, and they were still not there! I started to panic. At that moment, an announcement was made that another Alitalia plane was landing on the other side of the airport that had been delayed an hour. I ran over there quickly. The plane had just gotten there. After another moment, the doors opened, and the first passengers I saw getting out were my father and mother! Most of the people came out from the customs office but not my parents. As it turned out my father had brought a box of laxative salts with him that he often used for relief from constipation. The customs officer, however, concluded that it was probably cocaine! Then there was a skirmish of words—the officer in English, my father in German and Polish. Finally, some older worker licked the "cocaine" and determined that it was in fact Epsom salt.

Amidst all the words and statements in which we tried to capture our whole odyssey, we went to the old, cockroach-infested Wales Hotel. I rented a small room with a kitchenette. My parents were completely exhausted. I turned on the air-conditioner and went to the closest store for some food as well as some knives, forks, spoons, and dishes.

I can still see how we laid out plates of food on that dirty little table, how my mother made tea, then got a bottle of Italian wine out of the suitcase that they had gotten just before their departure. I remember that first meal together on American soil.

It was undoubtedly the happiest day of my life, for to this day, nothing comes close to it!

I stayed the night in my room at the hospital and then took care of what needed to be done in the morning at the hospital before going back to the Wales Hotel. I saw them now well rested, full of enthusiasm. Slowly, the questions began—so now what? First, we had to get an apartment. I solved this problem by renting an apartment on the eleventh floor of the building facing Metropolitan Hospital. The apartment had a great view of Manhattan's skyscrapers. But it wasn't furnished. I went to the flea market. I bought two armchairs and a small table, and the living room was furnished. Earlier, my mother had managed to send the painting by Jerzy Kossak, "The Return of Napoleon from Moscow," and some other things from Poland. I found the cheapest mattress I could and a foldout bed. I separated the mattress in two for me and my father, and my mother took the bed. I bought the cheapest dinette set. Then I brought from the hospital my small air-conditioner, which was essential for my parents who were not accustomed to the New York heat.

We bought my mother two summer dresses (costing a total of six dollars) in the poorest neighborhood, because besides her fur and the dress she was wearing, she didn't have anything else. Well then, something to keep her spirits up—for five dollars a month, I rented an old, run-down piano. My mother could play. My father took care of grocery shopping. There was a small store run by a German Jew on the corner—they could communicate well. My father was very run down—with a damaged heart and atrial fibrillation—and my mother weighed only eighty pounds. She had problems with recurrent pyelonephritis. On top of this, my future here on Washington's land was quite unclear. We did know, however, without having to say anything, that no one and nothing would ever be able to separate us again. We were at home, and we finally had a sense of freedom and safety. All other obstacles seemed irrelevant and small.

After work, I no longer went back to my hospital room but instead went "home," where my parents were waiting. We were so happy to be sharing what is tritely called family warmth. My mother played the piano from memory, because we didn't have any sheet music. The silvery tones of Chopin or the might of Beethoven filled our "home" with familiarity and the illusion that we were able to bring part of our Polish life across the ocean in the notes of the old ragged piano.

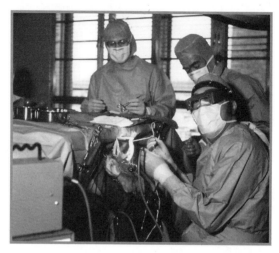

OPERATING ON A BRAIN TUMOR, LOOKING
AT VIDEO RECORDING THE SURGERY

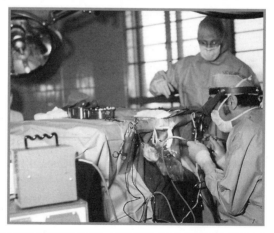

IN THE MIDDLE OF ACTION FOR BRAIN SURGERY

3

Gaining Credentials

F ROM MY FIRST days of residency at Metropolitan Hospital, I tried to find a way out of my one worrisome dilemma, which was not having the right to take the medical license exam so as to be able to practice medicine independently. I also didn't have citizenship.

I started working with an Underwood, an old typewriter. I translated my diplomas and grade books into English on it and wrote up a resume. I also wrote countless letters to various neuro-surgical programs on it.

Remembering that my teacher in Poland, Professor Choróbski had been a student of Professor Paul Bucy in Chicago, I wrote to him, among others, asking for help. But I didn't get any response from him. I received responses now and then from other places, but they were all negative. Professor Tarlov was still trying to work things out so that the residency program at Metropolitan Hospital would be recognized as valid by the board of neurosurgery.

One day, Professor Gurdijan, a well-known figure in American neurosurgery and a member of the board, came to visit us from Detroit. He was supposed to evaluate our neurosurgical depart-ment. I spent the whole day with him. He asked me a lot of professional but also personal questions. In the end, he was very interested in my predicament. Unfortunately, he couldn't help me because Metropolitan Hospital still didn't perform the required number of brain surgeries.

Then, I remembered Mr. Murphy's information about Washington—that I could take the licensing examination there despite not having permanent residence. I sent in all my documents and then learned that I had qualified for the exam! It was made up of two parts, each of which lasted three days. Quite a nice marathon! The first part focused on theoretical subjects, such as anatomy, pharmacology, biochemistry, etc. The second was centered on clinical subjects. Each subject contained 180 questions. You got forty-five seconds for each question.

I spent all the hours that I wasn't at work studying textbooks. I felt that my knowledge of anatomy, obstetrics, gynecology, neurosurgery, and even general pathology was pretty good. I had the most trouble with biochemistry, pharmacology, microbiology, and immunology. These fields had experienced incredible advances in the last few years. I spent the greatest amount of time on these, often into the late hours of the night.

The week before the exam, something strange happened. I was so exhausted that I simply couldn't think, couldn't connect thoughts. So I threw aside my books, and for the last 24 hours before leaving for the exam, I rested.

I traveled with my friends—one Japanese, one Italian. There were 113 of us amateurs seeking certification who were exactly like me—"refugees" from all over the world. I felt more at ease around them—we were all in the same situation, with the same chances.

After those three days of examination, I lost about five pounds. I was worn out and convinced that I had not passed.

After a few weeks, the response came in the mail; I had done well on the first part, known as "Basic Sciences," and was qualified for the second round. Delighted, I went back to Washington. It turned out that of those 113, there were barely sixteen of us left! More showed up for the exam, though, because they were the ones who hadn't done well the first time and so were taking this round of tests a second time.

The clinical subjects were easier for me. I answered the questions fairly quickly. I got to a part that was rather illogical. Namely, the answer to the question was written into the question. "That's impossible!" I thought. "I don't understand something here!"

I skipped that question and answered the next one. I went back to it again. And again I made the same conclusion. Despite this, I wrote down the answer I thought to be correct.

After the exam, I met up with my Italian friend.

"Janusz! I hope you didn't let yourself get taken in by those questions," he said. "Of course the answer can't be written into the question! I wrote down whatever else!"

Well then, as it happened I passed, and he didn't.

At that time, I didn't know that those exams were the first FLEX exams given in the United States. Up until that point, each state organized its own exam giving someone the right to practice only within that particular state. Moreover, for the first time, this exam allowed someone to practice medicine in all of North America. That's why some of the questions were supposed to test not only knowledge but also the shrewdness and critical thinking ability of those taking the test. There were sixty such questions with the answer obvious if you used common sense.

My financial situation wasn't getting any better. Fall came, and our needs began to surpass my earnings. I had to look for additional work. And as it often happens, I was helped out by a coincidence.

Strolling along the pavement of Manhattan, I ran into Dr. Stas Toczek. Our surprise was immeasurable! I knew that he had left the Warsaw Clinic on a Rockefeller scholarship, but I had no way of knowing that he had "chosen freedom," meaning he had not returned to Poland. He had married a doctor, an American woman of Greek descent, while he was here. He had been accepted for a neurosurgical residency at Georgetown University in Washington, D.C. I told him about my situation. He thought for a minute.

"Listen, Janusz. I know that they need someone to perform not only clinical work but also experimental scientific research at the Oncology Institute in Buffalo on the neurosurgery ward. The pay is good, and they also offer free housing. The one disadvantage is that the ward is not recognized by the board of neurosurgery as work towards the specialty. Still, you could work there for a year, earn more, and then look around for something better. Maybe even write an article in the meantime, too." I thanked him profusely.

I called Dr. Owens, the chief of neurosurgery in Buffalo. Indeed, he needed a neurosurgeon for all the aforementioned roles, and the job promised a good environment. The salary was seven hundred dollars a month, and the three-room apartment was on the block close to the Institute, and it was free. I sent out my documents. A few days later, I received a positive reply. I was to begin working there in January of 1966.

Professor Tarlov wasn't thrilled about my departure. Still, he didn't really have any arguments to keep me from going. He knew about my financial situation, especially now, with my parents.

It came time for our first Christmas on American land. We bought a Christmas tree, and my mother prepared a traditional Vilno Christmas Eve dinner. We did not exchange gifts for obvious reasons. The holidays were joyful, though filled with various reflections. We were together, though not in an easy situation, and our perspective had shifted towards the future. My mother and I played Polish carols and all the now familiar Anglo-Saxon carols.

It was soon time to move. I stopped two shady characters, Arabs with curly black beards, in a dilapidated van in Manhattan. Not really thinking about it, I went up to them asking if they would want to take my things to Buffalo for a fee. They agreed willingly.

Then we got into lively negotiations about the cost of this service. But we quickly came to an agreement. We were to leave before the New Year.

At the same time, my mother fell ill with pyelonephritis. The high fever dropped after antibiotics, but she was very weak. Still, there was nothing we could do—we had to go. The van came early in the morning, and proved to be unreliable. Though we had returned the piano to the renter, the van was overloaded. Our movers started speaking in Arabic. One of them got out and began pushing the van. After a few dozen meters, the engine finally revved and started. We were off.

We drove for a whole day through snow-covered mountains, fields, and forests. Dusk fell. The settlements and towns were lit up with thousands of colorful lights in holiday decoration. We ate some sandwiches, warmed up with some tea, got gas, and went further on our way.

We reached our destination in snow-covered Buffalo at night. The apartment was nice, functional, cozy, warm, and freshly painted, with a well-equipped kitchen. The ninth floor we were on promised a great view.

Our movers managed to get our things inside, then we made the beds, I paid the movers for their service, and my parents and I fell fast asleep.

Roswell Park Memorial Institute in Buffalo was, at that time, one of the larger centers in America involved in research in the fields of etiology and pathology of malignant tumors. It was located in two large buildings. The first was utilized as the clinical center, the second was for laboratories and research.

One of the groups at work was studying the role of phenan-threnes—the chemical component of cigarette tar—and its role in stimulating tumor growth in the lungs. Another group did viral studies. It was a period of great interest in slow viruses—viruses that were good at coexisting in the human body for years until they would cause mutation in cells and the growth of a malignant tumor. Still, another group worked on testing the immunology of cancer. The head of the institute was Dr. Moore, an oncologist who was well known in all of America.

The patients did not have to pay for anything. The Institute was financed by federal funds. In order to be admitted for treatment, however, patients had to agree to experimental treatment. New pharmacological remedies were first tested on cancer cell cultures, and then on animals, mainly mice. If the results were promising at these stages, they were given to the patients.

My chief was a neurosurgeon, Dr. Owens. Dr. Benvenuto worked with him, as did a neurosurgeon of Arab descent. Owens didn't engage in experimental work in the laboratory. He was implementing new therapeutic methods for malignant brain tumors in the third stage of research using appropriate protocols on the patients. This therapy was rather doubtful. At that time, a new anti-cancer drug named Vincristin was delivered to a patient through an injection to the carotid artery, so that it would reach the brain directly. The first attempts were awful; they ended either in death or in necrosis of not only part of the brain but also the scalp.

Another responsibility of the department of neurosurgery was the treatment of pain—a nightmarish part of cancer. One of the methods was cutting of the sensory tracts of the trigeminal nerve in the upper part of the brain stem. This served to alleviate the terrible pain in cancer of the throat and face. We performed also chordotomies—the cutting of sensory tracts in the spinal cord in tumors of the middle body region. At that time, a procedure was introduced to destroy the pain tracts of the spinal cord using an electrode placed into the spinal cord under X-ray control. In brain tumors we performed standard procedures with complete or more often partial removal of the malignant mass.

No one in the neurosurgery ward performed experimental work on animals. I was hired for this purpose. After the first conversation with Dr. Owens, I figured out that he didn't have any established plans in this regard. I felt that he was waiting to hear a concrete proposal from me. Already, during my work with Dr. Cooper I came to the conclusion that the flow of information from certain centers in the cerebellum had a significant influence on a patient's results of surgical treatment for Parkinson's disease. The spreading of these impulses in the area of the nuclei of the basal ganglia was never accurately identified. Almost all the information in this field was based on old experimental work that was rather primitive.

This puzzle really interested me. I presented Dr. Owens with the whole project, which would be done on anesthetized cats. He seized on the idea immediately and suggested that I contact an electronics wizard, an older Dutchman with a Ph.D. in physics, who had worked at that institute for years. I got my own lab and a technician. I was cut off from clinical practice completely, which worried me immeasurably—after all, I was a neurosurgeon.

My experiments were focused on the stimulation of brachium conjuctivum—a bunch of nerve fibers going from the cerebellum to the nuclei of the brain stem—and then recording the spread of these impulses. The localization of recorded potentials was confirmed by a histological evaluation of the brain. It was not an easy task. The evoked potentials oscillated in an area of millivolts, and any, even minute, interference in the magnetic field, caused for example by a passing police car with a siren on, ruined the results of the experiment. I also didn't have any of the appropriate electrodes, a proper stimulator, or adequate electronic equipment on which to record the evoked potentials from the nerve cells.

In other words, I was basically starting from scratch, having no knowledge of electronics.

I went to that Dutchman. He was of high general intelligence and, as many inventors are, an eccentric. He welcomed me in his own way—that is, not very politely, and added that I shouldn't bother him, because he had more important and more interesting puzzles to solve. In the end, however, he let himself be convinced to help me in the field of his specialization. Soon, he had created a system that allowed me to record potentials in the brain caused by the movement of a single hair! They were also carried by a speaker. As a result, by moving even one hair, you could hear the following sounds in the speaker—shoo-shoo-shoo. These were the sounds from a few irritated nerve cells.

I now had the necessary technical possibilities to undertake the proposed task. With the technician, we put a cat to sleep and placed its head in the stereotactic apparatus, which allowed for precise placement of the electrodes. Then, I removed most of the skull to uncover the brain and the pathways leading from the cerebellum to the nuclei of the basal ganglia. Performing this procedure was not easy. You couldn't damage anything. We were not supposed to allow for blood loss for the animal. I removed the bone with a drill that was similar to one a dentist uses, though of a higher caliber. Thanks to performing these craniotomies on cats, I learned a new skill—using a drill with precision, a skill that really became useful in my later neurosurgical career.

My first experiments were unsuccessful. The cats died before I could register anything. We also had to build a copper cage around the experiment site to isolate ourselves from external influences.

I was to begin the experiments in February, and all of January passed by simply in preparation. Finally, I was able to record the evoked potentials on several animals in March. We then preserved the brains and then cut them into fifteen-micron cross sections in which the irritated areas were localized.

We began work in the morning just after seven. If the experiment was going well, we couldn't take a break, or else the information we had just collected would be incomplete. Sometimes, we didn't finish working until just before midnight.

My main problem was that we had to kill the cats. Though they really did not suffer during the experiments, as they were put to sleep, I always felt guilty that I was destroying the life of a defenseless and innocent creature. To this day, when I close my eyes, I see cages of cats in my subconscious. And to this day, I haven't been released of that feeling of guilt.

The work was moving ahead quickly in terms of results. I already had some that were in accordance with my hypothesis in April. Owens was thrilled. He told me about an upcoming neurosurgery conference. Knowing about my uncertain immigration status, he also proposed that the Institute, through the Department of Education, should go to the immigration authorities about getting me permanent residence in the United States as a highly wanted specialist.

I was doubly shocked by this proposition that I was so well regarded and that it would mean a permanent stay. The necessary formalities were fulfilled, and after a month, I got a green card. My joy was difficult to describe. It was a strange thing that my parents came to the United States as refugees, so they already had the right for permanent residence, while I was in limbo until this point. At the same time, I received a document from Washington granting me a license to practice medicine. I was now a full-fledged American doctor with the right to have an independent medical practice. Still, I was not yet recognized by the American Board of Neurological Surgery as a specialist in that field.

To my amazement, I had already received a raise, evident in my next paycheck. Then, I understood the significance of getting a license in the United States.

Soon thereafter, I also began working at the neurosurgery ward. I performed many surgeries, mainly removing brain tumors and operating to relieve pain. I learned the technique of percutaneous chordotomies, in those years a new technique. This created great relief for the patient. A percutaneous chordotomy was performed by placing electrodes into the spinal cord under X-ray. The patient remained conscious and worked with the surgeon. The post-operative damage to the surrounding tissue is minimal in comparison to that following an open surgery.

Dr. Owens was also the chief of neurosurgery at the Veterans Administration Hospital, a federally funded hospital for war veterans. He offered me part-time work running the ward with him in that hospital. This meant a radical improvement in my financial situation. Of course, I accepted the offer, though the problem soon arose of how I would get to the hospital. In Buffalo, at that time, there was no public transportation system; everyone drove his own car. I decided along with my parents that I could buy a car with the money from the part-time work. And that's what I did. My first car was a Dodge Dart. The price was two thousand dollars.

This purchase greatly improved my mobility. During the weekends, we would go for brief visits with nature to the national parks around Buffalo. We were amazed by the variety of birds, different from the ones in Poland, and the striped squirrels on the trees. Now and then, we would see raccoons, though they were night creatures and could only be seen in the beam of the headlights.

I made myself go for my first dentist visit in a while, as I had an urgent problem. I also bought a small piano—the one way to lift my mother's spirits, who desperately missed Poland.

Our first guest in Buffalo was Mrs. Fema Fleszar. I still remember her as a young woman studying chemistry in Poznan. As the younger sister of my aunt Janka's husband, she would often come over to our house then. During the period of the occupation, we lost touch with her. We learned that she had worked in a fish shop in Warsaw and was able to make a living from that. She lived with a friend of hers from school; her view from the window opened up onto the ghetto wall. She was a witness to horrifying scenes. Her descriptions of events really caused the satanic character of the German Occupation to stick forever in my mind. She told me that in the ghetto, there was a Jewish police force—supposedly to keep order—that was armed with clubs. The policemen, in order to survive, had to torment their brethren. Fema saw many times young Jews mercilessly beating the older men to death.

The Jewish police were told by the Gestapo they could only survive another day if they murdered a fellow Jew. This was beyond the objective of just killing Jews. It was an experiment in how dehumanized an individual could become. The Nazis were cruel in this way beyond comprehension.

Near the end of the occupation, Fema married a vaudeville singer. The marriage turned out a total disaster. She was left again alone with a daughter, Ola. Her husband's parents had emigrated from Poland to the United States long before the Second World War. They worked hard and returned to Poland just before the German invasion. Fema's husband had an older brother who was a doctor in Warsaw. Taking advantage of his American citizenship, the brother managed to return to the United States. After a few years, he brought his wife and daughter, Eva, over, then his mother and brother. That's how Fema ended up alone with her child in Warsaw. Still, her mother-in-law, the mother of those two sons, was an upright and just woman. She demanded that her older son invite Fema to the United States so as to "join" the family. She ended up in Buffalo, not knowing the language and not having work, and her brother-in-law didn't go to any trouble to help her. She worked two jobs at the same time so as to earn enough to pay for a tiny apartment and to send her child to school. After two years, she managed to get work at Millard Fillmore Hospital as a lab technician. Shortly thereafter, she was recognized as an excellent chemist, despite difficulties with the language. She could finally get better apartment and pay for Ola's schooling. During all this time, she was incredibly in love with her ungrateful husband and was patiently awaiting his return. He, meanwhile, was living in the same city of Buffalo!

We always welcomed her into our home; she was the first really close person to us in a foreign land.

Our apartment in Buffalo was strange. There was a Kossak and two other paintings by Polish artists on the wall. These had been sent earlier by my mother from Warsaw. A nice but small table, two chairs, and my radio made up one room. There was even less in the remaining rooms—a bed for my parents in one, mine in the other. And that was all. The furnishing and equipment in the kitchen were quite scanty. There was a striking ambience of temporality and emptiness. This didn't, however, bother Fema. She had been through a lot and was quite flexible with such things.

Her brother-in-law, Dr. Fleszar, was intrigued by our arrival. He was at that time licensed to practice medicine and was also a Diplomate of the American Board of Surgery. One day, he came by with his wife and Fema. He turned out to be a braggart. After skeptically looking at our more-than-humble apartment, and after learning about my status as a doctor, which at that time was still uncertain, he frowned and said coolly, "Don't think that you'll ever be an American doctor. It's impossible to get your license. The earlier you understand that, the better off you'll be!"

I listened to his bragging oration without making a comment. At that point, I already knew that I had passed the exam in Washington and that I had my medical license! To this day, I cannot understand that man—his egoism and boasting in a situation in which I think he should have been encouraging me.

Not all our confrontations with "Polonia" were so unpleasant. Soon, through Fema, we met a soldier from the Second Corps who had come to America alone. He was Captain Dabrowski who worked in our institute as a lab technician. His little apartment was above a garage near a large villa. He earned very little, and what-ever was leftover after necessities went to his family in Poland. Having to cook for himself, he really appreciated my mother's cooking. However, on one occasion he asked my mother to make for him stuffed cabbage. My mother prepared this dish and he was very disappointed. They were made Vilno-style, stuffed only with meat, and they were in a spicy tomato sauce.

"My dear, you haven't made the stuffed cabbage as it's supposed to be! It shouldn't have tomatoes and should be baked Ukrainian style!"

I also recall survivors of a concentration camp. There was a Polish Jewish couple, the Falenskis. The camp numbers were tat-tooed on their forearms. There were also two cultured, lonely older ladies, who were very kind and intelligent. I grew to like these two ladies very much. We also became close with the Falenskis. Our circle of friends of Polish-Americans was growing larger. I learned a lot about the Jewish diaspora from the Falenskis. He was a can-tor in an Orthodox synagogue. He sometimes complained of the taxes he had to pay to the Jewish congregation, 10% of his gross earnings which were low to begin with. Falenski was a well edu-cated intellectual. Yet he could only get work doing physical labor in a factory. His wife's earnings were also meager.

During that period, I didn't run into any agents from the Polish Peoples' Republic, who were functioning within and penetrating the Polish-American diaspora. One day I received several phone calls from Professor Wald, a Stalinist who worked at the psychiat-ric institute in Poland and did experimentation on prisoners. He was in Buffalo and wanted to meet up with me. I was sure that this was an assignment that he had been given. He probably had to put together some kind of information at the UB, with which he was closely tied. I didn't answer any of his many phone calls, and we never met up. I'll add here that after getting political asylum, I received two letters at the same time from the Polish Academy of Science. In the first one, I was informed that I was discipli-narily discharged from work by seeking asylum. I'm curious by what channels they so quickly found out about the asylum I was granted. In the second letter, they demanded that I use my own money to buy some laboratory equipment. I still have those two letters. These letters and those phone calls from Dr. Wald were the last contact I had with the "people's government."

I was still trying to get approval as a specialist in neurosurgery. After receiving the license from Washington that allowed me to practice medicine, I was very happy to find out that I had the same privileges in the state of New York on the basis of that license without having to take an additional exam. I went with my father to the state capital in Albany, and took care of the formalities in the course of one day. But whether or not I would get approved in my specialty was still questionable.

The professor of neurosurgery at the University of Buffalo was Dr. Bakay, a Hungarian. During the memorable Hungarian uprising, he had managed to get across the border and escaped to the United States from Austria. I went to talk to him about my situation. He greeted me coldly. He said that, truthfully, there were no real possibilities of getting a residency, because all available spaces were taken. He really turned me off, all the more so because in the days of the Hungarian uprising a team of doctors from Warsaw and Poznan, including myself, planned to go to Budapest to offer medical help. The Soviet puppets forbade the trip, however, and nothing came of it. I was puzzled, even greatly disappointed, by his lack of friendship for a fellow refuge.

That's how the winter of 1967 passed. Spring came. My parents were my mainstay. I noticed that my mother played the piano much better than she had before my first departure to the United States; she had spent the years of separation by the piano. She played Beethoven, most of Chopin's works, and Scarlatti's sonatas without much difficulty. We felt somewhat settled. My work at the Institute and at the Veterans Administration Hospital allowed us to save a bit of money. Our goal was to make more pilgrimages, for we all agreed that I couldn't stay permanently at the Institute where I couldn't pursue my specialty.

I didn't stop trying. I sent all my documents, including information about my fellowship with Dr. Cooper and my work at

Metropolitan Hospital, to Dr. Odom, who was then the secretary of the Board of Neurosurgery, asking for the exact requirements to become eligible for the neurosurgical board exam. I waited a long time, but I never got a response. I had the right to a response. Finally I took a day off from work and flew to Durham, North Carolina to Duke University, where Dr. Odom was the chief of neurosurgery. I went to the secretary and told her who I was and what I was there about. I was soon brought into a large office; Dr. Odom sat behind the desk. He made a kind first impression. He greeted me politely and, not giving me the chance to say a word, started speaking.

"Listen, as if you were my son, I advise you, leave this alone. You can, of course, practice neurosurgery without having taken the board. Why go through all this? You have the practice; you have the knowledge, so I advise you—let it alone!"

While I was listening to this "fatherly" tirade, I began to feel quite angry. I spat back rather sharply, "Doctor, sir, I know very well what I must do. I came here for a reply, to know what the board requires of me, so that I can take the exam. I have the right to know this just like anyone else."

Odom didn't get angry. He looked at me with interest. He said with a note of esteem, "My God! You look like someone who really wants to do this! You know, so many people come here and bother me that, as a rule, I try to dissuade them. But, if you really want this so definitively, then I will send you a response. You will get a letter in two weeks with the specified requirements to fulfill."

He smiled and said, "Well then, I wish you luck. I can see that you know what you're doing."

He kept his word. After two weeks, I got a response. The American Board of Neurological Surgery stated that I would only need two years of residency in a senior position because of my professional background. This condition was practically impossible to fulfill because it was outside the flow of a normal five year residency.

And so the year passed. War broke out in Vietnam. I wondered whether I should report as a volunteer, so as to fulfill the conditions established by the board in that way. My parents agreed to it. They would somehow survive in Buffalo, and I as a neurosurgeon would work in Japan. I reported to the recruiting command station. They looked at me as if I'd been hit on the head—they really hadn't seen even one other person volunteering to go. I heard them say that, for now, they did not need me.

A few months later, a rumor went around that Dr. Owens got a professorship in one of the smaller universities; he had had enough of working with hopelessly sick patients. We speculated as to who would take over as chief after him. I started operating at that time at the Veterans Administration Hospital. I remember my first rounds with the neurosurgery residents. I determined that five of the patients needed surgery. I informed the chief resident, who was finishing up his specialty residency, that these patients should be prepared for surgery next week. He was really shocked. "We never operate on that many people in a single week, but over a month!"

Indeed, this hospital run by federal bureaucrats functioned at a slower pace. I didn't give up. During the course of one week, we performed the monthly limit of surgeries.

I particularly remember a certain patient who was a veteran from the Korean War. A grenade had torn out a piece of his skull, the bridge of his nose and his orbit, and, of course, his eye. He was shockingly disfigured and unhappy in his crippled state and appearance. I always liked doing plastic surgery. I decided that I would use metylmetacrylate—a plastic formed on the operating table from two components that then polymerizes and develops into a hard matter. Using this material, I could patch the missing parts of the bones, not only of the skull but also the bridge of the nose, as well as reconstruct the missing upper part of the orbit.

He agreed without hesitation. I got to work. The results were terrific, though he was missing an eye. I spoke with a young and intelligent ophthalmologist. He reconstructed the upper and lower eyelids from the skin folds and put in a glass eye! The patient looked rather mediocre after the procedure, as he was black and blue and swollen. The swelling quickly went down, though, as did the black and blue marks. We gave him a mirror.

"Amazing!" he cried out. "Finally, I can screw again!..." This was the best compliment I ever received.

There was a clinic in the veterans' hospital where I saw patients once a week. They were usually chronically ill patients, most often with epilepsy. One of them was an Indian chief. He lived in Canada but was still an American veteran. He suffered from epilepsy and would come periodically for prescriptions for Luminal and Dilantin. I gave him a prescription. He looked like a big fat old woman with the remnants of soft hair on his head. I made an appointment for him in a month, but he came back after just two weeks. He asked for another prescription. He explained dully that he had lost the bottle of Luminal tablets. I didn't believe him and didn't give him any more Luminal. I called a doctor in Canada with whom the "chief" also had contact. It became obvious that he had also used the same trick of the lost bottle there.

After a week, I received information from Canada that the "chief" had poisoned his wife with Luminal and was now sitting in prison!

One day in the fall of 1967, after Owens left, I was given word that Dr. Moore—the director of the Institute—wished to speak with me. I quickly ran through my medical care history looking for any big faults. I couldn't remember anything.

Dr. Moore mentioned Owens's departure briefly and then went into the matter at hand. "We need someone who can run the neurosurgery department with the ability to also organize research. We have decided that you fulfill these requirements. I am offering you the position of chief of neurosurgery with a salary of $35,000 a year. You can also earn more with your work at the Veterans Administration Hospital, another $14,000. What do you say to that?"

I was dumbfounded by this proposition. I had never even dreamed of such a salary, not to mention the prestige at the Institute. It meant that I would be able to settle down comfortably, buy a house, and live in completely different conditions. There were, however, some shortcomings. I would never be a Diplomate of the American Board of Neurological Surgery. I would also be sentenced to work with incurable patients, which was very depressing. If someone happened to show up with better qualifications, I would be defenseless. I replied that I thanked him for the trust and honor and that I would give him a reply in a few days. I knew, however, that I would not take this path.

After getting home, I heard my mother say, "Don't even think about it! Your first task is to get fully licensed in your specialty. There is nothing to discuss!"

My father said something similar.

The rumor about my promotion quickly spread throughout the Polish-American circles in Buffalo. Most of them couldn't believe that I had been so lucky. Everyone was sure that I would accept the offer.

The war in Vietnam was getting more and more intense. Chief residents in neurosurgery were being drafted into the Army, as the number of wounded was rising drastically. Many neurosurgery centers were lacking chief residents. This created a new demand to be filled as quickly as possible. Thus, new possibilities of getting a residency suddenly opened up for me.

I turned down Dr. Moore's offer, saying that I hoped to get a residency. He understood my arguments completely. I wrote letters to the larger training centers, and then concluded that calling them would be much faster. I got a list of all the phone numbers of universities and hospitals approved by the board to train neurosurgeons. With a map of the United States on the table, we wondered in what order I should call. Without thinking, my mother pointed her finger at Portland, Oregon on the other side of America, on the Pacific.

I dialed the number. I heard, "Who's speaking?" I described my situation and presented my qualifications. The voice on the other end of the phone sounded confused. "How did you know that I have a position open?"

"I didn't know that. I am just looking."

Then, I heard, "They just drafted my chief resident. I don't know anything about you, but if you are telling the truth, then send me your documents, and you'll be hired. A chief resident gets six thousand dollars a year and takes call every other day."

I assured him that I would send my documents immediately. I had been speaking with the chief of neurosurgery at Good Samaritan Hospital, a well-known training center. His name was Dr. Raaf.

And so, on the last day of December in 1967, we left on a long voyage—over 3000 miles west of Buffalo. We left our contacts, the Polish-Americans we knew, among others my cousin Andrew, who had come from Poland on my invitation. He already had a doctorate in chemistry and wished to work here in his field. I arranged a grant for him at Roswell Park Institute. He was to receive five hundred dollars a month. When he got there, though, he found out that the grant had been taken by an immunology worker, unfortunately, also a Pole. Andrew was disappointed and felt quite displaced. I suggested that he work voluntarily as a lab technician for Professor Laskowski. He agreed to this, though unwillingly. He was a very capable and intelligent scientific worker and proved to be very efficient. After a few months, Professor Laskowski asked me if I would approve a scholarship for Andrew at five hundred dollars a month. I agreed very happily, and Andrew's joy was infinite.

I sent our belongings and car to Portland in the early morning. We sat around in an empty apartment the rest of the day. In the evening, we took a taxi to the train station so as to take the train to Chicago. We planned to make the whole trip by train. We knew that the trip would be incredibly beautiful and also comfortable, as we had a sleeping compartment all to ourselves from Chicago to Oregon. We rode the entire night towards Chicago. After breakfast, we took a taxi to another train station, from which we would take our transcontinental train. We settled into our compartment; it was comfortable with a luxurious bathroom and a large window. American Pullmans were somewhat bigger than Polish ones, so were more comfortable.

We left in the afternoon. First, we passed by Chicago's suburbs and slums. Then there was more and more space, limitless fields, and clumps of bare trees here and there. After an hour, the landscape changed and settled. Fields covered in snow, flatness without the slightest hill. This was the central region of agricultural production in the United States. Near evening, the landscape changed again. We rode into the steppe. Clumps of dried grass peeked through the white snow. We moved through such emptiness until twilight. We ate supper in the dining car and went to bed.

When I woke up, the sun was shining. The train continued to crawl through empty terrain. The whiteness stretched on endlessly. At one moment, I saw a group of dark dots moving in our direction. I recognized them as a herd of bison. After a while, there was a herd of wild horses—mustangs. They were digging in the snow looking for grass.

We reached Cheyenne in the evening. We were in the middle of the "Wild West," the land of Westerns. I noticed an absence of black people on the platforms. They were instead full of thin silhouettes of men in short, sheepskin coats and ten gallon hats. They were mostly local ranchers.

The second night of our voyage came. The next morning, the same emptiness surrounded us, though soon the landscape began to change again. The terrain became slightly hilly, there were clumps of fir trees. Then hills became mountains covered in a dark wall of fir trees. We rode into the Rocky Mountains. Gorgeous views appeared one after another as in a kaleidoscope. The mountains seemed wild and threatening, black granite with caps of snow on the peaks. Here and there, we could see small communities buried in the snow. Around noon, we suddenly rode out of the mountains into a terrain somewhat similar to that of the Beskidy Mountains in Poland. Then we came into a huge valley, in which there were a lot of households, chimneys, and streets. We were in Portland.

We hadn't reserved a hotel, so I decided to go straight to the hospital. Outside the train station, I was greeted by a person's statue on a tall pedestal. I read the plaque; this was a monument to a hero who had been the first to make the cross-country trip, mainly on the Columbia River, to reach the Pacific Ocean. The west coast had been then known to people living on the east coast only through tales told by whalers. These men often spent the winters there among Indians, spreading syphilis.

We took a taxi to the hospital. My parents waited inside while I told them about my arrival. We left our things there and went to look for an apartment. One of the homes nearby was advertising an apartment for rent. It was a basement apartment, furnished with a few chairs, beds, and a table. The price was appealing, as we were still counting every penny.

I brought in the suitcases, and we ate a warm meal and fell asleep. I went to Good Samaritan Hospital in the morning. It was a huge, red-brick building. On the other side of the street, a vast parking lot filled with cars stretched into the distance. I found Dr. Raaf's office and, from there, the secretary led me to the hospital ward where the chief operated. He was a tall, thin man with a narrow head covered in gray hair. He inspired respect, as well as kindness. He moved slowly and spoke quietly in a voice characterized by authority. He evaluated me with a careful glance.

"I don't know anything about you, and that's how I'm going to treat you."

After this statement, he turned around and continued making rounds. The greeting was stiff but to the point. I understood immediately that I was dealing with a real man. There were a few residents near him. One of them had an injured hand. There was also a gray-haired woman circling around the residents with a sharp look on her face. She was Dr. Raaf's personal nurse—his right hand and overseer of everything. She handed Raaf instruments during surgery, often with a younger nurse, who then had a hard time. She greeted me in a style similar to her boss's. "I'm Ruby Waterstone. I am also known by the name 'The Witch of the North.' Be careful, or you'll have to deal with me."

I didn't let them get me off track. Despite a caustic disposition and an overt admiration for Raaf, she seemed to be a just and fair person.

I found myself in the operating room the same day. It was very well equipped. From the get-go, I appreciated the way the surgical team functioned, as well as Raaf's excellent technique. He was operating on a parasagittal meningioma of the brain—the tumor was pressing on the brain tissue, ingrown in the sagittal sinus (the large vein in the middle portion of the vertex of the skull). He performed the surgery quickly and precisely, without any unnecessary blood loss. I was happy. I was finally working with a real surgeon. Raaf wasn't interested in publishing articles about clinical cases. I got the impression that he actually couldn't stand it. His vocation was clinical work and surgery.

Because his chief resident was drafted and ended up in an Army medical hospital in Japan, I took over his position. The other residents were under me. I was thus responsible for all the practice of neurosurgery. The daily schedule was as follows: in the morning before seven, I met on the ward with Ruby. We made rounds on the patients, becoming familiar with their actual states and then determined the course of further treatment. Raaf came punctually at seven o'clock. After five minutes of discussion with me about the state of the patients, and a few remarks from Ruby, we rounded on the patients. Raaf made the ultimate decisions and gave orders to me and to the ward nurses. At eight o'clock, we were in the operating room. Surgeries lasted until the early afternoon. I ran home to eat something and came back equally fast to admit patients during the afternoon who were going to have surgery the following day. They needed to be examined, the history and physicals had to be written up, all orders had to be done, and they were prepped for surgery.

I got home late at night. This wasn't, however, the end of the day's work. Every other day, I was on home-call. We lived just next to the hospital, so I could be in the emergency room or in the ICU at any moment. There were a lot of traumas, often requiring surgery in the middle of the night.

Raaf quickly recognized that I had a sufficient supply of knowledge and surgical technique and, as a result, I most often operated on such emergency cases alone.

Raaf had a large private practice. He had a rule that only he operated on his "own" patients, while the patients admitted by the hospital were patients for the chief resident, so they were mine.

That didn't mean that I decided for them independently, but I did operate alone after getting the chief's opinion.

Besides Raaf, there was another, younger surgeon—thin, black-haired, calm, and often sporting an ironic smile. He was Dr. Mason, a Serb. I worked for two months under Dr. Raaf, then two under the direction of Mason. He was kind, lightly sarcastic, with excellent surgical technique. He grew to like me. He often let me operate on his own cases, assisting me and sometimes, though not overbearingly, making suggestions. Like Raaf, he was not inclined to academic writing to the *Journal of Neurosurgery*, but instead was doing good clinical work in his medical profession. Young Dr. Smith worked with him; Smith had just finished his residency, though without yet having taken the specialty exam. We got to be good friends.

Our belongings arrived very late, especially the car, without which you really couldn't get around, and the valuable new piano. Our apartment was warm, functional, and close to stores. I used to buy an incredibly large steak at the butcher shop that was big enough for three servings. It was the best meat I had ever eaten; it came from free-range cattle living all year-round in a herd under the open sky and feeding themselves. Some of them were bred with bison.

Loneliness surfaced again. In Buffalo, we had a circle of friends. Here, I didn't find a single other Polish person! A Polish priest in Vancouver, nearby in Canada, found out through I-don't-know-what channels that a Polish doctor was working in Good Samaritan Hospital. He came specially to meet me! We spent a few hours with him, learning about Canada and beautiful British Columbia. He was also interested in hearing about our past.

I had every other weekend off. Oregon has a completely different climate from other places sharing the same geographical plane. One reason for this is the proximity of the Pacific. In the winter, it rained constantly, only sometimes interrupted by wet snow. The fullness of spring came at the end or sometimes the beginning of March. The mountain bases—with Mount Hood crowning over

the other mountains—were covered with flowering blue rhododendrons growing in the wild. It was an unbelievable view: the
peak of Mount Hood, drowning in clouds, was covered in snow,
while a sea of flowering rhododendrons at the base created a mag-
nificent contrast.

On the weekends, we took the car into the mountains. After
an hour, we were already in a total wilderness. We got there on
a winding, narrow road that ran along a precipice. The majestic
Columbia River was at the bottom of the huge canyon, with tall
walls of rock on either side. There were steep slopes at the top
covered in fir trees and rocks. You could see ranches laid out here
and there in the valley on the river, as well as a white church with a
sharp spire and a long perch fastened to two poles. This perch was
used to tie up the horses of the parishioners coming to Sunday
Mass. In the entranceway to the church, there was a large shelf on
the sidewall. That's where you put your weapons; a sign above the
shelf reminded people about the need to be rid of these murder-
ous tools during the time of communion with God!

The patients I saw were very different from those in New York.
They were ordinary, hardened, and upright. They had been raised
in physical labor, making them resistant to pain and suffering.
There would often be a large felt hat on the bedside table and a
pair of tall cowboy boots next to the bed. This was a world of different people—closed, foreign to the foreigner, but kind and simple like an extended hand in greeting.

As the chief resident, I performed all the smaller procedures
that came onto the ward. I did a myelogram—an examination that
involved the injection of dye into the spinal canal through a lumbar puncture; an arteriogram—a test of the arterial circulation of
the brain under X-ray after an arterial injection of dye; and I often
had to perform a tracheotomy—an opening of the trachea on the
neck to improve breathing. This last procedure was only done in
an emergency scenario in which there was no time to lose, because
the patient was choking. I did this procedure in a flash on the
patient's bed using a minimal number of instruments. It became

known in the hospital that I performed tracheotomies well. As a result, I was called in to see patients who weren't even there for neurosurgery, simply making the nurses' jobs easier.

Dr. Raaf didn't go to the trouble of learning how to pronounce either my first or last name properly. He settled the problem in the following way: "Because your name begins with a J, that's what you'll be called."

With time, I got used to being called "Jay" and it no longer bothered me.

Sometime during the third month of work, after treating me sharply and watching me carefully, Dr. Raaf turned to me during rounds one day and mumbled, "You are okay."

This was a huge complement coming from those lips. And from that day forward, though nothing was ever said about it, he and Ruby treated me much better.

As a frequent visitor to the emergency room, I had a lot of interesting experiences. One day, a young girl was brought in with a head injury. She was conscious, and she had only vomited once. I examined her. I didn't notice anything in particular. She was still conscious and was behaving like a normal child her age. I asked for an X-ray of her skull and a report of the results, and I went home to get something to eat. Just when I reached the door of my apartment, I heard the phone ringing. I picked up the phone.

"Doctor, that little girl lost consciousness!"

I ran as fast as I could. Yes, she was unconscious, and one of her pupils had dilated—a sign that there was acute intracranial bleeding on the side of the dilated pupil, usually from the meningeal artery. There wasn't a moment to lose—damage to the brain stem could be irreversible. As she was lying on the gurney, I drilled an opening in her skull on the side of the dilated pupil without administering any anesthesia. Blood spurt from the artery, and the pressure lessened to the point that we could take her to the operating room and calmly perform the proper procedure. The little girl left the hospital without any neurological complications.

During the sixth month of my work, my chief really seemed upset about something and started treating me in a manner that was almost rude. He spoke in half syllables, from time to time barked some advice. I couldn't take it for very long.

"Doctor," I asked. "Why are you treating me so badly? What did I do?"

He looked at me for a long time in silence. Finally, he said, "You haven't done anything wrong. I made a colossal mistake. I sent to the board of neurosurgery a good opinion about you, and they shortened your residency from the previously required two years to one. In six months, I will once again be dealing with the same problem!"

I was incredibly happy despite my chief's ill fortune.

During the second half of my stay in Portland, my father fell ill. He started coughing and losing weight, and there were threads of blood in his phlegm. An X-ray revealed disseminated tuberculosis in the right lung; there were Koch mycobacterium in the phlegm. The recommendation was that I put my father in an infectious disease hospital. I opposed such a move and kept him at home. He didn't know how to speak English. Still, we had to quarantine him. He was treated with PAS and streptomycin. After a month, he started to improve. By the end of the year, we stopped the treatments.

Fall came, warm and sunny, followed by a rainy and cloudy winter. My residency was reaching its end. In December the board was organizing a written examination for finishing residents. This was the first part. The second was an oral examination to be taken later.

There were only two doctors qualifying for the exam in Good Samaritan Hospital—Dr. Smith and myself. Dr. Raaf got two thick sealed folders containing the entirety of the written exam. Smith and I were put in a conference room with each of us at either end of the long table. One of the administrative workers was to watch us to ensure that the exam was taken properly. It was a timed exam. At a certain moment, we were told to open the folder and respond to the questions. It was a multiple-choice exam. For each question, there were various answers, and you had to choose the correct one. The material was broad. It encompassed not only the surgical aspect of neurosurgery but also the diagnostic and neuroradiological components. Most of the puzzles didn't cause me much trouble, though there were a few that I couldn't answer. I marked those answers randomly, counting on the fact that at least some of the guesses might be right.

I got a response from the board very soon. I had done better than most of those taking the exam. Thanks to that, the board didn't require me to wait the usual two years before taking the oral exam, which was required to become board certified.

So, I had to think about finding work. I was offered a lucrative practice in Oregon in a beautiful neighborhood. I knew, though, that I had to be better prepared for the oral examination. In order to do it I needed to be employed at a university center. I chose New York, as I was now familiar with the city. The department of neurosurgery at New York University, as it was throughout America, was linked to a network of hospitals that were at the proper professional level of work and training in neurosurgery. One of them was St. Vincent's Hospital located in the heart of Greenwich Village, a neighborhood in Manhattan where, in those days, mostly artists, painters, and sculptors, the "gypsies" of New York, lived. I got a position at that hospital as a neurosurgeon, a "full-time attending in neurosurgery," with a rather low salary for the title—$25,000 a year. The chief of the department was Dr. Rovit.

The day came to say goodbye to Dr. Raaf, Mason, and the "Witch of the North"—Ruby Waterson. They said kind farewells. I was sad to leave, especially Dr. Raaf. He managed to put forth some humor and kindness. He said jokingly, "Well then, I gave you a beating, right?"

Years later I met up with him at one of the conferences on the west coast. I went to him with reverence; he was truly my mentor, as Dr. Choróbski had once been. We went for dinner. He told me a lot about the circumstances in Oregon and about his personal activities at the university. He asked how I was doing, how I was managing. It got late, and I had a flight to the east coast in two hours. He didn't pay much attention to this.

"I'll take you to the airport," he decided suddenly.

We took a taxi. After getting out, I again starting saying good-bye to Raaf.

"I'll go with you. You have to wait anyway, so we can keep talking."

He took me all the way to the gate and waited until the moment when I had to board. I saw him then for the last time.

My farewell from the "Witch" was also kind. For the next twenty years, we exchanged Christmas cards. Ruby wrote long letters full of the latest gossip from Good Samaritan Hospital. She died of breast cancer with metastasis. I learned about it in a letter from Dr. Raaf. He knew that I had always stayed in touch with Ruby.

Now, already old, I often think of them. I have one special warm place for them in my heart, which will be there until my last breath.

Our return to New York happened in very different conditions. We had left behind most of our old things from the New York flea market, much to the delight of the old retired woman who owned the house. We sent the piano, radio, and car by train. And again, we went on our way, this time by plane.

For the New Year of 1969, we again stayed in the same old, cockroach-infested Wales Hotel. I had to find a permanent apartment close to the hospital. I soon found a nice three-room place with two bathrooms on the eleventh floor of a building on Broadway, close to St. Vincent's Hospital. The building was new and had an underground garage. As I had begun to earn more we could shop, finally, for furniture. The living room was connected by a wide entryway to the dining room. My mother sewed a curtain to divide the two rooms. Our furnishings now included two couches, a dining room table with nice chairs, and some good mattresses. We also had a redwood table that I refurbished myself; it was an antique and looked quite elegant. The picture was completed by a piano and curtains on the windows. The view from the eleventh floor was impressive. It was also relatively close to Times Square, which shone at night with the lights of advertisements and was full of movie theaters, stores, and restaurants.

I started working at St. Vincent's Hospital—for the first time as a fully licensed American neurosurgeon. The chief of the ward, Dr. Rovit, was the opposite of Dr. Raaf. He had a vast amount of theoretical knowledge. At a patient's bedside, he could fluidly cite all the pertinent literature on the subject at hand. His one fault, however, was that God hadn't given him much talent as a surgeon. We had five residents. Since Dr. Ravit was primarily involved in theoretical aspects of neurosurgery all major decisions were made by the chief resident. He also would perform most of the operations. Of course, from the beginning, Dr. Rovit and I clashed. We simply didn't like one another. He treated me sarcastically, though he didn't interfere with my clinical work. I operated mainly on the hospital patients, not private cases, and took care of all the consults. I had my own office, a secretary, and a team of residents at my disposal—and for my needs, very little work. The hospital was pleased with me, however, because I worked much more productively than my predecessors. I shared call with Dr. Rovit. I had to be by the phone and, when the chief resident called me about an admission, I had to determine the orders with him and, if need be, go to the hospital to operate together.

My position at St. Vincent's Hospital qualified me to be a neurosurgery instructor at New York University. Each week, I would go there for meetings in which we discussed atypical and rare clinical cases.

During my first stay in New York, I had picked up a little bit of Spanish, as there is a large Latino population there. I could even do a neurological examination in that language, gathering the basic information about the patient. Still, I couldn't understand regular conversations, which showed me that my knowledge of Spanish was not that great. At one of these weekly meetings at New York University, a patient was brought in who didn't speak a word of English. I managed to somehow communicate with her. All those who were there thought that I spoke the language fluently and asked for all the details of the patient history. I was not able to do it, but the people around me wouldn't believe that my Spanish was so limited.

My daily responsibilities at St. Vincent's Hospital usually took me about three hours. I had the rest of the time to myself. As an attending on salary, I had to stay there for the rest of the work hours. That forced free time was a saving grace. During these hours, I studied neurosurgery and neuroradiology articles. I looked for old articles in the library at publications going back to the '30s. I got through several large volumes of surgical technique, diagnosis, and therapy. I knew that the oral exam awaiting me in May was made up of not only neurosurgery but also of neuroradiology, neuropathology, neuroanatomy, and general surgery. While I was pretty well oriented in subjects surrounding neurosurgery, I had weaknesses in general neurology, particularly in hereditary and inflammatory viral diseases. This material was especially troublesome for me, because, in practice, I didn't come into contact with these illnesses. General surgery was even worse, especially surgery of the abdomen. I was just plain weak in this area.

One of the pluses of this hospital was a huge, rich library, as well as one of the best collections of microscopic histological samples of all the diseases of the brain in the United States. Preparing for the exam, I spent hours staring into a microscope, evaluating characteristic traits of various illnesses. Among other things, I was struck by the deterioration of brain tissue in alcoholics. I knew that alcoholism was destructive, but only then did I see the extent of the damage done.

The exam was to take place at Northwestern University in Chicago. The supervisor of the committee was Dr. Odom, the same one who had given me "fatherly" advice. I went a day early. I reported to the exam at eight o'clock in the morning. From the early hours of the day, it was hot, humid, and sultry. The building didn't have air-conditioning. I saw a group of people sentenced to the same chore in the exam rooms. Odom came out to us and gave each of us a card with a schedule of the various segments of the exam. At nine o'clock, I was to report to room five, at ten o'clock to room eight, etc.

In the first designated room, I had to take the radiology portion of the exam. I was harassed by three examiners; when one got tired, another would take over, and then a third. I was shown dozens of X-rays and asked for diagnoses in each case. The cases were not obvious. If they seemed easy you might be sure there was something hidden that was easy to miss. For example, I was shown an image of a subdural hematoma—an obvious diagnosis on the basis of the performed arteriogram. Knowing that there weren't any easy answers here, and seeing the obvious hematoma, I suspected there was some kind of trick. I didn't say anything, just carefully analyzed the film. And then I glimpsed an aneurism that wasn't that easily visible on one of the arteries. My diagnosis was correct.

Then, I was shown a radionuclear image of a sagittal tumor with all the characteristic features of a meningioma. With a quiet, crafty voice, I was asked if this test would be sufficient. I responded that I would also do an arteriogram. It turned out that the mass was not a meningioma but a rare cerebrovascular accident only visible on an arteriogram.

I have only recounted a few illustrative moments from this exam. There was an overwhelming amount of diagnostic material shown to me. After an hour, they courteously thanked me, and I knew that I had answered all the questions correctly. It was ten o'clock, and the next torture-room awaited me. I went into the neuroanatomy exam. The same situation awaited me—three to one, an hour of battle. One of the professors, with clearly Semitic features, nearly jumped on me, "You Pole! Maybe we should examine in Polish?"

This was a provocation. I responded calmly that I could answer in English. He told me to draw the anatomical cross section of the spinal cord. He said something else under his breath. Without hesitation, I drew that cross-section on the board.

"Wrong!" he said. "You don't know what you're doing! I asked you for the cross section at the level of the first cervical vertebrae. You don't know anything!"

Not saying a word, I drew the cross-section for which he asked. After all, I knew neuroanatomy pretty well.

This lover of Polish people continued to attack me.

"So, let's see what else you don't know!"

We were speaking in English, so the other two understood everything. One of the examiners got up at a certain moment and said quietly, "Professor, sit down. I will examine this candidate."

Only then did the real exam begin. I responded to all the questions with no mistakes! He thanked me, and I again found myself in the corridor. This time it was neuropathology. Samples of various parts of the brain were on the table. There were also several microscopes by the window. I was confronted with three big-shot examiners ready to devour me. We went from one sample to the next. I was to describe them and determine the nature of the illness. It was going rather smoothly. We got to the microscopes. There was one sample after another.

I heard, "Don't describe it. Give a diagnosis."

And that part of the exam also went smoothly. I recognized some of the samples immediately, as some were the same as those that I had studied at St. Vincent's Hospital. At the end, I got another sample and new instructions, "Don't give a diagnosis; just describe exactly what you see."

I got through that test without a problem.

Then it was time for general neurology. As usual, there were three examiners and endless questions.

"Describe possible neurological complications of labor."

I immediately started speaking about eclampsia; I was rather well oriented about most of these complications.

"I'm not asking for the complications for the mother; I'm asking for complications for the fetus."

For a moment, I was stuck. But I quickly remembered and recited everything that I knew on that subject. The second examiner asked me for the classification of viral infection of the brain and a detailed description of various anatomical and clinical changes in the brain. I got through that obstacle.

Finally, I got to the exam in general surgery. The first question was about shock. Without hesitating, I started describing and discussing the mechanism of shock and its complications. The next question was in reference to ulcerative colitis. And I got through that one okay, too—the night spent studying the surgery textbook at the last minute had really helped me with that one. Then, I got the following question.

"Please describe the detailed surgical technique of excision of the large bowel in this illness."

I had never performed such an operation, though I had an idea of what was involved.

Luckily, another examiner interrupted. "Listen! What do you want from this poor guy? After all, he's a neurosurgeon; he has never done such a surgery in his life, nor will he do one!"

So, in the end, I didn't have to linger on the large bowel.

I still had to take the exam in neurosurgery. Among the three examiners was Dr. Love—his last name really went against the nature of its owner. He was a professor from Boston, from Massachusetts General Hospital. He was dreaded by all those taking the exam. Before the exam, I had to put together a complete list of surgeries that I had performed over the years. I had done a lot of percutaneous chordotomies in Roswell Park Institute and at St. Vincent's Hospital.

Dr. Love, older, withered, with a penetrating and shrewd glance, began first. He glanced at the list of my surgeries.

"I see that you have done a lot of percutaneous chordotomies. Describe the technique of this surgery."

I calmly described the whole procedure knowing, however, what this old fox was leading towards. It just so happened that while I was looking through all that old literature, I came upon his old work about anatomical variations of the localization of the dentate ligament—the main anatomical marker of these surgeries. I played along, knowing what was at stake. I purposely lingered on the description of the procedure, going into the details of all the elements. I saw how impatient Love was getting.

In the end he asked, "Your marker is dentate ligament, right?"

I didn't have any doubt for what he was going.

"Of course," I replied. "Unfortunately, we don't have a better reference point."

"So, you think that the dentate ligament is the right anatomical marker?"

Then, I put my ace on the table.

"Professor, how could I even think that? After all, you wrote in your article in the '40s about the anatomical variations of this ligament! It would not make any sense not to take these variations into account during a surgical procedure—you have to rely mostly on physiological data!"

The other two burst out laughing.

"Bill," one of them said, clearing his throat from laughter. "You wanted to get him on that one, but he got you!"

Love smiled. He turned to me and added, "Don't be such a smart-aleck, or you might not be able to save yourself!"

He was, however, pleased in the end with my response. The end of the exam was almost relaxing.

The marathon reached its end at two o'clock in the afternoon. After four o'clock, I was to report for information about the date of the exam results. Meanwhile, the whole committee deliberated. I was so exhausted that I barely made it to the nearest restaurant to use the bathroom and finally eat something. I went back before four. The committee session had already finished. I saw only Dr. Odom.

From the time of our encounter in his office in North Carolina, he had a soft spot for me.

"Professor, please! Did I pass?"

It was obvious, as the supervisor of the committee, that he couldn't openly tell me my score.

"You know, you scoundrel, that I can't tell you that! Don't bother me!"

I didn't give up. I insisted, this time on just a hint, "yes" or "no." Finally, he smiled.

"Go home and know that you have nothing to worry about."

I thanked him profusely. He just waved his hand and walked off.

After a few weeks, I got a document stating that I had earned the title, Diplomate of the American Board of Neurosurgical Surgery.

So finally I had reached my ultimate professional goal. How long and bumpy the road was to that title! Three elements came together to lead to this success—work, perseverance, and a big dose of luck. Yes, luck, amidst human misfortune—for if the war in Vietnam had not broken out, I never would have gotten a neurosurgery residency. When I look back now in hindsight on the chain of fortunate events that surrounded me, I am deeply convinced that if it wasn't the whole hand of Providence caring for me, then it was certainly a finger pointing me in the right direction.

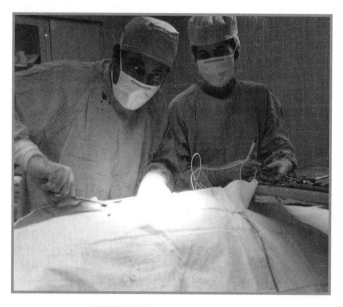

OPERATING ON THE SPINE

After two years of work, I had the right to apply for the next step—the title of "Fellow of American College of Surgeons" or FACS. It was a prestigious title, as well as proof of full acceptance, in terms of "He's one of us now." I sent out the necessary papers and documentation of the surgeries I had performed, which was one of

WITH DR. SIDHU DURING RESIDENCY AT
METROPOLITAN HOSPITAL IN NEW YORK

the conditions of being accepted, and waited for a response. After
a few months, I got word that I was to report at Mount Carmel
Hospital in Detroit at a particular time to go before a committee.

The secretary led me to the conference room. About eight surgeons sat at the long table, among whom were two neurosurgeons
I knew. They asked me to sit down and began asking me exam
questions about neurosurgery. I was dumbfounded, as I had not
expected to be walking into an exam! I collected myself quickly
and began answering the questions in turn. It didn't last long.
They thanked me, and I left the room. After a few weeks, I got a
letter saying that the formal initiation would take place in Chicago
in six months.

4

A Brush with Disaster

CONTINUING WORK AT St. Vincent's Hospital was quickly becoming a road leading to nowhere. It was not developing my professional ambitions or my skills in surgery. I wanted to be active, to work at full force. My wish was to find myself in a large university center, though the chances of that were slim. I asked the secretary at Cornell University in New York if I could speak with the chief of neurosurgery; I was referred to the senior resident!

The only chance I saw was to join a neurosurgery group in private practice. They were self-employed and had income not from a salary but only if they had work. Income was proportional to performance. This didn't bother me. I wanted to work intensively. The one problem with going in this direction for my career was that I would again be outside a university setting, in which the work could be much more challenging. For example, it is very difficult to organize a team to operate on temporal epilepsy in a private practice. In a university center, it is incomparably easier.

Looking at some advertisements in a neurosurgery bulletin, I found a few places that were looking for a new hire. Among them was an ad from Dr. Berke in Detroit. He wrote that he worked with another neurosurgeon, had a large practice, and needed a third, because they could not handle all the work between just the two of them. He was offering $35,000 a year, as well as full participation in the corporation. I knew that there was a large Polish population in Detroit, as well as a climate that was similar to the one in which I grew up. I went.

Dr. Berke was the son of a doctor. His building was in a shady neighborhood, but it was very well equipped. Berke was Jewish, thin, agile, with dark eyes and curly hair. He was convincing in saying that the three of us could work in the best hospitals, that we would create competition in the medical field, and that one day we might create our own neurosurgery institute. These were quite optimistic visions, but his plans appealed to me. Dr. Rotter made a very good impression on me, too. He had recently been able to remove his army uniform. He didn't look Jewish, though that came out later.

I signed a contract and left St. Vincent's Hospital in the middle of October 1969, much to Dr. Rovit's dismay, as I had been very helpful, operating on patients even during the night. The administration was also sad to see me go. I had a reputation as a good and honest doctor.

And again, we were on the move. We sent the furniture, and drove from New York to Detroit through the mountains in Pennsylvania. I drove into some unbelievable fog. I could barely see the hood of the car. I couldn't pull over or I might have driven off a cliff or got hit from the back by another car. Fortunately, I could see the lights of a huge truck in front of me. At a certain, really the last, moment, I saw an exit from the highway and the lights of a motel further on. I was covered in sweat from long hours of worry. The next morning, we reached Detroit. I called Berke, and arranged to meet him.

I listened to his advice and rented a large, third-floor apartment on the block.

Berke and Rotter worked in several hospitals and got surgical cases through consults in hospitals or by admitting patients in their offices who were referred to them by doctors in other specialties.

I was given a good room in which to work, provided with a secretary, and began to operate, mostly in Holy Cross Hospital, located on the border of the Polish neighborhood. I quickly figured out that the functioning of this neurosurgical corporation was rather strange. Rotter was unhappy. He told me that he didn't want to have anything to do with Berke and that he was going to leave. He didn't give a concrete reason for his decision. Berke mostly stayed in his own office. Patients would come to him who didn't look like they were seriously ill. His office had an EEG room and a nuclear scan. All the patients would undergo these two tests. The cost of these tests and the money they brought in was much higher than the cost of a regular doctor's visit. I also noticed that there were discussions with individuals who had nothing to do with medicine in Dr. Berke's office! These were other Jewish people who were working with him.

Soon thereafter, he told me that it would be good if I would send him patients who had experienced injuries in car accidents, even minor injuries; they would undergo tests on that moneymaking diagnostic machinery. Then, he said that I should get in touch with a lawyer who handled indemnity claims for such injured persons. And the indemnity claims were enormous. If the diagnosis proved a more severe injury, the indemnity claims were even higher. The lawyers working with them were paid very well!

I understood that I had fallen into a quagmire. I was horrified. I didn't know what to do, or how to get out of it. I was really impeded by my financial situation. I had just gotten a small house, and the payments were big. With a pang, I remembered the high ethical standards at Good Samaritan Hospital in Portland.

Amidst these conflicts, a saving anchor fell straight from the sky in the form of a phone call from Dr. Gurdijan.

"It's Gurdijan. I wanted to get together with you. I'd like to invite you to lunch at the Athletic Club. Does that work for you?"

I quickly remembered that Gurdijan was that representative of the board of neurosurgery who had evaluated the neurosurgery ward at Metropolitan Hospital. I had taken him around that entire day serving as the main source of information.

I agreed to the lunch meeting. Gurdijan, whose family was from Russian-occupied Georgia, was an older man of about sixty years with a hefty frame. He was a well-known senior among all the neurosurgeons in Detroit. After ordering lunch he came right to the point. "Jan, I know that you have gotten yourself into a mess! Your reputation could be completely ruined! You have to leave Berke in the quickest possible way. He is known throughout Detroit as an individual capable of the worst things. I brought you here to this meeting only for this reason, so that you know what you've gotten yourself into!"

"What can I do?" I asked hopelessly. "I have a contract."

"I suggest that you leave there immediately and open your own office. As for the contract—you have to break it! I know that you will do fine even though you are an unknown Polish man here in Detroit."

I talked to my parents about it. They had the same viewpoint—leave the crook immediately, regardless of the consequences.

I got a loan for ten thousand dollars at the bank with no collateral because of my professional qualifications—something that was really unheard of at the time. I rented some office space in a building that housed other doctors' offices. I bought the cheapest and most essential furniture and hired a young woman as a secretary. Then, I went back to Berke's building, took my diplomas off the walls, put them in the car, and drove away.

"Why are you doing this?" they asked.

They heard, "The answer is obvious, so I will keep it to myself."

At the time, I was working in two hospitals, Holy Cross and Saratoga. I informed both of them about my departure from Berke's practice and put together a formal application for surgical rights in those hospitals—for individual rights, not as Dr. Berke's partner. Silence fell. Four days later, I got five consults, among them one surgery. I relaxed. I knew that I would not be broken. Dr. Berke was furious. In the beginning, he demanded that I be removed from the physicians staff of these hospitals, because I had gotten there as his partner and now no longer was. The hospital administrations and staff refused his demand. Then, he filed a complaint with the public prosecutor that I had stolen his surgical instruments!

Indeed, because the hospitals didn't have several of the necessary tools used mainly in surgeries of intervertebral discs, I carried them with me. They weren't worth a lot at all, and I had simply forgotten about them. After receiving a summons from the prosecutor, I was referred to a lawyer, a kind German named Waldman. He calmed me down. He told me to give him the misappropriated instruments for safekeeping and made an appointment with the prosecutor.

We stood in front of the prosecutor.

"I have here before me a complaint that you stole surgical instruments. Is this true?"

Waldman replied, "These instruments were not stolen. I have them with me and can immediately turn them over to you."

"If that's the case," said the watchman of law, "then the matter has resolved itself. Thank you both."

Berke's maneuver was unsuccessful, though it cost me and my parents some health. And that was, of course, all that vengeful crook intended.

A few days later, I got a formal notice that a lawsuit was being filed against me for breaking my contract. Berke wanted financial compensation. I don't know what arguments Waldman used to convince Berke to drop the claim. I wonder if he threatened to reveal his swindle with the indemnity claims.

Holy Cross was a hospital run by nuns. Many of them were of Polish descent. They treated me very warmly. I received similar kindness at Saratoga Hospital, as no one there was fond of Berke. They most often called in Dr. Granger—a neurosurgeon with an office in the same building as mine. We were competitors, but our encounters were always friendly.

My practice grew larger. I was doing two, then five major surgeries a week. The money from the insurance companies that was supposed to come after the surgeries was not coming. I didn't know why. In order to get the fees, you had to fill out the proper forms and send them to the insurance companies. My secretary didn't know how to do it, so I filled them out myself. And one day, I saw her take these forms and put them in one of the desk drawers, which was already filled with similar forms. I ran over to her. I opened the drawer and took out all the bills that should have been paid long ago!

"Why are you doing this? For God's sake, why didn't you send them out?"

She got red in the face. She cried, "My husband and I are communists! We have to destroy capitalism always and everywhere as much as we can!"

I don't need to add that her desk was emptied the same day. Soon, the money owed me was sent. The loan which I obtained in November, I was able to repay in March.

5

The Final Days of My Father

AGAIN, SPRING CAME. In the back of the house was a small garden full of flowers. I can still see my father warming himself in the sun on a bench. Our quickly growing dachshund, Dar, was at his feet.

Dr. Zukowski would visit us quite frequently; he was of Polish descent, born in the United States and able to speak perfect Polish. He was an old bachelor and a colleague of mine from the operating room. I most often operated with his assistance. In this stage of life in Detroit, we didn't have any other Polish friends. Every once in a while, we would go to the Polish neighborhood, which was now becoming increasingly black, called Hamtramck. Going into the Polish stores, we would buy bread—Polish bread!—cold cuts, and "krowki" (fudge candies) from the old country. My mother constantly missed Poland. She didn't feel well here. My father, worn out by his difficult life, was able to find peace and appreciate America much better. He would always say, "You are now responsible for everything, and I am here as a permanent tourist!" He suffered, however, from atrial fibrillation, easily got tired, even after fairly minimal exertion. He was also mildly incapacitated by hemiparesis after the stroke. He appreciated my accomplishments, our status, and our home and garden. He could call it all his own.

His inseparable companion was a puppy dachshund that he just adored. My father had a certain ability to befriend any dog, even the most dangerous ones. Years ago, when we were on vacation, a huge dog tore off his chain and ran towards us. The owner was horrified. My father put out his hand to the beast, let him smell it, then started talking to the dog, and in a few minutes, they were best fiends.

Using an outdated phrase from the communist jargon one could say that the meeting was "in the atmosphere of full appreciation and understanding."

My father was also strange in another way. He wouldn't even kill a cockroach. He shooed flies from the house with a piece of cloth, usually unsuccessfully. How was his relationship to his only son? On the one hand, he had a lot of admiration that I was managing in such difficult circumstances in a foreign country and that I continuously got through difficult times. On the other hand, he said that I was a "butcher," because I could "cut people up!" This mix of feelings—positive and critical—created a unique father-son bond between us.

He loved the garden and knew what it took to maintain it. He was also an expert at planting and grafting trees. While working in the garden, he would sit on the bench and direct me through the process from there.

But, my father's life was irrevocably reaching its end.

And now this is what my typical workday was like. I went to the hospital in the morning. I was then on the staff at three hospitals—Holy Cross, Saratoga, and St. Joseph's. If there happened to be a surgery scheduled, then I would be in the operating room around 7:30 a.m. After the surgery, I would do rounds in each hospital, as well as consults for patients who had been referred to me by other doctors. At three in the afternoon, during the week, I saw patients at my office. These were postoperative patients and also new patients referred to me by various doctors. I had a standard history and physical report for each patient. The secretary collected basic information, and then during the time of interviewing the patient, I added to and corrected this information. I also documented neurological examinations. Then, in the course of things, I would have a conversation with the patient and the family. If I had determined that surgery was needed, I explained the surgical procedure using proper models, talking about the expected results and the potential complications. I also told them about statistical cases of fatality in the area of this illness and procedure. I then dictated a letter to the referring doctor in the presence of the patient or the family. It was usually two full typed pages. The letter presented the full documentation of the diagnosis of the illness and proposed treatment. A modified form of this letter could be used as a report for the patient's insurance company.

I made it a rule that all of the documentation had to be taken care of immediately at the present moment. An additional benefit of this rule, that I hadn't originally appreciated, was that the patient and the family heard what I was dictating to be recorded.

Seeing patients usually lasted late into the evening. During breaks, I took care of the many phone calls from hospital nurses and patients. After getting home and having a late dinner, I still wasn't on my own time. I was on-call twenty-four hours a day for emergencies. I received phone calls at the latest hours of the night. My body got used to being able to fall asleep immediately after giving orders, though I often had to go into the hospital at night to scrub in on an emergency surgery, as after a car accident injury or a gunshot wound to the head or back. The next morning, another normal workday awaited me. I was often unbelievably exhausted.

The closest person to my mother and me in Poland was Prelate Stanislaw Klimm, my mother's uncle, who christened her, married her, and later christened me.

He was a rather uncommon person. He was very intelligent, speaking fluent French, German, and Russian, with wide interests and great tolerance. He didn't try to persuade anyone in the family who visited him to go to church, but when he turned around from the altar, he was always pleased to see us at mass. A patriot and an activist from before the First World War, he worked with youth organizations. He often spoke more about Poland than religious subjects from the pulpit.

Despite the great age difference between us, we were tightly linked. We understood each other. When I was leaving Poland, Uncle Klimm, already a prelate, was the parish priest of the Ujazd parish near Lodz. It was very hard for me to say goodbye to him. He didn't say anything to me, but I knew that he did not approve of my departure. He saw it as a shunning of my responsibilities as a Polish patriot and also a sort of depletion of educated minds from Poland.

While I was working at Roswell Park Institute, I received word from one of the members of our family that Father Klimm had been transferred in retirement to an apartment in Lodz. A nun, Sister Roma, took care of him. I knew her and liked and respected her. The modest pension was not enough for all the priest's needs. My cousin added that no one in his family had the means to help the priest financially. This surprised me. About five people working in various places had been educated either through his efforts or at times through the priest's personal financial help. It became obvious to me that the responsibility of giving my uncle help was being thrown onto me. I was happy to do it. I could send the priests monthly sums that would be enough for him to safely and comfortably live out the rest of his difficult and just life.

One night in 1971—I don't exactly remember the date—I woke up knowing that Uncle Klimm had died right at that moment! This wasn't a nightmare. No, I knew that that's what had happened, that he had passed away. I woke up my parents and told them that "Uncle" (that's what we called him) had passed away. They didn't want to believe me, especially the next day when we received a letter from him and nothing in it indicated that he was feeling at all unwell. I called Lodz. I found out that he had died at exactly that hour when I had woken up with the full conviction of his passing! Years ago, I experienced a similar situation; just before the sudden death of my patient, I had a foreboding that he was no longer alive, though at the moment I got the premonition, he was standing on his own two feet talking to a nurse with me next to him!

In April of 1972, having saved some money, I started looking around for a larger house. The one we had was hot in the summer and cold in the winter. It didn't have air-conditioning, nor was it possible to install central air.

The prices of the better homes in Grosse Pointe were not what I could afford. But, on the same street where my house stood (on Washington Road), closer to the lake and in a more exclusive area, I found a huge house built with very fine-quality brick on a large property. An older woman lived there, and after she died, her sons, who were scattered all over America, decided to get rid of the trouble of having it and sold the property. The price was favorable.

The interior was awful—gray ceilings, dirty walls, warped windows, a thick layer of old grime in the kitchen. The floors were covered with disgustingly dirty old rugs. My mother didn't even want to consider buying it. My father, however, quietly walked around all the rooms, looked at the walls, floors and installation, and said, "Janusz, buy this house. There will be a lot of work to do and a lot of extra costs, but it will be a beautiful residence."

And my father's word was final. I bought the house taking out a mortgage and selling the old one for not much of a profit. I hired carpenters and bricklayers. We tore the dirty curtains off the windows, and suddenly the house began to look very bright. It had large windows on all sides. The bricklayers tore down two walls combining some small rooms upstairs. They built a wall in the dinette area, a room alongside the kitchen. I set up a new bathroom upstairs, the carpenters changed the cabinets in the kitchen, and a painter got to work painting the walls.

We moved in during the month of May, in the middle of the renovations. Two rooms were ready for us to live in, and the kitchen was restored to proper function. I put in the windows, refinished the floor with a rented machine, and lay down the fireplace tiles myself. This took up any free time I had outside work.

The yard seemed to be small and unkempt, covered in weeds and bushes, with a few old fruit trees. There was no landscaping. I put up a wire fence. Then my mother and I got to work digging up trees and shrubs. My father was getting more and more weak.

However he would sit on a chair, directing me in the landscaping work and enjoy the company of the puppy.

My mother indeed had good reasons for her opposition to this investment. The house required an incredible amount of work. My father was also right, however, in that the place was really beautiful, and it was in a good neighborhood with a lot of property. Years later, I was left alone in this large, beautiful house with its yard, fountain, and central statue that symbolized youth and life. I was left alone, but it was always full of memories, feelings, experiences, and thoughts of those who shared my joys and sorrows, and who were gone forever.

Christmastime came. We celebrated Christmas Eve, and some friends came over the next day. Then, my father suddenly fell ill. At first, he began vomiting. Then, the following day, he developed progressive paralysis. His condition was getting worse by the hour. I took him half-conscious in an ambulance to the hospital I trusted most—Holy Cross. The next day, he lost all consciousness. He was breathing, but he didn't react to voices and barely reacted to pain. I knew that he had had a stroke in the area of the basal artery of the brain. His condition was terrible. The nurses, who liked me a lot, cared for my father as best they could. He was fed by a nasogastric tube and given oxygen; he looked like he was peacefully sleeping. I stood over him and looked at his face, in which there was neither pain nor suffering, at his closed eyes, at his hands, so familiar to me, lying motionless on either side of the blanket. I was powerless—I, an accomplished neurosurgeon and his son—and I could not help this patient, my very own father!

I was very shaken up. At the same time I had to function within my work frame. My father's condition didn't change for several weeks. Each day, I would go to his room. I would stand there powerless and then move on to take care of patients. One of the days, I had to perform a particularly difficult and complicated brain surgery. On the way to the operating room, I went in to my father's room. The same image as always—closed eyes, calm breathing, seemingly asleep. I went closer to him. "My God, this is hard for me," I breathed. "How can I do this surgery? Where will I find the concentration to do this?"

And then, suddenly, I had the feeling that my father understood and was sharing my burden. The feeling was incredibly strong, almost tangible. I knew that the barriers that had once divided us no longer existed. I did the surgery well, and Dr. Zukowski, assisting me at this surgery, noticed, "Janusz, you had especially little blood loss!" In other words, the patient had not lost much blood. From that day, "my" surgical blood loss was significantly lower. Even the nurses and assistants noticed.

My father died on February 7 at around four a.m. A phone call from the hospital woke me up, informing me of his passing. I went to the hospital with my mother. The body was still lying in the bed, but my father was not there anymore.

I had to take care of the funeral arrangements. There was a funeral home in Grosse Pointe named Verhayden. My father's earthly remains were taken there. I went to the office of that large funeral home. A polite man with a routinely sympathetic look plastered on his face wearing a black, somewhat beat up suit and similar tie, led me to a room where there were coffins on display. He praised them. First, he showed the most expensive, with a comfortable mattress on springs! I was shocked. Advertising the comfort of the dead seemed like a sadistic joke to me. I chose a proper coffin that was made of metal, so as to keep out humidity.

I saw my father the next day. He had been preserved, his hair was combed, and his face had been visibly retouched. We buried him in the tuxedo that I had brought from Poland and had only worn once to the Warsaw Philharmonic ball. The coffin was set up in a large room, surrounded by elegant chairs. I stood there frozen, looking at my father, at his so familiar hands, at the motionless face covered in lofty peace, at the sharp line of his nose. It was him, handsome in the majesty of death—and yet not him, because he didn't have his usual smile, movements, mannerisms—all of that had disappeared, had fallen behind the dead mask of his face. I couldn't even really pray. I saw as people knelt down to pray at the foot of the coffin and listened to their condolences; all of them seemed like a group of people from some unknown reality. I looked at my mother, standing at the side of the coffin, dressed in black. She looked at my father with a peaceful glance that was fixed infinitely further away.

The priest came and said the rosary. Evening was falling, and the mourners began to leave.

I went home with my mother after the funeral. The silence of the walls of the house was striking. Even during the weeks when my father had already been lying unconscious in the hospital, I was kept company by the feeling that he had just stepped out for a moment but was still around. Now, there was nothing left of these illusions. Now, there was only memory, the invisible wall of time—memory and remembrance—the soothing shadow of destiny.

We buried my father at a small cemetery called the Sacred Heart of Mary. In all the other cemeteries, there was a rule that there could be no tombstone, just a small sign lost in the grass. On this old, mostly Polish cemetery, I had to buy five spaces in order to erect a monument. The coffin was not immediately lowered into the grave, only after the funeral, when it was placed in a cement crypt that had already been dug into the ground.

After getting home, we were greeted by our dog, who was also sad, feeling the seriousness of the situation with his faultless perception. He missed my father's presence terribly for he had spent most of his life with him.

I could cope with my father's death much better than my mother could. I had to return to work the following day to take care of my professional responsibilities. My mother stayed inside the walls of the house, alone with her thoughts and sorrow. She wished to put a monument on the grave as quickly as possible. I sketched a model for the monument of my own impression of Sorrowful Mary. I presented the project to a large firm. They hired a sculptor from Chicago, a Czech. He carved the figure of Sorrowful Mary out of granite. Being a talented artist he was able to capture in stone, the quiet suffering of a Mother who will never forget the sight of her son on the cross.

6

The Vultures Circle

A FEW MONTHS LATER, I received a desperate phone call. Dr. Granger's wife was calling—he was then a close friend of mine. Her husband had a heart attack and had been clinically dead but they had resuscitated him. She asked me to take care of his practice. I agreed willingly. Through an agency, I found a secretary, Doris, a lady of hefty stature with a look on her face that was somewhat reminiscent of a bulldog. She was in her late forties. She worked well and honestly, didn't steal some of my money like her predecessor, nor did she "fight against capitalism" with the same results for me. Her one fault was that she lacked patience with respect to some of the more capricious patients.

Dr. Granger regained his health slowly over a long period of time. He always worried about his practice, if he would even have any patients left, or if I wouldn't ultimately appropriate some of his sick little lambs.

I found out on what day he planned to make his first visit to the office after his illness. Doris and I tried to arrange things so that the moment he walked through the waiting-room door, he would see five patients waiting for his arrival. Tears welled up in his eyes. From that day forward, we became even closer friends.

Dr. Granger's illness meant that St. John's Hospital, the largest hospital in the eastern Detroit metropolitan area, was lacking a neurosurgeon for the trauma rotation in the emergency room. Haddad, Latimer, and Scratch were the neurosurgeons working there, though the two latter ones worked mostly in the northern part of the city and could not take on responsibility in the emergency room as they lived too far away. There was a moratorium in place at this hospital against hiring neurosurgeons onto the staff. It had to do mainly with protecting the interests of the neurosurgeons already working there. Granger's illness created an opening. The hospital asked me in writing if I would agree to have surgical privileges there and to admit my patients for surgical treatment. I had always wanted to work in this hospital and would sometimes look with sorrow and envy. St. John's was then a large, well-renowned medical center, training residents in various specialties.

I was accepted onto the staff of St. John's Hospital in a matter of a few weeks. The emergency room was active, and being called in at night was not a rare occurrence. I didn't get any consults from the practicing doctors for a while, because everyone referred to Dr. Haddad. They simply didn't know me. I had to earn a good reputation for myself first.

A woman in a serious state was admitted to Holy Cross. She suffered from obesity and swelling of the legs. In the emergency room, to which she had been directed, her blood pressure was 260/220! She had a long history of high blood pressure and severe kidney damage. She was brought to the hospital because of a subarachnoid hemorrhage caused by a bleeding aneurism. We moved her to the ICU and lowered her blood pressure, and then we lessened the swelling of the brain with steroids. The aneurism was no longer bleeding; otherwise, she would have died long ago. She regained her health slowly, but her basic illness, which was high blood pressure and kidney illness, along with the beginnings of diabetes, didn't improve. I performed an arteriogram of the brain that showed an aneurism in the frontal part of the brain, in the place connecting the left and right anterior cerebral arteries. The aneurism was large and difficult to operate. The fatality rate for surgery in such cases was about thirty percent at that time.

An article by a neurologist from New York named Schlosberg appeared during that period that was based on a rather vast amount of material in which he showed that maintaining a much lower blood pressure could, to a great extent, prevent the recurrence of bleeding. This patient was getting better. I called in her husband to talk about the situation. He was a train conductor. I explained extensively the whole complicated situation concerning his wife. An obvious deduction with a brain aneurism is surgery, because a second bleeding is almost always fatal. But in the case of this woman, the risk of surgery was much greater because of her basic illnesses and obesity. I presented the husband with two alternatives—either treatment to lower the blood pressure, or surgery. He chose "breaking down" the blood pressure. The patient went home in good condition. After a few months, she was again brought to the emergency room with high blood pressure. She was also drunk! It became apparent that she was not taking the medication given to her and neglected the regular visits to her internist. The emergency room doctor renewed her medications and sent her home.

Another few months went by when she again landed in the hospital in a serious state with a recurrent subarachnoid hemorrhage. I brought her out of it, but this time I was convinced that surgery was essential. The husband agreed to the surgery. I clamped the aneurism without much difficulty. The patient came out of it with no neurological damage. Then, I learned that she spent three months in a psychiatric hospital. In the end, however, she returned to a normal life and raised five children.

I always envisioned the treatment of my patients as a battle for their life and wellbeing. My enemy was incapacitation and the ultimate enemy was death.

In 1973, I was seeing patients in my office as usual, when my secretary informed me that some man wanted to speak with me immediately. Though several patients were waiting, I said to let him in. A young man came up to me and, without saying a word, handed me a pile of papers. He still didn't say anything, turned around, and left. Silently, I looked at the papers. This was documentation, formally compiled and submitted to the court, accusing me of "malpractice" in the case of treating that woman "S." A Jewish lawyer, Mr. "L," the owner of a large law firm—whom I remembered from his frequent visits in Berke's building—was the one representing her. The lawsuit against me stated that Mrs. S unnecessarily suffered and experienced an undeserved injury, because I did not operate on her during her first visit to the hospital!

It's worth adding here that this type of case, about which I didn't know anything at that time, was based on an agreement between the lawyer and the plaintiff for a "contingency fee." According to this agreement the patient didn't pay any costs for the law suit, but if the lawyer won the case, he would take half or one third of the settlement, to which he would also add the costs of service. A client only had to pay thirty dollars to take the matter to court! And in this case, I was being sued for millions of dollars in damages! I was shocked. I tried to convince myself naively that Mrs. "S" survived from her almost fatal situation by a miracle; after all, her husband had decided during a conversation with me and with her that they didn't want to operate at that point. And finally, that she didn't follow the internist's orders, drank, and didn't take her medication!

I had a feeling of overwhelming baseness and pain. The danger of the situation was worsened by the fact that, as a doctor, I was barely insured for $100,000, and here they wanted millions! If I lost the case, I would become a beggar, working to repay the damages.

I collected myself with difficulty but enough so that I could properly see the patients who were still waiting. It was mentioned in the summons that I had to notify my insurance company about the lawsuit filed against me during the next twenty-four hours. And that's what I did. I was put in touch with a lawyer, Mr. "R." His first task was to put together documents for the court in which he denied the allegations on all grounds in my name.

That's how a few months passed. After that time, I got a notice that my defender and I were to report for a deposition led by the lawyer of the opposing side. I didn't know then that this fully documented interrogation was already a part of the judicial case. I was questioned by Lawyer "L's" partner, some Mr. "O," who was also Jewish. He was an incredibly arrogant and ruthless individual. He had carved out a goal of angering me so that I would more readily mess up my statements. I calmed down and understood that I was being threatened and that I had to resist with all my strength. I listened to the questions carefully and answered them calmly, at the same time renouncing and discrediting all the lies that were in turn wrapped up in them. And I was replying under oath!

As a result of this, the lawyer questioning me fell into a complete fury, and the meeting was interrupted.

After some time, I got another notice that there would be a similar meeting. It was very similar in nature, with the one difference being that we completed the deposition.

And so a year went by. In that time, I received summonses for four additional lawsuits, accusing me of more malpractice. The accusing party was the same lawyer. And so, I had five lawsuits at once, and it was becoming obvious a vendetta was at work here. They were simply trying to destroy me. During that time, Dr. Berke became a member of the disciplinary committee of the state office, which gave out the right to practice. He brought forth a case suggesting my professional incompetence, and that legal body got to work. I didn't give up. I worked each day as I always had, though I felt as though my life had been awfully poisoned, as well as my mother's life, who obviously knew about everything that was going on.

One of these summonses was dismissed immediately. I had been accused of causing a stroke by performing an arteriogram through the carotid artery. It turned out that the plaintiff's lawyer had made a small mistake. Namely, that stroke happened on the same side of the brain where the arteriogram was done. Strokes always occur on the opposite side from the lesion and thus it was clear that there was no connection between the procedure and the stroke.

Still, four cases hung before me like the sword of Damocles. In that time, the period lasting from the moment the case was brought to court to its final resolution, lasted several years. I had to live through those years under incredible duress and anticipation of possible catastrophe. It was obviously extremely distressing.

The first positive information I got was the confirmation by the state office that the case brought against me had yielded a negative result, and so that there was no reason to take away my professional privileges. Then, over the course of two years, two other lawsuits were similarly dismissed, as it became clear to Mr. "L" after hearing my responses that he didn't have any chance of winning against me. He preferred not to lose time or incur greater costs for himself. Two summonses still had to be resolved—one in the case of Mrs. "S" and the other, the death of a young woman who had a tumor in the posterior fossa in the cerebellum.

Finally, it came time to go to court. From the beginning, I figured out that the judge's position was not wholly objective. He clearly favored the plaintiff's lawyer. It was well known that lawyer "L," had made a donation of forty thousand dollars for this judge's campaign fund. There were six jurors chosen who were to give the general verdict. The trial began. I also figured out that my lawyer, who was intelligent and quick to react, couldn't really defend me. I imagined the situation simply as a boxing match. I was in the ring, my opponent was Lawyer "L," and my defender was present in the ring, but he could only help me or intervene when the opponent hit me unfairly. My acceptance of this tactic from the very beginning was a saving grace. Despite lawyer "L's" many attacks, I didn't let myself get down or irritated. At one moment, he started yelling in a harsh voice, "You were busy making money; you didn't care what would happen to my client, isn't that true?"

I reacted calmly to this provocation. "In my time, I took a Hippocratic oath obligating me for my entire life. I always do my work in accordance with the principles of this oath as much as I possibly can. I am not a peddler of money like you are!"

He started yelling, this time to the judge, "Your Honor! He offended me! Please, your honor, intervene immediately!"

This time, the judge calmly replied, "You heard what you deserved."

You can imagine what kind of impression this response made on the jury.

The trial went on with some breaks for two weeks. On the second or third day, Mr. "L" brought in his "expert neurologist," who was also Jewish, to testify against me. He was a character free of any moral principles, though he was intelligent; he twisted the facts so as to discredit me. His testimony was undoubtedly damaging for me. The next day, my lawyer had the right to do a cross-examination, to give him questions in my name. I went home with a heavy heart. My lawyer was a good professional, but he didn't know much about all the nuances of medicine. I knew then that I could only get to my persecutor if I could question him myself. But I didn't have the right to do this—only my lawyer could act on my behalf. I spent most of the night making a list of more than one hundred questions, logically following one from the other. In the morning, I gave the list to my lawyer in the courtroom telling him to ask the plaintiff's expert witness only questions from the list—even if he didn't understand them. He agreed willingly. It came time for the cross-examination. The respected expert started speaking loosely, sarcastically, and arrogantly. After the fifth and sixth question, touching on essential details, he starting squirming in his chair, which was somewhat lower than the judge's podium. You could see that he had not expected such an attack.

It all had to do with the fact that Mrs. "S" suffered from hypertensive encephalopathy, which with the existence of a subarachnoid hemorrhage greatly increases the risk of surgery—a key issue in this case. After several more questions forcing the "expert" to describe that very fact, he couldn't stand any more. "Well then, I see that you would like me to say that Mrs. 'S' suffered from hypertensive encephalopathy, right?"

My lawyer, who had a rather good sense of humor and knew about the drama of a trial, bowed to him politely and said, "That's the answer we wished to hear from the professor's mouth. Thank you very much."

This statement nearly brought the expert to hysterics! He muddled through his responses to the following questions. It was obvious, even to a layperson, that he had been lying and twisting facts before. My almost entire night's work did not go to waste. By chance, it also came out that Mrs. "S" had previously suffered from psychosis that had manifested exactly the same way to that which showed up after surgery—so the surgery had nothing to do with it.

There was still one small matter—around eleven a.m., after two hours of trial, the judge called for a ten-minute recess. I had already quit smoking, though I had never really smoked that much. My nervous tension needed some kind of release—even just smoking one cigarette. I was overwhelmed by the desire to have one. But I told myself, "You have to be clear-headed—a cigarette after such a long break could make you dopey!"

So, instead of going for a cigarette, I went to the bathroom. It happened that Lawyer "L" was in there—he was in the process of relieving his bladder. He was small and thin, even sneaky to look at. Seeing me, he immediately stopped peeing and left. I wonder if he didn't wet his pants! He must have thought that, when I was looking at his balding head surrounded by black curls, I might be overcome by the desire to grab him by the neck and break his back.

After two weeks of this suffering—while I had to take care of patients and be on home-call in the evenings and on the weekends—it came time for the jury's deliberation. A verdict was to be presented. The deliberation lasted a surprisingly short amount of time. They came back to the courtroom, and the foreman, who was delegated by the other jurors, reported that the jury found no grounds for prosecution. In other words, I won the case!

Through all the days and stages of the trial, I had been level-headed and fought the best I could. But when I heard that the nightmare was finally over, like a bad dream, I just broke down. And to my embarrassment, I cried in the courtroom.

My tears didn't surprise anyone there. Everyone knew what had been at stake for me.

Six months later, there was another case brought on by that

same lawyer-friend of Dr. Berke's. In this case, I was accused of actually causing the death of a young woman who had a tumor in the cerebellum. This time, I knew what awaited me and could defend myself well. After three weeks of this torture, I won the case.

And so, the many attempts to destroy me, first as a neurosurgeon and secondly as a Pole, came to nothing. Supposedly, lawyer "L" said that he would never take on a case against me again, because the damage to his health, nerves, and income wasn't worth it. The well-orchestrated action of annihilating me as a neurosurgeon by inciting my patients to sue me for medical mistakes came to nothing. The experiences tied to these cases undoubtedly didn't improve the health of lawyer "L." And only God knows how much health and nerve it cost my mother and me.

During the period of the trial brought against me by Mrs. "S" under the auspices of lawyer "L," I set up a meeting with my lawyer at eight o'clock in the morning at his house. We wanted to go to court together in one car so as to have less trouble finding parking. We would then also have half an hour to discuss the case during the ride. He lived close to me in Grosse Pointe. I knew that he had a large family, four or five kids. Just before eight, I stood in front of the door to his house. I rang the doorbell. No one answered. I rang it again. It was hard for me to believe that no one was home—after all, we had arranged to meet. Finally, impatient, I tried the doorknob. The door wasn't locked. I found myself confronted by a large dog. His upper lip was quivering—a sign of the impending aggression. There was a growl coming from deep in his throat. I knew that I shouldn't move or show fear. I wasn't especially afraid. I had inherited a love of four-legged creatures, especially dogs, from my parents. There was no way out; I stood there like a pole, while he growled threateningly.

After a moment, however, I started talking to him, "Maybe you'd like to sniff my hand?" I put my right hand forward the way you're supposed to—palm and hand down—so that the movement didn't seem at all aggressive. He reacted positively. After the necessary sniffing of my hand, he concluded that there really wasn't any cause for fuss. I asked if he would let me scratch him behind the ear. And he agreed to it. And then, the most difficult question—"Will you let me into the house?" He agreed and led me to the living room. I sat down in a comfortable chair and petted him to his great pleasure. But the house was empty. Suddenly, my lawyer was standing speechless in the doorway!

"How did you get in here? How could this happen? Why did he let you in?"

I told him with pleasure about my taming effect on beasts.

"We didn't have any real problems with each other, or any reason for a fuss!"

Then, I found out that the dog had a rather unusual past. He once bit a passerby in the calf, and the matter ended up in a trial over damages at the courthouse in Grosse Pointe. Lawyer "R" enthusiastically defended this creature for which he cared.

"Your honor! This is a large but truly gentle dog that is friendly to children. He has never caused anyone harm before!"

At this point, the judge's face reddened. "Don't you lie to me, scoundrel! It was your dog that once bit me!"

After this outburst of the personal injury the judge had experienced, there was no more discussion or chance of defense.

After long months of working together, this lawyer and I became friends. During one of our free moments together, he told me an interesting story about his life. He came from a poor family, and had finished law school at night while working during the day. But even this work was not sufficient to pay off all the costs. He joined the National Guard. The pay wasn't great, and weekends were spent in training. In addition it was always possible that his unit could be called to active duty. Just before the eruption of the Korean War, his financial situation improved and he was able to discharge himself from the National Guard. A few months later, Korea found itself under fire. His battalion was called up and was one of the first to go into combat. They suffered very high casualties under Chinese gunfire. He had managed to evade the fate of his colleagues in that battalion.

And then again, here is another experience I had with the vultures. I was just finishing rounds in Holy Cross when I was told that Dr. "W" needed me for an urgent consultation. It concerned a young woman who had just given birth. During the delivery, she experienced sudden paralysis of the proximal muscles of the right lower extremity with partial numbness. I saw her in bed; the child was healthy, the delivery normal. She didn't have pains, but it was certain that the fourth and fifth lumbar nerve roots on the right side were permanently damaged.

I got the details of the incident from Dr. "W." Near the end of the delivery, when the cervix was completely dilated, Dr. "W" had performed an epidural through lumbar puncture, and then he went to wash his hands to be ready to get the baby at any moment. While washing his hands, he heard the woman cry out, "My leg! My leg!"

He ran up to the table—the head of the baby was already out. He quickly got the baby out, but the patient still didn't stop complaining about the pain and then the absence of feeling and partial paralysis of the leg.

I couldn't figure out what had happened. I was sure, though, that delivery had led to the damage to those two nerve roots.

Dr. "W" was sued for malpractice. An expert doctor was going to testify for the prosecution, a doctor who prostituted himself testifying in courts for money. He was going to accuse Dr. "W" of damaging the nerve roots during the lumbar puncture. I started thinking about this. Damaging even one of the roots was rather difficult, and never to such a degree that had been determined in this patient, while damaging both of them was practically impossible. One of the statisticians told me that the chances were one in a billion. If Dr. "W" really made a mistake and injected the anesthetic into the end of the spinal cord ("Conus Medullaris"), which was really unthinkable, then the damage would be symmetrical on both sides and would also include the sacral nerve roots. This would mean that the patient would have impaired control of her urination and bowel movements. But, in this case, there was no sign of such problems.

This whole matter bothered me, because I couldn't understand the mechanism of the damage. Dr. "W's" lawyer hired me to speak as an expert for the defense. The prosecuting attorney asked for my deposition under oath which meant that it was fully obligating for the trial. To the question of what had happened, I replied that I didn't know and that I would try to figure it out. I only knew that it was totally impossible to cause such neurological changes by performing an epidural. That's how my explanations ended.

I started digging through the literature on the subject. I didn't find anything. I came to the conclusion that something about this topic would be somewhere in obstetrics literature. I borrowed the thickest volume on obstetrics from the hospital library, and I found what I was looking for! Amidst the thousands of pages, I came upon half a page that explained my dilemma.

And so, during delivery, the sacro-iliac joints open slightly. The nerve roots, especially the fourth and fifth lumbar, are strained at that time. If the delivery is quick and the head of the baby is large, it may result in ischemic damage of the nerves on the side of the rotation of the head. The pressure on the strained nerve roots may deprive them of blood supply thus resulting in permanent damage. This lack of circulation leads to what is called irreversible ischemic neuropathy.

The next day, I looked over the history of that patient's labor and delivery. Indeed, the delivery was very quick, the head of the baby was large, and the labor happened in such a way that the baby's head was pressing into the right side of the pelvis—and so right on those lumbar roots!

I knew everything I needed to know, and the cause of the injury was now completely clear.

I was to testify in court the day after I had this revelation, for the trial had already begun. I didn't even have a chance to familiarize Dr. "W" or his lawyer with my findings.

I knew that I was the only one in the courtroom who knew the essence of the matter. The lawyers for the prosecution—there were two of them, one "imported" from Chicago, as the case was for a lot of money—immediately began cross-examining me, the only expert witness for the defense. I was to them the hostile witness meaning I had been hired by the defendant's lawyer. The purpose of questioning the hostile witness is to break him down and prove his incompetence.

I knew all these legal tricks like the palm of my hand from personal dramatic experiences with these hyenas. Besides, I was confident, because I knew what had really happened. The lawyers had placards from anatomy atlases displayed on the walls that showed those lumbar roots as well as their location.

The cross-examination began with routine questions—name, education, qualifications, etc. Then, we got to the heart of the matter. To what degree was the patient handicapped? Was the damage permanent? I calmly replied to these questions. The judge requested a ten-minute recess. Dr. "W's" lawyer came up to me.

"You know, I can see it, feel it, that you're about to go in a particular direction. But I don't know which! Am I right?"

"Yes," I said calmly. "But don't bother me about it now; just watch and listen to what happens in the next round."

Everyone went back in. More questions. Isn't it true that Dr. "W" made a mistake and damaged the nerve roots during the lumbar puncture?

I calmly explained the probability of this happening based on the statistical data that my friend had given me. I demonstrated the impossibility of such damage on their very placards.

At wit's end, they asked, "So, what exactly happened?"

Calmly, again using their placards, I explained the whole mechanism of damage, giving evidence from the labor and delivery documentation.

Silence fell. It was obvious that I had ruined their case. Then, the prosecuting lawyer, knowing that he had lost, decided to try to discredit me in the eyes of the jury, to show that I wasn't "objective" and that I was only taking the side of the accused doctor.

"Don't you believe in justice? Don't you think that this unfortunate young woman, who will be handicapped for the rest of her life, deserves justice?" he called out dramatically.

I put on a dignified face.

"I believe in the need for justice for all, including that doctor sitting there being unjustly accused!"

Then he asked craftily, desperately, "What is your opinion of lawyers?"

He wanted to get me to say some rash word that would offend the court. I got a happy though risky idea. I took on an even more righteous posture and said, "My opinion about the law profession is the same as Mario Puzo's!"

He was completely dumbfounded. He didn't know what to say. Mario Puzo, the author of *The Godfather*, came up with a venomous maxim in one of his books: "One little lawyer with his black briefcase can do more harm than the whole criminal New York mafia!" I had decided to quote this opinion. The judge turned out to be an intelligent enough man. He leaned over to me from the height of his throne—I was sitting beside him, lower than his podium, on the witness stand.

"If you're planning to say what I think you're going to say, you better not say it!"

Now, I took on the look of a humbled braggart, and the jury was almost beside themselves with laughter, because each of them understood what was going on. The lawyer blushed.

"I don't have any more questions for this witness!"

I bowed to the judge and went back to my seat. The case was obviously in favor of Dr. "W." He said to me in the doorway of the courtroom, "Janusz! I can't thank you enough! But why did you go to so much trouble?"

"What do you mean? Don't you care that you won the trial?"

"Yes," he said. "But it doesn't make much difference. All that I earn will still go to alimony!"

And that's what happened!

7

On the Front Lines

I BEGAN TO SEE more and more patients, not only in Holy Cross, but also in St. John's Hospital. Private doctors referred their patients on whom I would later operate. I performed about 250 surgeries a year, more than the whole department of neurosurgery did at the Polish Academy of Science. I also had above-average results, so I had a good reputation. My patients were Americans of various backgrounds, though mostly Anglo-Saxon. I also operated on a lot of Italians, Germans, and a few Poles.

I appreciated having Italian patients. They keep close ties and stick together. When it came time to discuss the need for surgery, the whole family, often numerous, would show up. They could appreciate my effort and results. I remember a certain, rather humorous, incident from that period that could very well have ended tragically. An older Italian woman was referred to me with degenerative changes in the lumbar spine and pressure on the nerve roots. She was really suffering. She had sons and daughters and a countless number of grandchildren. She spoke English poorly and was much more comfortable in her Sicilian dialect. I operated on her. The result was very good, and her symptoms went away. She was very grateful to me. After a year, she came with new symptoms. This time, there was some paresis (partial paralysis) of the lower extremities with the beginning of sensory deficit. It turned out that she had a tumor growing in the spinal canal that was compressing on the spinal cord in the thoracic spine. I had to operate once again. The results were excellent, and all the symptoms subsided.

After months, she showed up again at the office, this time hysterical. She cried out that someone had killed her! Amidst her cries, I was able to get at the truth. She had driven to a large shopping center in her car. She parked, did her shopping, and got behind the wheel. Then she heard a voice from the backseat, "Go where I tell you, you damned old bitch, or else I'll bash your head in!"

She fell into shock, floored the gas pedal, and after a moment, drove straight into a telephone pole, crushing the front of the car. Nothing happened to her, but the thug sitting in the backseat hit his head against the windshield. She started crying hysterically, and a passerby ran over and the police showed up. They recognized the guy—he was very dangerous, a serial killer who had been sought by the police all over Michigan! The police inspector was thrilled with my patient's reflex action, because causing that accident was about the only way of saving herself from certain death! Knowing my patient, I would doubt if this was a well-thought action but rather a plain panic. My role became that of comforting the Italian woman. I am sure that, from that moment for the rest of her life, she checks to make sure no one is lurking in the backseat before she gets behind the wheel.

Near the end of a long and draining day of work at the office, one of the last patients I saw was a young and pretty woman. She sat down and said, "My doctor thinks I am an idiot and wants me to go see a psychiatrist. In my opinion, my problem has nothing to do with my head!" I asked her what was bothering her. "My right leg near my foot. The outer part is cold, while the inner part is hot."

I had no idea what kind of illness could present itself in such a strange way. We went into the examining room. I asked her to remove her pantyhose and lie down on the examining table. The center part of the leg, just above the anklebone, was in fact warmer and lightly reddened, but there was no evident inflammation. The outer part of the leg around the bone and somewhat above was clearly cold and much paler. I racked my brain wondering what could be causing this. Now, I knew at least one thing—it was her previous doctor and not this woman who should be seeking psychiatric help. Hastily, I went through all the syndromes that could cause dysfunction of that kind. She didn't smoke and was rather a shining example of health and youth. I asked if she hadn't injured the leg in any way. She hadn't.

After a moment, she added, "This can't have made a difference, but over the summer, while swimming in the lake, I stepped on a sharp piece of a broken beer bottle. It bled a lot, but then it stopped."

The wheels in my head started turning. I grabbed a stethoscope and placed it on the small, white scar located in the middle of her sole. I heard the characteristic "Shoo, shoo, shoo"—right in rhythm with the heartbeat. And I knew. Under the skin that had been cut rather deeply, there were also a small artery and a vein that had been cut. They had healed improperly, and the blood of the artery flowed into the veins of the inner part of the leg making it warm, while the outer part was lacking adequate arterial blood supply, making it cold and pale. The treatment was rather simple; it involved a small incision and then the tying of the arteriovenous fistula. I explained the procedure to her and sent her to a vascular surgeon.

As a farewell, I heard, "Please know that I'm not only grateful to you for finding out what was wrong, but even more so for proving that I'm not an idiot!"

I liked my work and my contact with people. Several things became very clear to me. I refer to these as my three unspoken rules. Rule one is to understand and be aware that everyone who shows up to see a surgeon, usually with a very serious problem, is afraid and anxious. It is important to be conscious of and respectful of their anxiety. Rule two is to understand that each patient, regardless of age or social status, doesn't differ at all from a four-year-old when it comes to a crisis situation, like an illness that can often be life-threatening. They can tell in a heartbeat if you are evasive about their situation. They deserve to know the truth, told in a respectful way. Finally, the third unspoken rule, and the most essential, is establishing an emotional contact with the patient, a mutual understanding of trust and cooperation. If these elements are lacking, one should not proceed with surgical treatment, but rather send the patient to another specialist. I still claim that this hard-to-describe contact even has an effect on the surgical results and the postoperative recovery process. After surgery the patient is obviously drained-out and anxious. They don't know if moving around will cause them to hurt themselves, and they don't know what threatens them. Often, a patient in a panic will imagine that something terrible is happening, while in reality it's not terrible at all. If he doesn't move, though, the breathing gets worse, the gastrointestinal tract works less efficiently, the diaphragm goes up, and the patient generally feels pretty bad. When you add the effects of Morphine or Demerol—both of which slow down the peristalsis of the intestine—to this situation, you can easily imagine that the frame of mind of this unfortunate person is quite negative.

That is why, as I mentioned, my rule was to get the patient moving again as soon as possible after surgery. Then the patient gets air to his lungs, the gastrointestinal tract goes back to normal function, and he doesn't get blood clots in the legs or pelvic area that can often be dangerous. I remember one incident in particular. One of the older doctors referred his secretary of years to me. The surgery was simple, without blood loss and with good results. I wrote the postoperative orders and went home. In the morning, I found the patient almost unconscious with a distended belly. I was horrified and feverishly looked through the patient history, glancing at the orders.

Well then, it turned out that the "good doctor" who came to visit his secretary at night changed my orders and pumped her full of drugs out of the goodness of his heart! I was furious. The results of this carefree attitude could have been very dangerous. I dragged her out of bed. She was already swaying on her feet. Right after I lifted her up, she burped loudly, passed some gas, and her belly returned to normal. I forbade that doctor from writing out any kind of orders for her. I think he was offended, and probably took me for a sadist refusing to give the patient some "simple relief." After the drugs passed through her system, the patient quickly recovered.

One of the internists referred to me a patient who was from Yemen and didn't speak a word of English. Her husband was the one who decided everything, as it often happens in that cultural circle. But he also didn't speak English. The Arab doctor who referred her to me showed up to translate. She suffered from a herniated lumbar disc. She needed a relatively simple surgery, after which she can walk almost immediately. I operated on her. I came by to see her the next day. She was lying in bed. In my usual way, I grabbed her by the arm and began pulling her up. "La-la-la," she started yelling. Thinking this was a cry of joy, I also started saying, "La-la-la." Suddenly, I heard someone's loud laughter out in the hallway. The laughter was coming from that Arab doctor. After a moment, he told me that, in Arabic, "La-la-la" means "No, no, no!"

The advances made in neurosurgical technique in the 1970s were enormous. One of the causes was a newfound understanding of the pathophysiology of illnesses that required surgical intervention. There was also the development of CAT—Computerized Axial Tomography—and later MRI—Magnetic Resonance Imaging. All these things together revolutionized surgical possibilities.

One of the main reasons for better results and expanded surgical possibilities was the use of the microscope. For a long time, I had used a magnifying glass—first enlarging one-and-a-half times, then two, and finally three and a half. The microscope, however, allowed incomparably greater enlargement, more than twenty-five times greater. When you operate under a microscope, the operative field is right before your eyes, though the hands doing the operating are actually much lower. In other words, you need to disassociate your vision from your hand movements. It is not easy to master. Playing the piano from sheet music requires mastering the same skill. Since I did play piano I had no difficulty with operating with the microsope. I went to several courses performing anastomoses—connecting cut arteries that were one millimeter in diameter in rats. This type of procedure required a twenty-five-time enlargement of the operative field. My hands never shook, though under such magnification, a surgeon might think that he suffers from Parkinson's disease, as the physiological trembling is that much more enlarged. Having a cup of coffee before such a procedure can ruin it completely. Mastering the technique of anastomosis of small arteries enabled surgeons to improve the blood supply to the ischemic area of the brain, and it also made various procedures possible on the base of the brain, procedures that neurosurgeons had never even dreamed about before.

It's worth mentioning some of the atypical clinical cases I encountered during that period of my work.

A sixteen-year-old girl with a head injury was admitted to Holy Cross after a car accident. She was unconscious and in a very serious state. We began by doing the standard procedure at that time of lowering the intracranial pressure caused by the swelling of the bruised brain. I had already determined that she did not need surgery. Caring for such a patient is difficult, because the patient can easily get pneumonia from being bedridden, along with a bladder infection and pyelonephritis, as well as bedsores. It's important to change the position of the body often and to do physical therapy that involved movement of the extremities as well as preventive treatments for the respiratory tract.

I was always a proponent of getting patients to move around very soon after surgery. In the case of a coma—a state of deep unconsciousness and loss of reaction to most stimuli—there was no possibility of overt movement, but it was possible to perform passive movement—in water. The head nurse didn't hide her surprise, bordering on shock, when I suggested putting the girl in a large bath full of warm water. She must have thought I was an idiot! She still had to do what I ordered. I helped to carry the continuously unconscious girl to the bathroom and put her in a tub. Here, the Law of Archimedes went to work; it was rather easy to put all of her joints in motion and to do full movement in all the extremities, preventing the development of muscle constrictions. The nurses on the floor understood the sense behind this "bath." From that day forward, none of my suggestions surprised them.

For several weeks, the young woman lay in a coma without any visible improvement. The hospital ordered to move her to a "nursing home," a home where she would not receive any further treatment and would undoubtedly die from complications. I didn't give up. I moved her to St. Joseph's Hospital and continued full treatment with physical therapy. The Christmas holidays were drawing near. The nurses decorated the ward with garlands, stars, and a Christmas tree. Suddenly, I noticed that their enlivened comings and goings started registering in the consciousness of the unfortunate young woman. She awoke and looked with understanding at her surroundings. She was also able to tolerate oral food intake at mealtimes. After two weeks, she could communicate with us relatively well, soon even call her family! Of course, her condition was still very serious. She had to come back to life really beginning at zero, learning how to walk, finding her balance, communicating with the environment. I sent her to a rehabilitation institute. Her condition improved to the point where she could, practically speaking, live almost independently.

I would "throw" patients out of bed who had surgeries on intravertebral discs from the first day after surgery, to the surprise of the nursing personnel. The concept of keeping such patients in bed for two weeks, which was required, for example, at the Warsaw Neurosurgery Clinic, was also upheld in the United States. Meanwhile, mobilizing the patients had key significance. You could avoid various complications that were caused by long-lasting immobility, the first and most often of which was pneumonia. Moreover, the patient would rid himself of fear and anxiety, would need much less pain medication, and usually on the third or fourth day, would return home. After a while, the surprise of the nurses faded. Additionally, I made their work easier—it was easier to care for a walking patient than one tied to his bed.

One night, at three o'clock in the morning, I got a phone call. I woke up, asking what was going on.

"This is the doctor from the emergency room. We have a five-year-old patient who was in a car accident. She's in a coma."

I ran to the hospital. I had an image in my head of that girl with the epidural hematoma at Portland's Good Samaritan Hospital who I was able to save at the last minute.

I went into the emergency room. Behind the curtain on a gurney lay an unconscious, beautiful little girl with long eyelashes. She lay there calmly, breathing normally. She blinked at the sound of my footsteps or the light—so she wasn't in a coma! I leaned over her.

"Mary, how do you feel?"

"Fine," she said.

Hearing this, the emergency room physician virtually screamed, "Why didn't you say anything to me?"

"Because I don't like you," she replied calmly.

Well then, this young woman already had her preferences, sympathies, and antipathies so typical for her gender. The situation would have been comical had it not been almost four in the morning. On the way home, I braked at the last minute so as not to hit a black child wandering in the middle of the road. It became the dilemma of that evening for me—what was he doing at night wandering in the middle of the street?

One of the doctors called me into Holy Cross for a consultation to a patient suffering from acute sciatica. On Saturday, I performed a myelogram; it showed a complete herniation of the disc between L5 and S1. She had to have surgery. On Sunday morning, I found myself next to her bed explaining the problem and necessity of surgery. She was in a very bad mood.

"You didn't tell me anything about this before! I don't like such treatment. I can't trust you."

I couldn't allow her to tell me what to do. I said as calmly as I could, "You're right. The relationship between a patient and a doctor should be based on mutual trust. You do not trust me and I do not trust you. As far as I am concerned you can go to hell!"

She fell silent, and I turned on my heel and continued making rounds on patients.

I was seeing patients in my office on Monday afternoon. I saw that woman's husband in the waiting room. He asked to speak with me.

"Doctor, I know that witch needs to have surgery! Please, would you agree to perform this procedure? I promise that she will not flap her gums at you anymore."

I agreed, and the surgery went well. The patient recovered. And truly, I didn't hear a single negative word come out of her mouth.

One of the doctors practicing at Holy Cross admitted a patient who was about fifty years old with the same exact problem. I did the myelogram, and it was obvious that he needed surgery. During my rounds the next day, I found him standing near his bed all contorted, with awfully horrified eyes.

"Doctor! It's gotten better! Nothing is wrong with me! I'm going home!"

He was lying. It couldn't just "get better." He was lying for fear of having surgery.

"If you have healed so miraculously, that's wonderful! You can go home immediately."

"Yes, yes, I want to go right now!"

He was discharged, and I went to my office to see patients. A corpulent woman showed up; she was the wife of that "healed" man. She looked at me angrily.

"I have known for a long time that my husband is an ass, but that you're so stupid . . . well, that makes me wonder! You have to admit him immediately and do the surgery!"

Well then, there was no way out.

One sunny Sunday, I was called urgently to Holy Cross to a patient who had jumped out of a first-floor window and crushed his first lumbar vertebrae with serious neurological consequences. He needed immediate surgery, this time with the participation of an orthopedic surgeon, for we had to fuse the spinal column with the implantation of metal elements. Our patient did such a desperate thing, because the husband of the woman with whom he was in bed unexpectedly came home.

The surgery was long; it took us most of the day. I had to perform a laminectomy in that area, and then we built the support structure for the spine together. The results were promising. During the surgery, the orthopedist said to me, "I hope that he is insured. If not, then this whole Sunday is forsaken—we've made nothing!"

After the surgery, we found his insurance card. What we didn't know was that his romantic lady friend had given him her husband's insurance card—the lover had been admitted under the husband's name! The lover didn't work anywhere, didn't have any insurance, and was a typical, lazy bum.

From the multitude of the admissions at Holy Cross, one sticks out in my memory. I was informed there was a middle-aged man who had fallen down the stairs, injured his head, and was in a critical state, not reacting to the deep pain. I found him still in the emergency room. Indeed, his state was awful. He had dilated, fixed pupils, didn't react to pain at all, and his extremities were totally lax. What was curious, however, was the lack of any surface injuries. Falling down the stairs had to cause some minor bruises, black and blue marks. There weren't any. Looking at his head, I saw a small hole near the right temple. I saw brain tissue coming out, but there was no blood in the hair, though the hair on that side was wet, as if someone had wiped it with a wet towel. I ordered an X-ray of the skull, thinking about what might have happened. The X-ray showed the presence of a revolver bullet. The "affectionate" wife and family "friend" were sitting in the waiting room. I called the police, and they took them away in handcuffs. They were deluded in thinking that no one in the emergency room would figure out that a murder had been committed—and they almost did get away with it!

The focus of my work slowly began to move from Holy Cross to St. John's Hospital. The reason was rather simple—it was a larger hospital that was better equipped and developing dynamically as the main medical center in the eastern part of the Detroit metropolis. Dr. Haddad, who was then the chief of neurosurgery, and I slowly established a solid diagnostic and surgical foundation.

One of the most difficult, but also most often required, brain surgeries is the treatment of ruptured aneurysms resulting in a subarachnoid hemorrhage. It involves placing a metal clip at the base of the aneurism in order to eliminate it from the circulation in a way that the blood flow of the artery is still preserved. The procedure is difficult and dangerous. It requires significant magnification, appropriate anesthesiology, and strong nerves on the part of the surgeon. Advances in this area were significant at that time, though my experience with them was rather limited. The surgical team with which I worked didn't understand the demands required by this surgery so as to get the best possible results. My task was to change this situation and to make the team aware of these demands.

I went for a special course that had been organized by the American Neurological Surgery Society. I took the head of the operating room at St. John's Hospital with me. Terry, who was of German descent, distinguished herself in her intelligence, devotion to her work, and forthrightness in her opinions, a quality that didn't appeal to everyone. She would lash out at me sometimes, but when I needed a room and proper surgical team, she was faultless at bringing it about. I had also treated members of her family, so she trusted me.

Our showdown began when we met up at the airport. Terry was in an awkward situation outside of her comfort zone. Pretty soon she adjusted to the situation and started bossing me around, as she often did with her husband. Our excursion was a great success mainly because Terry understood what was essential for a well-performed surgery. I learned a lot there too. The course covered an enormous amount of surgical material. After coming back, I didn't have any more trouble gathering the instruments necessary for this type of surgery, including a high-quality microscope.

Over the coming years, I operated on a lot of brain aneurisms, sometimes doing two a week. It was very hard work and definitely put a strain on the surgeon's nerves—the surgical risk was high, and the result depended in large part upon the surgeon. My mother always worried when I had to do such a surgery. She expressed more than once that she thought these procedures were too detrimental to my health.

8

Secretaries, Secretaries

A FTER GETTING RID of my first communist secretary, who fought against capitalism in such a unique way—against the money that I was owed for performing surgeries—I hired another one. Claudia was the older sister of a nurse at Holy Cross. She was intelligent and faultless in relation to patients, which was of course very important to me. She took care of her responsibilities quickly and effectively.

After a few months of such idyll, I noticed that there was a certain fault in the functioning of our practice. My income was decreasing instead of increasing, though I was performing more and more procedures. I heard some alarm bells go off in my head. I started suspecting that there was some kind of void into which some of my income was dropping. I looked over the bookkeeping of which Claudia took care. It was faultless. The inflow and out-flow of money was recorded exactly and was up-to-date, written in nice and clear penmanship. When I asked if we were receiving checks from the insurance companies for work I had performed, she always confirmed their receipt. And what I saw was that the amount was much less than I expected. In that time, Claudia bought a new, rather expensive car. I came to the conclusion that she was stealing from me, and her shrewdness and intelligence allowed her to conceal the means by which she was a thief.

I decided to set a trap. I asked one of the patients to pay Claudia right after his visit, not with a check but with cash. It was a larger sum of money, as this patient was paying for a part of the bill that was not covered by the insurance. He agreed immediately, aware of what I was trying to do.

After finishing up my office work and admissions, I asked Claudia to present the day's income to me. In the column of figures, the payment from this patient was missing! I asked her then if that patient had paid his bill. She replied that he had not and had asked to wait!

I had the proof in my grasp. I told her that she should leave my office immediately and never come back! I also added that I wasn't going to press charges but only because of her sister. She understood. She took her bag, coat, and a few of her personal things, and she left in silence. She stole between five to ten thousand dollars from me. The exact sum of this embezzlement was never precisely established.

A neurosurgeon's life is not only made up of surgical work and patient diagnosis. A large part of it comes down to the administrative side of running a medical practice. During the period when I was operating the most at St. John's Hospital, Doris was my secretary. She was a stout, heavy built woman with abrupt manners, husky voice and the personality of a bull dog. One day when I was seeing a patient, I heard him say, "Your wife told me to come in today for a visit, even though I had an appointment scheduled to come see you next week."

I was surprised by this sudden "marriage," as I was a committed bachelor. It turned out that Doris had decidedly raised her status by posing in front of the patients as my wife! I had nothing else to do but fire her. She didn't want to leave and protested greatly, but I didn't change my mind. Years later, she became a patient of mine. She had been diagnosed with a brain tumor, a benign meningioma. She had asked her doctor to refer her to me for surgery. I removed the tumor without a problem, and she went home in good health with a routinely shaved head.

Lucille, a kind, cultured Italian woman, took her place. She performed all the duties rather well. Her problem was that she couldn't handle the workload, as my practice was constantly growing. I hired a young woman, Liza, to help her out. She was supposed to help type up the medical reports I dictated. Well then, Liza managed to sit for hours by that typewriter doing nothing, lost in reveries, perhaps of fairytale kingdoms. The material I dictated wasn't typed, the reports weren't sent out, and the doctors who referred patients to me were annoyed, because they hadn't received any letters giving them my medical opinion. After a week, I let Liza go. She was in a stupor, not even realizing her own incompetence.

Lucille couldn't handle the difficulty of working overtime, because she had her own obligations at home with a husband and kids. She resigned as my secretary. I then hired an American-German woman named Ann, and I hired Judy in place of Liza. Ann did her work very well; she was well organized and responsible. Judy was Scottish and tall, with a hefty frame; she was rather pretty and worked fairly well. I breathed a sigh of relief. Finally, the work in my office was well organized. Unfortunately, the idyllic time didn't last long. Judy got pregnant. With whose baby? Her fiancé's cousin! She left work, too. I ran into her years later. She came by to show off her second child. She had married yet another man, who adopted her first child and had a second one with her. She was happy, and the marriage was working out well. So, after a stormy youth, she finally settled on calm waters.

After Judy, I hired one of my colleague's daughters, a Filipino woman. Her name was Susie. She really reminded me of a porcelain doll—small, with beautiful olive skin and large, narrow eyes; she was kind and efficient. But after a year, she got married, and I was again left without a secretary. What's worse, Ann, my main support, had had enough of hard work. One day, she told me that she was leaving, but that she would wait until I found a replacement.

You usually looked for a secretary through a hiring agency. After a candidate was hired, the agency would collect its fee from the first month's salary. One late afternoon, a new candidate came to see me. She was Italian—her parents had come over from Sicily, and she had been raised in Brooklyn. She had a typical New York accent, and she could also get by in Italian. She was a kind and compassionate woman with two kids. Her husband had left her, and she really needed work to provide for herself and the children. I looked at her—impoverished, with a kind smile and wide eyes. Her name was Joann. When I looked over her CV, I saw that she had a lot of experience in bookkeeping, but she had no idea about the responsibilities in the field of neurosurgery. I knew that without knowledge of the basic terminology she wouldn't be able to do her work. I also wanted to get an idea of her general intelligence level. So, instead of asking her how fast she could type and do bookkeeping, I asked her to name three well-known American writers. She responded immediately, without hesitation. Then, I asked her to name three Italian writers. And she had no trouble with this. I went into history. What was the main cause of the Civil War in the United States?

Without hesitating, she responded, "Money."

In the later part of this exam, I asked her several terms in Latin ending in "-itis," which means an inflammatory state, and "-ectomy," which means an excision. After a short break, I threw several other Latin terms at her, mixing them with these suffixes; what do these terms mean? She answered perfectly! Now, I didn't have any doubts that we would work together very well. Her aunt was waiting for her downstairs. "Well, how did it go? Did you get the job?"

"Yes," she said, "but I think he's a totally crazy!"

To this, the aunt said, "Joann you're in a tough spot—you can't complain! Even if he is a lunatic, at least you'll have a job!"

When Joann reported to work, Ann was still reigning over my office. She didn't treat her very well. After a few days, Joann said tearfully that she didn't know what to do. I also knew that she was going through a horrible divorce and that she didn't even have a car—which makes living in Detroit almost impossible. I asked her to sit down.

"Joann, I want to make a private agreement with you. I'll guarantee to help so that you can raise your kids without worry. You'll see to it that my work goes smoothly here and that everything is done as it should be done and promptly. If you promise, I'll give you half the money you need to buy a car right away so that you won't have trouble getting here."

She looked at me with eyes filled with tears and gratitude. She promised to uphold her end of the deal. For the next twenty-five years, she ran my office and was not only my right hand but also one of my closest friends.

After Judy left, I hired Denis. Joann and Denis, who was petite and shrewd, worked together fairly well. Denis did her work without making mistakes, but she also left eventually. She married a widower, who had three children, and she later had her own—she definitely had her hands full. This widower thanked God that he found such a wife and mother for his children, because Denis loved kids. She came to visit us later on with one of her many kids. Still, Joann couldn't do it all alone.

Then I hired Terry, a young Greek woman. She worked well and was kind and quiet. Sometimes, a young Greek guy would come by to see her. One day, she told me with joy that she was going to get married. They had a small ceremony, but after a few months, she was sitting at the computer with red eyes and a red nose. Her beloved was in prison, because he had been in the States illegally, and what's more, he had a wife in Greece and another wife in New York—Terry was the third! She asked me to let her go to court and post bail for him. Of course, I didn't object. I fully sympathized with her personal tragedy. She returned after a few hours, almost beside herself with tears. She found out that this very well-traveled individual had already been let out—another young woman had posted bail for him! Terry left; she decided to go stay with her family to recover and get through it. I ran into her years later. She was working in a doctor's office. She didn't get married again.

And I still needed a good, intelligent, and consistent typist. Doris was sent from the agency; she was almost forty, an Arab-Italian mix with dark eyes, dark skin, and dark hair. I asked her to do a typing test while I dictated. She turned her head to me so as to hear better and started typing at an incredibly fast speed! Then, she gave me the text to correct it. I didn't find a single mistake! I hired her on the spot. Joann and Doris worked with me until I retired. My practice was taken over by two young neurosurgeons who continued their employment at my request.

MY UNERRING SECRETARY, JOANNA MARIA
VINCENSINA-GIRIMONTE, WITH WHOM I SHARED
MANY YEARS OF WORK AND FRIENDSHIP

9

Useful Idiots of the Communists

IN THE WINTER of 1980 I met a Polish lawyer, Mr. Gruszkiewicz. He was a representative of the Solidarity Movement, just developing. He had been designated to generate the support of the Polish Americans, and hopefully, obtain some funds. As far as I know his actions were totally futile. I was greatly surprised by his hope and conviction that Solidarity could peacefully overturn the occupational Soviet regime in Poland. I wanted to warn him and invited him to my house where we had a long discussion. Soon after marshal law was announced in Poland and Solidarity was crushed.

I came upon an article written by Krzysztof Rac in a Chicago newspaper. He portrayed the crimes happening in Poland clearly and called people to determined action. I found his phone number and called him. I told him that I fully agreed with his position and that I also wanted to participate.

"That's good," I heard. "We run an organization named POMOST. You can organize a cell of this organization in Detroit. I'll send you an envoy to take care of all the details."

Rac sent me the organization's statute, which also completely met with my approval, as well as other publications that maintained this same spirit. And that's how I became the coordinator of POMOST in the state of Michigan. POMOST held an uncompromising position. It regarded the regime of the People's Republic of Poland (PRP) as a regime of the Soviet Union, the PRP "authorities" as tools of the Bolsheviks, serving to terrorize and subordinate the Polish nation, and the Yalta Agreement as a betrayal of allied Poland by Western Europe and the United States. There was no room for something to be left unsaid, no room for compromise, only the naked truth.

Through all the years that I spent in the United States fighting to establish myself in my profession, I never let go of the thought that I was, of course, and still am, a Pole, and that I should help Poland in every possible way I could. Father Klimm's tradition or rather family tradition of patriotism never left me. I treated the United States as a second fatherland that I treasured and that was close to my heart, but still, my roots and moral obligations to Poland always remained present with me.

I pondered ways of further spreading the activism of POMOST. I thought that one of the real ways to reach out would be through radio programming—ten-minute broadcasts that spoke openly about Polish reality and concealed nothing. I started working on this idea almost immediately.

A Polish radio program had existed for years in Detroit. Mr. Kreuz led the program, and his wife did after he died. Jerzy Rozalski bought that program from Mrs. Kreuz at a time she was already an older woman. Before the state of war was declared in Poland, a group of black people bought this radio station, which was then owned by a Jewish man and ran programs geared towards minorities that focused on various ethnicities and broadcast in many languages. These radio programs then stopped. Meanwhile, all the minorities, especially the Polish-Americans, largest of the minority groups, wanted these programs to continue. The directors of particular national programs created a joint stock company with two hundred thousand dollars in capital with the participation of the Polish American Congress, which bought forty thousand dollars worth of shares from donations collected from Polish-

Americans. Then the "preferred shares" were put on the market. These were shares that did not offer any voting rights in the company, but they were first in line to receive dividend payments. The capital value of the preferred stock was $490,000. Also a loan was taken from the bank of around $650,000 to buy the radio station, WPON. Polish programs again appeared on the radio, this time presented by Rozalski.

My ten-minute broadcasts began to appear on this very program. I spoke clearly and openly about the whole truth of the crimes that were being committed in Poland. Almost immediately, there was a great deal of movement among the Polish-American listeners. A group of combat soldiers from the Polish National Army got in touch with me offering their support and cooperation. At that time, they were putting out a monthly brochure that overwhelmingly focused on the events of forty years ago. Still, they did hold a decidedly anti-regime and anti-Soviet position.

An engineer named Lacki also got in touch with me, suggesting that we work together. And so, we organized these programs. Then a scandal erupted. We learned that the "Radio Station of Nations" was going bankrupt! I also learned that this bankruptcy had begun on the first day of this "Station of Nations" existence. The main reasons were complete disorganization in the station's management and systematic theft by certain "directors" of radio programs. How did it happen? Rather simply. The money from advertisers went into people's pockets, though the payments appeared to have been made in the station's account books. Even after selling the station building, the station was still almost forty thousand dollars in debt to the bank. This led to bankruptcy. The bank was to take the station over as collateral for the debts and then sell it on auction. This meant that hundreds of poor people would lose all the money they had invested in the station and that there would be no more ethnically geared programs.

Mr. Bashara, who was an American Arab and former judge, appeared on the horizon. He offered to buy the station, paying ten cents for every dollar. And the Polish American Congress in Detroit agreed to such a "business venture!"

This upset me greatly, though I wasn't the only one. We called for a meeting, in which we were able to gather $140,000 during several hours. I was the one who proposed this collection, warning everyone that our money might go completely to waste. We then immediately created an investment corporation and registered it, and then as a corporation, we put together a formal offer to buy some of the shares of the station that would give us some say in deciding its future functions. I became the chairman of this investment company. There was a meeting between me and my representatives and the station's board. Because they didn't have any other option, they agreed to our conditions.

And that's how I became the head of the board of radio station WPON. Of course, I resigned from the position of chairman in the investment company, as that would have been a conflict of interest. Then, I negotiated with the bank to spread out the debt over a longer period of time with an immediate payment of twenty-five thousand dollars. And so, I became the chairman of the bankrupting radio station WPON. I didn't wish for this at all, but it was necessary so that the poor investors who had been deluded by the promise of large rewards wouldn't lose all their savings.

I went to the building that housed the radio station. I was horrified! Everything there was an unbelievable mess—there were unpaid bills in the drawers, and pieces of recently purchased transmitting equipment were missing. I had never imagined that a group of relatively intelligent people could bring a station to such ruin.

Mr. Rozalski was then in charge of running the station. I immediately removed him from this position, and hired a bookkeeper through an agency to run all the billing and told her to clean up the books. This helped, but not for long, because she also ended up participating in a thieving venture. I got rid of the bookkeeper, and Mr. Chominski took her place; he was a sincere person for whom I am still grateful to this day. We started repaying the bank, and the deficit stopped growing.

While all these events were taking place, I was also doing political commentary for POMOST on Mr. Rozalski's program, which was the only Polish-language program. It's easy to guess that we quickly collided. My chairmanship was very inconvenient for Mr. Rozalski, as some of the transmitting equipment was to be found in his garage (it was later returned), and his programs were at the very least neutral and "light," if not pro-regime. After one of my commentaries, he decided that he didn't have a place for me on his program. I didn't really think much of it, but I understood with whom and what I was dealing. I had already purchased some of the shares, giving the Polish American Congress and me a larger number of votes in the joint-stock company. The representative of the Polish American Congress was Mr. Zmurkiewicz, a hardened conservative who later became my good friend; he had been an officer of the Second Corps who shed some blood on the slopes of Monte Cassino.

After cutting ties with Rozalski, I bought three hours a week of radio programs, working to spread the activism of POMOST. The POMOST group in Detroit had already grown a lot. The Majcher's had joined, Bolko Skowron had joined—he was an old member of KPN—with his wife, Jola, as had the Zawadzkis, Bochniakows, Dr. Niec and his wife, Mrs. Pruszynska, Mrs. Bukowska, and Mrs. Biermanska. We also found Polish-American firms that were no longer afraid to sponsor us. One of them, a travel agency named Darpol, was owned by the Plochockis and became a faithful friend through the years.

With the help of Mr. Zawadzki, an electrical engineer, we created a broadcasting studio in the basement of my house; it was totally professional, complete with a soundproof isolation booth for transmitting. We had a "mixer," which allowed us to give a musical background to the broadcast. I also bought a whole set of transmitting equipment for our broadcasts. Our announcing signal was a mighty fragment of S. Dworzak's symphony. The music for this signal had a threefold meaning. It had been created in America, so in the "New World," composed by the Panslavist that Dworzak was,[2] and it was also finally the signal of the under-

---

2. And I think that's why there isn't even the smallest mention of Dworzak in the "Great General Encyclopedia" PWN from 1964 (Volume II) or in the "New General

ground Radio Solidarnosc in Poland. We recorded the programs over the weekend, often late into the night. Only someone who has experience in this field knows how much effort goes into preparing one hour of radio programming. And we were preparing three hours a week. And, after all, each of us worked very hard in his own profession. I was always on home-call and sometimes had to interrupt the recording session to go into a surgery on an emergency case. But we somehow managed; the programs flowed in the air, and though in the beginning they were rather amateur-ish, they grew better and better in time. We also put forth original material that was easily accessible to us.

The symbol of the POMOST organization was the face of a young person with a gagged mouth. This was the symbol of Poland. Our task was to reveal this truth, which could not be articulated by the people in Poland. In doing so, I felt as though I was finally repaying a son's debt towards his nation and fatherland.

These programs became more and more popular and also sparked indignation! The source of this indignation could be found in the special services group of the PPR (the Polish Workers' Party) and in people who were cooperating with them for one purpose or another—some for material gain, some wishing to go for a visit to Poland. There were also those who publicized scathing slander against me. In reading one of them, I found out that I was supposedly a UB agent, and that during June's "Poznan uprising," I hadn't been operating on the wounded strikers but rather only on the wounded UB agents in the UB hospital! And finally, that I had not been an adjunct in the Polish Academy of Science. They ran so far so fast with all this that they didn't even think about the fact that a UB hospital didn't exist in Poznan in the '50s. But this didn't seem to bother the authors of all these lies—Mr. Rozalski and Mr. Baszczynski.

I decided to organize a demonstration for the anniversary of the Katyn massacre. There was one monument dedicated to Katyn in the city of Detroit. It stood in Orchard Lake on the terrain of

Encyclopedia" PWN in 1998, published by the Scientific Publisher PWN—they were completely run by Jewish people.

a Catholic seminary whose chancellor was Father Milewski. The monument was modest though symbolic—a mass of twisted metal with a sign that read "Katyn"—not a word about what that name means to a Pole or to any honest person. We gathered there in the morning with Polish flags and a wreath of flowers. There were quite a few of us, maybe even a hundred. After singing the Polish national anthem with those gathered there, I said a few words emphasizing the genocidal character of the Katyn murders and the role of national traitors present there who then tried to conceal this genocide. Our activism did not go unnoticed by the clergy of Orchard Lake. Father Peszkowski came over to us and asked what we were doing there. I replied that we wished to demonstrate our indignation and our protest on this day, the anniversary of the Katyn massacre, and to show that the criminal behind it was the Soviet tyrant that was occupying Poland. I also said that I couldn't understand why there was only the word Katyn on the monument and not a full explanation in English so that everyone could learn about the horrifying crime of communism.

Father Peszkowski was not thrilled in the least by our expression of patriotism. He said contemptuously that we were trampling the flowers, of which there were none, that he didn't know what we were really doing there, and that we should leave the area of Orchard Lake.

To my question as to why the monument only portrayed one word, Katyn, Father Peszkowski explained, "It can't be any other way. After all, the consul is going to come visit, so how would it look? It would hurt his feelings!"

Years have gone by since that moment, and Father Peszkowski is very active now in the Katyn movement, but I will never forget what he said that day, and I'll never forgive him for it.

10

Professional Courtesy

N 1977, DURING a surgery that I was performing in a standing position, I felt a sharp pain in the lumbosacral area radiating all the way down to my left leg. I also felt some numbness in the outer part of the calf, reaching down to the toe. I knew very well what was wrong. I had an acute herniated disc, between the fourth and fifth lumbar vertebrae. The pain was severe, and I finished the surgery with difficulty. The pain wasn't new to me, because I had already had several rather severe attacks. It began when I was still working in Poznan as a very young doctor. One day, while I was rounding on patients, I found one of them lying in his own excrement. I was indignant with the nurses; they explained that it was difficult to pick him up. Furious, I leaned over him and picked him up myself. Then, for the first time, I felt a sharp pain in my back—it almost broke me in half!

I usually got better after the period of sharp pain, often a week of rest was enough. But this time in 1977, the situation was much more serious. I knew that I needed surgery. I often saw Dr. Harvey Gass's patients in my office, and I knew him from professional encounters and neurosurgical conferences.

I called him.

"Listen, I have a herniated lumbar disc, L4–L5. I need surgery. Would you like to do it?"

There was silence on the other end. Then a question, "Janusz, are you hysterical, or do you really have a problem?"

"I know what I'm talking about. Really!"

"Fine. I'll operate on you the day after tomorrow. Tomorrow, go to Sinai Hospital for a myelogram (an examination with injection of dye by lumbar puncture)."

And that's what I did. The radiologist, an older gray-haired man did the puncture, injected dye into the spinal canal, and under fluoroscopy, he took the appropriate images. I wanted to know exactly what was going on in my back, so I turned around so as to look at the screen.

"Don't twist around like that!" he said. "I'm the one who needs to see this, not you!"

Indeed, there were no delusions to be had; I had a herniated lumbar disc, L4–L5. Harvey Gass, a small Jew with intelligent sparkling eyes showed up during the test. He admitted that I definitely met criteria for surgery. I don't remember him ever doing neurological examination on me—he took me at my word. He frightened my mother in explaining all the possible complications. He did this routinely because the number of lawsuits being brought against doctors for malpractice, which I almost fell victim to myself, was growing like wildfire then. It's worth mentioning here that Harvey, who was of Jewish descent, wasn't in union with his fellow countrymen who were practicing law in the accusing law firm. It was actually quite the opposite—he fought against them with all his strength and possibilities. He even created a special committee to fight against their underhanded practices!

I felt good after the surgery. Only then did I understand how much pain I had suffered over the last few months. I had simply and imperceptibly learned to live with the pain. Before the surgery, I was naturally somewhat nervous, so my blood pressure went up. The internist gave me some strong medication to lower the pressure. When the results of surgery were added to this, my blood pressure dropped significantly. I didn't feel it, because I was lying down. The nurse's words to me were amusing.

"Doctor, your blood pressure is too low. What should I do?"

I told her to give me plenty of fluids and to leave me in peace.

The next day, Harvey showed up. He didn't even ask me how I was feeling. He sat down on the edge of the bed and began discussing his own professional difficulties, cursing all shortcomings of the administration of the hospital and the legal profession, et al. We talked for a while on this subject, feeling sorry for our mutual fate. He got up and left, still not having asked me how I felt after the surgery. It seemed as though he'd simply forgotten I was his patient! Only on the third day did he recognize that this time I was his patient and not a colleague stretched out on a bed.

"Listen, Janusz! Did someone look at your wound?"

"As far as I know, no one did."

"We should throw out that bandage. But, then again, you can take it off yourself. It's healing beautifully," he said in a complimenting tone.

On the fourth day, I decided that I had had enough of the hospital. Harvey didn't object, knowing that I wouldn't give in anyway. I have a lot of warmth in my heart for him. And I was able to return the favor in the near future. After a year or two, I got a phone call.

"It's Harvey. One of these old devils is suing me for malpractice! I operated on her back, and it got better, but this old Jewish lady wants some money. Her expert is some guy Ziemnowicz from Washington. Do you know anything about him? And, could you be my expert?"

I agreed immediately. I knew much too much about Ziemnowicz. Before I started in Warsaw doing neurosurgery, Ziemnowicz was there. He didn't last long because Professor Choróbski threw him out. Then, he went to Wroclaw, where he pretended to be a neurosurgeon, operating on various cases, though he never had specialist privileges in Poland. He got to the United States in a particularly strange way. It is rumored that, on the day in which Khrushchev came to Warsaw after Gomolka came into power, Ziemnowicz paid a photographer to be there as he pushed his way to Khrushchev and put out his hand. Not knowing what was going on, Khrushchev shook his hand. The photographer took a picture. Ziemnowicz went to the passport office with this photo and demanded passports for his entire family. When the UB agent there acted surprised by his ruthlessness, Ziemnowicz pulled out that photo with Khrushchev and showed it to him. The UB agent was speechless. Ziemnowicz quickly got those passports.

Harvey's lawyer, Sullivan, who I also knew well, got me all of Ziemnowicz's testimony against Dr. Harvey Gass. Ziemnowicz's professional "qualifications" were tremendously exaggerated and mostly false. The trial went to court. Sullivan called me as the expert for the defense. It only took me about fifteen minutes to destroy "expert" Ziemnowicz, and exposed all his lies. The prosecuting lawyer had a right to do a cross-examination—to ask me questions with the aim of breaking down my testimony. He was arrogant, brutal, and provoking. He tried to twist my words, mock them. I was furious, but I answered calmly and politely. I was waiting for Harvey's lawyer, Mr. Sullivan, to react to these stunts. But he sat silent as if he had been cursed.

After several hours of this questioning, I left the witness stand, went to Sullivan, and asked, "Why didn't you help? There were many opportunities for you to raise objections."

And he said, "You know, when I was looking at your tousled head and how you were destroying the prosecution, I didn't want to interrupt such a feast for the eyes with an unnecessary interruption!"

Harvey thanked me, and he won the case.

After several years, I was the one needing an expert for a case that was brought against me by the well-known Lawyer "L." Harvey was supposed to testify in court, but he called me and said that he couldn't testify. He didn't explain, which hurt me a little. Instead he offered to provide a deposition the very same day. The deposition was lengthy and the matter ended before midnight. I later found out that Dr. Harvey Gass was going in for heart surgery the next morning at 7:00 a.m. That's the kind of man he was.

11

POMOST

POMOST WAS GROWING. We already had clubs in most of the large American cities. A periodical of the organization with the same name came out each month. We had radio programs not only in Detroit, but also in Chicago and Phoenix. Protests were written to congressmen, and demonstrations were organized.

The PAC (Polish American Congress) didn't approve of POMOST. They treated us like an inconvenient and embarrassing disruption of the status quo. And indeed we were. The "elite" of the congress considered themselves to be the only group with the right to represent Polish interests in the United States. At the same time they cooperated with the Soviet imposed regime in Poland. The POMOST-group of young people who held an uncompromising position irritated and angered them, inciting a reaction of, "how can they dare?" But this didn't bother our organization. Adam Kiernik came up with a proposition to work towards annulling the Yalta Agreement—it was unheard of, encroaching into an area that was taboo! We did have a lot of advantages on our side. After all neither the House of Representatives nor the Senate ever formally approved the Yalta Agreement. American conservatives, who were decidedly anticommunist, were in favor of doing away with this agreement. Still, the agreement had its obligations, and each president in turn acted in accordance with it.

Adam Kiernik, who was from California, was a friend of Congressman Bob Dornan. Dornan had been a fighter pilot for the United States, and he was a person of fearless nerve, upright through and through. He spoke openly about the betrayal of Poland by the United States that was made manifest in Yalta. I still have the videotape during which Dornan openly condemned maintaining the Yalta Agreement.

We decided that Kiernik was in the best position to lead the "Yalta action." We sent out the appropriate pamphlets with our plan of action. On a specified day, we were each, as coordinators, to organize a demonstration against the Yalta Agreement that would bring together enough people so as to draw the attention of TV and radio stations, which through their intermediary position could inform Americans of the diabolic aspect of this base agreement. It was not easy to organize such a demonstration. I had to get special permission in the city of Warren, a neighborhood of metropolitan Detroit that had a largely white population and a large Polish diaspora. Then, I began to advertise the event on the radio. We prepared the appropriate slogans and flags and brought in a small speaker's platform. Our whole group went to the designated square early and prepared the place of assembly. Minutes went by, then quarters of an hour. No one was coming! I was getting really worried, for the meeting seemed to be a failure. But, in the last fifteen minutes, the square started to fill up with people. First, some couples came one by one, then whole groups. The crowd grew larger. We waited another fifteen minutes; our speaker's platform was now surrounded by the crowd, and some American TV stations had shown up.

I made a speech about the necessity of doing away with the Yalta Agreement, about the necessity of our activism here on American soil. I called people to action against the UB agencies' infiltration of Polish American social circles. I heard some bravos and gave interviews to several TV stations. The demonstration was a success. On the way home, a large crowd of people surrounded us. The first question that came from them was, "How is it that you're not afraid to speak out this way?"

And then one woman, so typical of that time, said, "I wouldn't want for them to see that I was here! I have a sister who's still in Poland, and I'm on my way to visit her!"

The rally against the Yalta Agreement that day took place in all the larger American cities and didn't go unnoticed. Congressman Dornan brought forth a non-binding resolution that condemned the Yalta Agreement to the podium of the House of Representatives. The resolution passed in the vote. This was our first real political success, and it was all due to Adam Kiernik and Congressman Dornan.

The whole POMOST organization, not only its radio broadcast, became the brunt of furious propaganda attacks from the agent of the PRP (Polish Peoples' Republic). They were aimed at what were described as "diversionary tactics" within the organization, and all of it was done simply to discredit POMOST in the United States and in the PRP. It's important to remember that the main tabloids of propaganda, such as the *Trybuna Ludu*, the *Rzeczpospolita*, and the *Zolnierz Wolnosci* were distributed for free in Polish areas of the United States.

The headlines of the *Trybuna Ludu* usually fueled the fire. Then, like loyal hunting dogs, other tabloids undertook similar actions. Here is a brief glance at the attacks, sayings, libel, and misleading lies. It becomes apparent from them that the greatest fury was caused by our actions to annul the Yalta Agreement.

"POMOST—A diversionary link of the U.S.," ("119" 5 [VI] 1985.):

> [. . .] This organization, almost unknown to the general public, has its headquarters in Chicago, along with divisions in San Diego, San Francisco, and Los Angeles. We learned from sources in the West that, after a three-year period of organization, the POMOST group has presently undertaken an actively antisocialist and anti-Polish action. From the analysis of the individual leading activ-

ists of **POMOST**, it turns out that the directors recruit fanatical anticommunists (Yes, that's true, author!) who are capable of every traitorous act against their country. [. . .] The activists of the **POMOST** group have so completely lost any national ties that they actively support Western German revisionisms [sic!]. Lately, they are leading an action under the title "Renounce Yalta." Working to spread anti-Polish activism in this direction, **POMOST** established, among other things, a petition to the Congress of the United States demanding that the country "break with the spirit and letter of Yalta 45." This petition has been distributed to all the states in America. Its role is to influence public opinion and put a squeeze on the United States political authorities.

After establishing our anti-Polish role, the question immediately arose as to where the money for this big action was coming from and who was behind it. Such a betrayal of the "vital interests" of Poland obviously flowed from pleasant incentives. It had to do with money. From where? "Rzeczpospolita" clarifies this matter:

It is not a secret to anyone that the **POMOST** organization gets money. The speech made by Janusz Szymanski [sic], a member of the leading group of **POMOST**, is characteristic in this respect. In a conversation with one Western reporter, he stated the following: "They are even accusing us of being financed by the CIA, FBI, and finally the ECA, which is actually a transportation firm and has absolutely nothing to do with us."

Somewhat earlier (March 4, 1985), the *Trybuna Ludu* reported a convenient statement made by the Attorney General, speaking about the punishment that would be doled out for people who worked with organizations that weren't fond of the Soviet Occupation of Poland:

The Attorney General reminds you that cooperation with foreign centers threatening Poland is illegal; you will get the punishment prescribed in the rules of law and will be held responsible. This punishment—in defense of national interests and citizens—will be harshly and fully executed.

Stanislaw Glabinski, an unerring regime dog in the United States and a PAP correspondent in the *Trybuna Ludu* of August 27, 1982, singled out POMOST from all the other Polish-American political movements because of its radicalism:

The people on top have noticed an organization by the name of POMOST in the Chicago area whose activism gives an impression of how certain Solidarnosc radicals imagine work in a foreign country. POMOST is a grouping of extremists showing combative tendencies and is considered a fierce enemy of the People's Republic of Poland.

The Silesian *Trybuna Robotnicza* (January, 1983) published a lampoon with the title, "Dollars for Pirates." The subtitle read: 'Towards what station are the newest Polish immigrants reaching?"

It then clarifies what kind of pirates they are talking about:

The current actions being followed involve a Polish radio station in Chicago rented by POMOST that reported fundraising so as to legally defend hijackers of Polish planes who were on trial in Western Europe.

As POMOST was organizing a fundraiser to defend hijackers, it was clearly a terrorist organization:

The organization comes dangerously close to what we describe as a terrorist phenomenon, and in addition, it has unclear ties to various American institutions. No one knows exactly where POMOST gets it funding, but its progress in some directions suggests that it has a surprising amount of money for certain types of activism. [In reality POMOST did not receive any funds from any other source than members dues.]

"Polish Americans do not Support POMOST," *Trybuna Ludu* (27 [VIII] 1982.):

Where do they get the money for this kind of publishing activism? Obviously, no one knows. Older Polish-Americans did not admit to contributing a single dollar to a practice that inspires serious hesitations and doubts in them. New immigrants have no funds of their own to use.

The following day, after this singling out of POMOST from the support of "old Polish-Americans", the *Zolnierz Wolnosci* (28 [VIII] 1982) proclaimed the same thing, with the same PAP-ist-like phrases:

> Despite the well-known and loudly expressed position of the U.S. in Polish affairs, the new "political immigrants" from our (yes, right—your) country enjoy neither sympathy nor widespread support or recognition here.

On Monday, October 27, 1982, the *Express Wieczorny*, in relation to the POMOST initiative to do away with the Yalta Agreement, asked in the title of its article, "Who does this benefit?" And then answered, "Western revisionists!" The author of this jargon—Jerzy Janicki—called these attempts "delusions of various fanatics." These delusions are so unbelievable that a representative said, "The most extreme anti-Polish division is undoubtedly the group with the graceful name of POMOST."

The originator of these revelations, Mr. Adam Kiernik from California, is a member of the "board of directors" of the aforementioned organization and belongs to the second generation of Poles born across the ocean, who wasn't able to speak his predecessors' language and so couldn't do an interview for the radio broadcast, "Voice of America." In one conversation, he said among other things that POMOST is a political organization that tries to put pressure on the government and the American population [. . .]. "We are demanding to maintain sanctions against Jaruzelski's military junta and against Moscow."

Perspektywy on November 4, 1982 again hits against the "revisionists'" renouncement of Yalta along with POMOST. In the article "Blind Players and Poland," we read:

The POMOST activists collecting "signatures for the petition to renounce Yalta" want to present it to the U.S. Congress and [. . .] "Who knows," says Kiernik. "If it won't come to a vote in the House of Representatives and in the Senate after which the American government would officially confirm that it does not uphold the Yalta Agreement."

In the *Freedom Soldier* from February 9–10, 1985, there was a huge article by Henryk Kawki. The antisocialist and anti-Polish coalition will not leave any room for traitors, provoking people "with no conscience," who demand revision of the Yalta Agreement:

And we, Poles, so heavily experienced in war, are to come out as marionettes crying, "Down with Yalta! We want war!"

With the use of such compliments and the ammunition of such propaganda, the Jaruzelski-Kiszczak tabloids tried to discredit POMOST.

* * *

There was an ethnic festival held each year in Detroit's city center on the river in an amphitheater. All the minority groups in turn had their days, during which there would be folkloric performances and bands. You could also help yourself to the foods particular to a given ethnic group. Each such ethnic celebration was initiated quite ceremoniously. The Polish festival always enjoyed wide popularity. In those years, the PRP consul always came for the "Polish" day and sat up on the speakers' platform with the festival's organizer, a man by the name of Sobieraj who was a lawyer and a representative of the PRP in Detroit; the chancellor of the Orchard Lake seminary, Father Milewski, who was next to the participating bishop and the others so called representatives of Polish-Americans. I came to the conclusion that this symbiosis of Polish-Americans and the puppets of the occupying regime in

Poland had to be destroyed or at least seriously thwarted. Other members of our group felt the same way.

But how could we make this come about? During a speech on public land, you can protest loudly—so that's something we could do. We could also give out flyers demanding the dissolution of the Yalta Agreement. No one could arrest us for such an act. I felt, however, that this wasn't good enough. I got in touch with a pilot whose small plane carried advertisements into the sky. I paid him what was then a large amount of money—$280. We arranged it so that at the moment the consul was to begin his speech, the pilot would be flying around above the crowd with a sign flowing behind the plane that read, "Renounce Yalta!"

The festivities began. I spread out my group around the whole square with piles of flyers explaining the baseness of the Yalta Agreement and the Soviet Occupation of Poland. When the consul was about to get up to the podium, we ran up to it and, using completely non-parliamentary words, demanded that he immediately step down from the platform. He was very angry and tried to speak anyway, but nothing came of it. He had to step down with his tail between his legs, and the whole festivity ended at that moment. We had our first local victory.

The next year, we decided to repeat this scenario. This time, Mr. Sobieraj rented his own black police force. We were completely surrounded. There were also some vehicles waiting nearby to transport us to jail. An FBI inspector told me that they couldn't do anything to us, because we had the right to protest and give out flyers in public space. And that's what happened. They didn't try to "gather us up," because they would have had to deal with a legal case of physical attack and bodily harm. Our actions went as planned without a hitch, and the consul didn't give a speech.

The following year, however, the organizers of this affair were more conniving. They arranged things so that the event was held in a spacious building, the underground space that was connected to the amphitheater. The building was normally designated for situations in which bad weather meant that the festivities couldn't take place in the open air. This time, the legal situation looked somewhat different. Here, Sobieraj could have us arrested if we were to yell and give out flyers. We had prepared banners that were tucked under our arms. Two or three black policemen were "stuck onto" each of us. One of them asked me what I was holding under my arm. I replied that he should try to take it from me and see for himself. Of course, he couldn't let himself do this, because it would be illegal. All in all, however, we didn't have the means to express our protest. All the ways seemed blocked to us. But were they really all blocked?

Then, I got a terrific idea! Bolko Skowron's wife, Jola, full of femininity and calmness, could be our aid in this company of mutual adoration. I asked her to go up to Mr. Sobieraj with our people behind her and ask him in the most polite voice in the name of POMOST for the PRP consul not to show his face there.

And that's what she did. Sobieraj reddened and barked, "He won't show up here! He won't show up here!"

Jola thanked him kindly, and the consul really didn't show up. Instead, a dancing couple came on the stage in Polish folk costumes.

* * *

Lech "Bolko" Walesa became the president of the "Third Republic." (Bolko was the code name given to Walesa by the regime security department. He was their agent.) Poland ostensibly became a free country. In plain truth, however, the terrorist structure of the PRP remained untouched, the Russian armies were still stationed in Poland, and even Walesa was an agent of the Soviets, disgraced and blackmailed by Moscow. His closest coworkers were Milewski, an officer of the KGB, and Wachowski, an officer of the GRU. Those working closest with "President" Walesa were also Soviet agents.

"Reconstruction," or rather the reanimation of "Solidarnosc," did not happen democratically but rather from the top, and the key positions were taken by Walesa's people. A parody arose, a mere image of a free country, while really the next suit of Soviet agencies took power. I had all this well documented information in my hand and could at any moment release it. I was asked to go to a meeting of the American Polish National Council in Boulder, Colorado. The organizers of the meeting were Professor Rozek and, of course, Colonel Kajkowski, a delegate of the Polish Government In Exile to the United States. I found out that the president of the Polish Government In Exile, Mr. Kaczorowski—the former president, Mr. Sabat, had died of a heart attack—was also supposed to come. The purpose of the meeting was to discuss whether or not the Polish Government In Exile should award the national insignia of authority to Walesa. The British Branch of National Council was opposed to this gesture. Kaczorowski was hoping that the Polish American National Council would express agreement, as he was undoubtedly counting on getting a position in the Polish government.

I went there deeply upset. I thought that even as emigrants we should adamantly strive for Poland's nationhood and not simply accept supposed freedom and supposed nationhood. I prepared an elaborate essay including all the evidence. Of course, this wasn't my position alone—it was also the position of POMOST.

I arrived in Boulder a day early. I wanted to speak privately with President Kaczorowski so as to convince him about the mistake that he was going to make with this course of action and to give him the evidence I had. I found out that he was already there, staying in the same hotel, while the meeting was supposed to take place the following day. I called him and asked to meet with him for an hour. He refused emphatically. Angered by this refusal, I called Colonel Kajkowski and presented him with "Mr. President's" arrogant response. He was not thrilled with this behavior. He promised to do something. Indeed, he called me just a moment later and told me that we would meet in the president's room and that I would have fifteen minutes to present my concerns.

Kaczorowski welcomed me rather impolitely. I also didn't feel like being so polite myself.

"Mr. President," I said, mindful of those fifteen minutes, "you were kind enough to give me the opportunity to familiarize you with my concerns in fifteen minutes after Colonel Kajkowski's intervention. Respecting your valuable time, I'll do it in five minutes!"

Having said this, I got out the evidence I had about Lech "Bolko" Walesa's cooperation with the occupational regime, including the testimony about his beating down the strike. I said, "Because of these facts, I was emphatically opposed to giving the national insignia of authority to someone like Lech Walesa. I think it would be a big mistake, if not a down right abandonment of our basic principles. This is the point of view I will take during my presentation time at the meeting of the National Council."

"I won't take any more of your time. I'm sorry for the few minutes I did take. I do this not for myself, but for the good of Poland. Good day!"

I turned on my heel and left. Kaczorowski stood in the middle of the room red-faced and furious, not knowing what to say.

The meeting of the National Council began the next day. If I'm not mistaken, it was initiated by Professor Rozek. He put forth that they had received the permission of President Kaczorowski to award the national insignia to Walesa. Some opposing voices arose, though not very many. With some difficulty, I got a chance to speak. I presented my argument, documenting the need to refuse this action, as the transfer of the national insignia would become an official recognition of the new Warsaw regime, which was still a Soviet agency. A heated debate arose. Professor Rozek did everything he could to stop or pacify me. But, I was getting more and more adherents. Seeing that there was a need for some kind of compromise, Rozek proposed that President Kaczorowski would make the ultimate decision, with the condition that the protocols of that decision were precisely highlighted with all the concerns put forth by Dr. Subczynski. I couldn't not agree to this; Rozek had most of the participants' support.

As a result of the vote a rather curious document arose. The Polish American National Council recognized President Kaczorowski as the one who would make the ultimate decision, but the document would also highlight Dr. Subczynski's concerns. The bullet points of these concerns summarized the criminal activity of the Soviet agencies in Poland and Lech Walesa's role in that activity.

Soon after that, Kaczorowski went to Warsaw and ceremoniously gave "Bolko" the national insignia of the Second Republic of Poland, which had been traitorously attacked by Hitlerist Germans and Stalinist Bolsheviks, bloodied in concentration camps and labor camps, befouled by both occupiers, and betrayed villainously by both supposed allies.

Walesa accepted this insignia rather arrogantly. Kaczorowski was disappointed. Instead of being rewarded for his service to Walesa and betrayal of Poland, he was ultimately dismissed and ignored.

We had a POMOST meeting at my house. We were going to discuss the strategy of further activism and organize ways to attract more members. The Zawadzkis immediately made a motion to remove me from the position of coordinator. I couldn't believe my ears! All of POMOST's work radiated from and happened in my house. After all, our recording studio was here. I was in the midst of all the action. No one else had these possibilities. A stormy scene arose. It seemed that they had formed their own "party." Most of the people gathered, however, were really angered, and the Zawadzkis had to leave the meeting, having hurt the unity of POMOST but not achieving much.

Disparaging letters about me that had been written by this couple started circulating around Detroit. I have these letters. During that time, a letter written by Andrzej Czuma to Janusz Szymanski fell into Krzystof Rac's hands. He was offering his suggestions as to what means should be used to break up POMOST.

We received unhappy news from Poland. We heard about the stifling of the Solidarnosc movement and that Kornel Morawiecki, who stood at the forefront of the Fighting Solidarnosc movement, was in hiding from the UB. Like lightning on a clear day, we got word that he had been "spotted," arrested, soon afterwards sentenced to exile, and sent to the Holy Father in Rome. After a few more weeks, the news reached us that Kornel was staying in London under the care of patriotic immigrants there.

I thought it was essential for Morawiecki to come to the United States and to reach out to senators and congressmen as a representative of the resistance of the Polish nation. I bought him a ticket (with my own money), and in the company of my late friend and POMOST activist Professor Krynski, we were soon greeting our guest at the airport in Washington.

A young Pole came with him, kind, and devoted to the cause. To my dismay, Kornel Morawiecki acted with visible reserve towards us. That same night, that young man secretly gave me a copy of a memorandum that had been a slanderous statement brought over to Kornel. It was written by Andrzej Czuma. Clearly biased, he wrote libelously about the POMOST organization and me specifically, quoting the opinion of the Zawadzkis! I understood then why Morawiecki had not trusted us.

Professor Krynski arranged a series of meetings for us with Republican senators and congressmen. They welcomed us warmly. They asked about the situation in Poland and expressed their support for the freedom movement of Poles. One of them suggested that we go to the Senate's director of finance—it might be possible to get subsidies for the freedom movement in Poland. The director was very kind. He told us that there was a possibility of getting support in the sum of around two million dollars. He undoubtedly believed in what he was saying. The appropriation however went not to the freedom movement but rather was received by regime-member Janusz Onyszkiewicz, a member of the Jewish junta controlling the post communistic Poland. That was the road that United States international politics followed with respect to the "Polish problem."

After arriving in Detroit, Kornel Morawiecki stayed in Zawadzkis home. I had only a short meeting with him at that time. Then he left for Chicago, where he met with Andrzej Czuma.

We couldn't tolerate the systematic destruction of our organization. Krzysztof Rac took the matter to court as illegal use of our organization's name and distribution of pamphlets under the same name. The matter went to trial. The judge called for votes from the entire organization.

Our group spent an entire night preparing ballots, to which a letter and return envelope were added. Hundreds of such letters were sent out to all the members of the organization. All the material from the voters ended up in the judge's hands. Seventy percent of the members supported the proper organization. Thus, the judge couldn't rule otherwise than to forbid the dissenters from using the name POMOST and putting out pamphlets under the same name. This battle lasted a long time and was very costly with the lawyer's fee. What's worse, it decisively damaged the fundamental goal of POMOST's existence—to unmask the Warsaw regime.

On April 25, 1986, the nuclear reactor in Chernobyl exploded. It just happened on the very day a Russian sporting event was taking place in a nearby stadium. The Soviet authorities not only did not notify the surrounding population but also did not stop the sporting event, knowing very well that all would die from radiation exposure. In Poland the nuclear testing center discovered very strong radiation, but it was not permitted to disclose this information. Sweden raised the first alarm.

I received some recordings at that time from a propaganda radio station named Warszawa I. It presented the Chernobyl tragedy rather curiously. In the first communication about the matter, it completely denied that anything had happened there, implying it was only evil propaganda from the West. In the next communication, Poles were told that there had been some "technical difficulties," but that the situation was fully under control and that no one was in danger. The next communication claimed that the radiation resulting from the explosion was minimal and that the situation was being taken care of. Each following communication was somewhat contrary to one that preceded it. After a delay of several days, the naked truth finally spread through the world like a nuclear wave. Not many people know that the Soviets sent a train full of army reservists from Latvia who, without any protection, had to cement the remains of the nuclear core. Their survival rate was less than two weeks. And not many may know that no measures were taken to protect people who lived in areas of immediate danger.

The radioactive smog moved in two waves. The first one went north, reaching as far as eastern Sweden and Finland, where the Laplanders live, and moving into present Belorussia, the former land of Eastern Poles. The second pass moved west, reaching as far as Germany through Southern Poland. It's worth adding that this radioactive wave reached as far as northern Canada.

During the first phase, the most dangerous substance was radioactive iodide, which was later responsible for hundreds of thousands of thyroid tumors and maldeveloped fetuses. Despite the rather short radiation period of this particular element, its effects last long, destroying everything that crosses its path. The effects of the radiation appears after several years or even several decades.

Cesium and strontium are even more dangerous than iodide. They actually radiate with much less intensity but for a longer period of time. Their half-life of radioactivity is fifty years. Thus, their "weak" radiation, spread over ten years, becomes unspeakably destructive in its effects.

I suspected that situation was far more dangerous than people thought. I quickly looked over the essential professional literature on the subject. Most experts estimated that the number of victims during the coming years would be about thirteen million people! Even now, when I write these words, the radiation continues.

From the information available, it became obvious that the explosion wasn't the main engineer's fault. The murderer was the communist party and its lackeys. They wanted to increase the production capacity of the reactor regardless of the danger involved. The stupidity of those apparatchiks was hard to even comprehend. This same authority also demanded that wheat still be collected from the nearby fields, and the flour made from it was distributed to the people of the Caucas Mountain region. Not many people know about this quiet form of genocide.

A few weeks after the explosion, the Polish-American community in Windsor invited me, as a creator of radio programming, to give a report on the subject of Chernobyl from a doctor's point of view. The first speaker was a physics professor from Poland. He tried to convince people that the Chernobyl catastrophe wasn't a threat to people, that the radiation effects were minimal, and that there was no reason to worry. In other words, everything was "fine"; the regime propaganda was apparently "radiating" here as well, in the very room we were in. In the second part of the meeting, I had the opportunity to present all the horrifying facts I had found in American literature on the subject. It became clear to everyone there that the professor, simply and openly, had been lying.

After the meeting, a lot of the listeners wanted to speak with me to find out further details and to give me their opinion of my radio shows. Kazimir Weber also came up to me; he had been a machinist from a steel mill in Stalowa Wola, thrown out of Poland for his activism in the Solidarnosc movement.

"I can't join forces with you right now, but when I figure things out, I'll contact you so that we can work together," he said.

And he kept his word. We spent many hours recording radio programs together.

The news of Father Jerzy Popieluszko's murder shocked us completely. We knew that the young vicar from the parish in Zoliborz gave fiery sermons for which he had already been threatened, but he continued to do his duty steadfastly as a chaplain and a patriot, serving God and Truth.

I organized a meeting of the Polish-American community in Detroit in the parish room of St. Mary Catholic church. The room was bursting at the seams from all the people. I spoke from the heart; it was hard for me to hold back tears. I called for us to continue Father Jerzy's work here on foreign land and, in particular, to continue having monthly Masses for the Fatherland as they had been conducted by Father Jerzy Popieluszko in Poland. Everyone there supported the project, and Mr. Stepien, the chairman of the veterans of the Home Army, offered to handle its organization. He kept his word. During all the years that I lived there, masses took place in which flags of the

National Army veterans and the POMOST organization appeared prominently in front of the altar.

The freedom movement in Red China was throttled by the massacre in Tiananmen Square. Millions of TV viewers in the United States and abroad looked in horror at the young man-hero who stopped a row of tanks with his own body.

The rather numerous Chinese population of Detroit organized a demonstration in protest. POMOST also participated. When the organizer of the demonstration saw us, he invited me up to the podium and asked me to make a short speech. What could I say to these desperate people? Still, the words that came from my heart found clear resonance. The Chinese people saw that we understood them, that we shared the pain and anger with them, and that they, the Chinese people on a far foreign shore, weren't the only ones fighting against this same evil that was being spilled all over the whole world.

Through the following years, nearly all the people of the anti-communist resistance movement made their way through my house. Mrs. Anna Walentynowicz spent a week with me. She told me the truth about the events that had led up to the strike in Gdansk stockyard. She also informed me about Lech Walesa's perfidious role in an attempt to suppress the strike. I had not known about these details up until that point.

Andrzej Gwiazda, who I admire and respect for his opinions, was also one of my guests. I admire his unbreakable, uncompromising position—his complete devotion to Polish affairs. There were moments when he seemed like Gandhi—he had something similar in him. I see him as he goes out on the terrace with the strongest and most stinking French cigarette in his mouth so as not to pollute the air inside the house, standing there, looking up at the stars. We stood like that for a long time, without saying a word, sharing unspoken dialogue and unspoken understanding.

A few weeks after his departure, I found out that he had been attacked and beaten up sustaining a broken jaw as a result.

Romuald Szermietew also came to see me. He was confident and authoritative. He didn't make a very positive impression on me. My feeling was confirmed by his later career in the Third Polish Republic.

DURING ANNA WALENTYNOWICZ'S VISIT AT MY HOUSE

I also remember Jan Parys's visit with his wife, Mrs. Bochenska. He made a kind impression on me. He was young, intelligent, and full of verve.

I have to clarify here that it was mostly my responsibility to organize meetings of the Polish-American community and to invite the luminaries of the resistance movement. The meetings were successful; there were always heated debates after several lectures. From time to time, provokers would show up, usually trying to offend our guest. The ones leading the meeting would always take care of them quickly and, as some have said, not always in the most polite manner.

Leszek Moczulski also came to Detroit, mainly to visit his coworker from the KPN, Bolko Skowron, who worked with me in POMOST. Moczulski didn't know about our work together. But he was well informed about POMOST's activism and agenda. Why does this make a difference? Well, Moczulski didn't want to meet me!

That particular day, the Skowrons had invited the Moczulskis to their house for dinner. Bolko called me and invited me to dinner as well. Moczulski was really shocked at the sight of me—he mumbled that he didn't want to have anything to do with me! When our host calmly asked him why, he didn't respond. He calmed down after a while and made some sensible conversation. Later on, we got in the car and went to a meeting of the Polish-American community. When Mrs. Moczulski found out that she was riding with the coordinator of POMOST, she fell into a rage.

"I don't want this to go on!" She cried.

Her protests didn't do much, simply because no one could get out of the car when it was moving at full speed.

Moczulski's later career and regime connections completely explained her dislike of anticommunist organizations in the United States.

People in Poland and throughout the world don't know much about the fact that during Brezniew's leadership, and Jimmy Carter's in the U.S.A., Poland was threatened by a fatal danger. Around 1974, for reasons that were unclear at the time, there was a reorganization of the administrative structure of the People's Republic of Poland. This change was actually transforming the administration of Polish terrain to Soviet design. Not able to break down the Polish resistance, the occupier decided that Poland should be divided, torn apart in the spirit of a "peaceful" systematic partition. Eleven million Poles would find themselves in terrain that was administered by Eastern Germans of the so-called Democratic Republic of Germany as an integral part of the German nation's hull. The remaining area—"the country around the Vistula," as if an echo of the czar's "country on the Vistula"— was to become an integral Soviet "republic." As far as we know President Jimmy Carter accepted this plan. In accordance with the obligatory Yalta Agreement's partition of Europe, the United States was not to meddle in this even greater expansion of Soviet dominion.

The unexpected victory of Ronald Reagan and advent of his administration in January of 1981 impeded the Soviet plans. In his speech, Reagan called the Soviet Bolsheviks an "Evil Empire"— a satanic empire. The world's "Marxist media," including the American media, took the real sting out of this metaphor by explaining and maintaining Reagan's "Evil Empire" as simply a "Bad Empire." This significant change was a real misnomer. Satan's Empire was replaced by an empire of unnamed badness.

President Reagan called the American people and the civilized world to "roll back the red carpet," which was engulfing both hemispheres like a creeping flame.

This speech must have seriously shocked and devastated the Soviet leader and his followers.

Two years prior to that in 1978, after the sudden death of John Paul I—who "died" in very strange circumstances while he was preparing a list that named cardinals and high-up Vatican officials who had links to masonry—a Polish cardinal, Karol Wojtyla, was elected pope. He then took the name John Paul II, in honor and a remembrance of John Paul I his predecessor, most likely murdered because of his ideological fight with communism and masonry.

Those ruling the Soviet "Satanic Empire" underestimated Karol Wojtyla's personality. I am convinced that they did not appreciate the creativity with which he fought communism, the religion of Satan's empire, ideologically. He had a reputation among the leaders in the Kremlin as a person who was weak and who confined himself to the subtle meanderings of Catholic philosophy.

How wrong they were! When they decided that such an opponent should be physically destroyed—with an order given by a Jewish man, Chairman Andropov—it was already too late, and the attempt didn't work.

To this day, there is evidence of the close cooperation between John Paul II and President Reagan in the fight against the "Satanic Empire." John Paul's visit to oppressed and beleaguered Poland in 1979, became the first blows to the Soviet "Satanic Empire." No one, not even the professional political analysts, knew then on what a crumbling, malleable foundation the giant of evil stood. Many firmly maintained that communism would wash over the entire world.

One of the shareholders of the radio station WPON, of which I became the chairman and main shareholder, was Father Panczuk— a Ukrainian who ran religious programs for his fellow believers. He was a Basilian Uniat monk who served under the Vatican auspicies. We rarely had any opportunity to talk. The shareholders' meetings were rather stormy, mostly for political reasons. Father Panczuk supported me discreetly, often silently but clearly.

One day, we happened to be on the same transcontinental flight across America. Coincidentally, we were also seated next to one another. A long flight with such immobile positions led to a deeper exchange of our points of view. Father Panczuk, who was then a general of the Basilian convent and who knew about my personal battle against the Soviet evil, familiarized me with the activism of the Basilians and the role that John Paul II played in their activity. I found out that a seminary ordaining Basilian priests existed in Poland. These priests were then secretly transferred to the Ukraine. The underground Uniat Church already had two hundred bishops, not counting the ordinary priests. Father Panczuk only revealed one unknown side of the Polish pope's activism. How many more were there, similarly unknown to general believers and his opponents? We are just now learning about the close cooperation that existed between the Vatican and Washington.

Ronald Reagan, by introducing the Strategic Defense Initiative (SDI), tilted the balance of power to the American side by destroying Soviet confidence in the old defense of Mutually Assured Destruction (MAD). The global state of "Cold War" was extended into outer space—basing U.S. defense on the "Star Wars" system of subduing long-range Soviet missiles immediately after they had been fired.

There was a conference of conservative Americans in the United States in the 1980s. As a member of the party, I went to this conference. I was able to meet the most exemplary people of those times. But Judy Sheldon, a young, attractive, and mostly unknown woman, made the greatest impression on me. She was the star of that conference. During her studies of political science, she wrote a doctoral dissertation about the economic situation in the Soviet Union. Capable, intelligent, and hardworking, she researched all the possible sources she could find. She demonstrated unwaveringly that the Soviet economy, mainly as a result of participating in a mad arms race and supporting communist insurgencies throughout the world, had a deficit of more than two hundred billion dollars! She came to the inarguable conclusion that this was the beginning of the end of that "Satanic Empire." She described it all in her book, *The Upcoming Downfall of the Soviet Union.*

At first, no one wanted to believe her, viewing with skepticism her statistics and synthesis. When in time, however, the data on which she based her work was checked, American politicians came to the conclusion that she had written the truth and presented the real picture of a wavering giant.

This made me incredibly happy. I saw a real chance for Poland to tear away from that Soviet "paradise." I have to pat myself on the back here and say that even before these revelations, I foresaw the downfall of the Soviet Union on the basis of economic erosion and indicated in several radio programs of POMOST.

Events quickly followed. In 1980, the Solidarnosc movement arose. It became the fatal wound in the flesh of the Soviet monster. Those who had for tens of years under the banner of, "Proletarians of every country unite!" against their own will and desire came out against the Soviet government and their apparatchiks. This blow from the workers in a workers' "paradise" panicked the Soviet "heads of state."

Here is an essential breakdown of several falsehoods and facts to this day maintained by the Polish-speaking soviet propagandists. Jaruzelski was a general of the Red Army and the head of the army-strategy ring of an area that was much larger than Poland! His direct military superior was Marshal Kulikow.

Another lie, propagated by Jaruzelski, was the need to impose martial law to avoid threat of direct Soviet intervention. From the documents of a KGB archivist named Mitrochin that were published by Christopher Andrew, it is clear that Jaruzelski was the one who wanted Soviet and East German military intervention. The Kremlin refused such intervention, however, and demanded that the Polish-speaking conspirators subdue the nation on their own.

This is the naked truth about Jaruzelski. Now, I can't understand Poles who still have a shadow of a doubt about Jaruzelski's role; he was a Soviet general in a Polish uniform! I am embarrassed by these fellow countrymen, who in their time stood in a long line patiently waiting for Solidarnosc's executioner to put his bloody autograph on their copies of his lie-filled book. I cheer myself thinking that these are the same kind of "countrymen" as this Soviet viceroy.

And one more clarification—when the Americans installed their medium-range missiles in Turkey, the Soviets still didn't have such missiles. The KGB colonel, Ogarkow, received orders to create a bold diversion. Using KGB channels, he spread false information to U.S. intelligence that the Soviets had the same kind of weaponry. Then, these missiles were rather awkwardly "placed" in Cuba. This situation led to the well-known Cuban missile crisis, during which war hung by a thread. The Soviets graciously backed down and "removed" their in reality short-range missiles from Cuba in exchange for the same gesture by the United States in Turkey! It should be noted that the missiles which the United States placed in Turkey were of a middle range and easily threatened the European part of the Soviet Union. Ogarkow was promoted to the rank of general for this masterful work. He soon became a marshal for the Soviet Union. His strategic assignment then became to work out a Soviet "blitzkrieg" that would allow for immediate conquest of Western Europe. And thus, we reach the position of Poland in all these plans. Poland was to be made a death zone for decades as a result of destruction and nuclear radiation. Russia had an enormous amount of conventional force at its disposal, including 40,000 tanks and divisions of *specnaz*—commandos who would infiltrate the enemy from behind—as well as a countless number of military helicopters. An attack was predicted for 1984. Colonel Kuklinski was the one who revealed these plans to America. The information delivered to U.S. intelligence led to the creation of a new type of military plane: it could destroy tank divisions from beyond the horizon. This stopped the expansive plans of the Soviets.

I heard a certain woman, as a representative of Polish culture, say rather recently that Colonel Kuklinski's role is still controversial and that it is really difficult to judge whether he was a traitor or a hero! The effects of systemic brainwashing are indeed amazing and frightening it its power!

GIVING A SPEECH AT A MEETING ORGANIZED FOR
POLONIA BY THE MICHIGAN POMOST CHAPTER

WITH MR ANTONI MACIEREWICZ, ONE OF THE LEADERS
OF THE OPPOSITION IN POLAND WHO VISITED ME IN
DETROIT. HE WAS LATER A MEMBER OF THE POLISH DIET.

DEMONSTRATION TO RENOUNCE YALTA,
ORGANIZED IN CANADA

145

I WAS HONORED TO BE AN INVITED SPEAKER AT AN ANTI-
COMMUNIST DEMONSTRATION AFTER THE MASSACRE
AT TIANANMEN. THE MEETING WAS ORGANIZED BY
LOCAL CHINESE AND SUPPORTED BY POMOST.

RELAXING WITH MY POMOST GROUP AFTER
PREPARING A RADIO PROGRAM

THE POMOST GROUP WITH ANNA
WALENTYNOWICZ IN THE MIDDLE

DURING A PARADE, HEADING THE POMOST
GROUP WITH ITS YOUNGEST "MEMBERS"

ONE OF THE DEMONSTRATIONS AGAINST THE
SOVIET OCCUPATION OF POLAND

THE KATYN MONUMENT AT ORCHARD LAKE, ON THE TERRAIN
OF THE RELIGIOUS SEMINARY. POMOST'S FIRST DEMONSTRATION
TOOK PLACE HERE. THE SIGN WITH THE INSCRIPTION, "SOVIET
CRIME 1940" WAS PASTED ON BY UNKNOWN CULPRITS.
AFTER A YEAR, FATHER MILEWSKI REMOVED THE SIGN.

12

More Tales from the Front Lines

NE BLACK CITIZEN of the United States apparently didn't have the best relationship with an also black criminal gang; he ran away from them as fast as his legs would carry him. He ran onto a bridge above a highway. He was halfway across when he realized that they were blocking his way on the other side. He had to have been very desperate, for he threw himself off the bridge onto the cement of the roadway below among speeding cars. By some miracle, he wasn't run over. He did have a crushed forehead and eyebrow arches. The impact of the injury was taken by the bones. This was the reason why the brain was spared. He made this suicidal leap in the middle of the night and I had to operate on him immediately.

I opened the anterior fossa. Fragments of bone were tearing into the dura matter and were pushing into the frontal lobes, which were in large part crushed. Practically speaking, there was no longer a base of the anterior fossa or the upper part of the orbit—it was just a bloody mass interspersed with pieces of skull. I removed them slowly, trying not to damage anything. I found the eye, which had an intact ophthalmic nerve and an uninjured vascular system. I managed to put it back in place along with all the muscles and their bone attachment to the orbit. I cleaned the frontal lobes, stopped the bleeding, and repaired the torn dura matter with a graft of fascia from the leg. The problem of the lack of the base of the anterior fossa remained—you could see one huge hole to the nose and the crushed ethmoid sinuses. I couldn't leave the matter as it was, because it could have led to infection. At that time, we had a semi-hard mesh called "mercelin" that was used as an implant in surgeries of inguinal hernias. I cut out an appropriate piece of that material and fit it to the configuration of the skull, then wrapped it with fascia taken from the thigh. I put a drain to the nose underneath it.

My patient healed in a matter of several days. We removed the drain. There was no leakage of cerebro-spinal fluid or any signs of infection. The huge indentation in the forehead and eyebrow arches made him somewhat of a monster. To my surprise, he could not only see out of the repositioned eye but even retained some movement of the eyeball.

After several months, I admitted him again and did plastic surgery of the forehead and upper part of the orbit. My patient had to have been happy with the results, because he sent me a photograph of himself later. Of course, he was missing a part of the frontal lobes, which could certainly have had an impact on his personality. I lost touch with him.

After a few years, he showed up again to see me.

"I'm not coming as a patient. I simply wanted to visit you. I'm now a well-known black politician in the Chicago area."

"Not surprising," I thought. He had excellent qualifications for a politician, having been uninhibited by a frontal lobotomy. I kept this knowledge to myself, maintaining politeness to my undoubtedly important guest.

Again, years went by. And then, I suddenly received a summons in which that black politician was suing me for malpractice. I was incredibly surprised, because fifteen years had gone by since that day. I didn't understand what was going on.

Soon, however, I learned the truth. That guy got drunk during a visit to Detroit, crashed his car, and was taken, bleeding and bruised, to one of the large medical centers in Detroit. There, he was given routine head scans, and it was concluded that frontal and ethmoid sinuses were inflamed since they could not see them. The radiologist came to a false conclusion that there was active infection in this area. An ENT was called in, who also didn't distinguish himself with a great deal of common sense, as further events proved. He started draining the "sinuses" through an incision in the area of the nose. After opening the scar, he grabbed something hard with the clamp and started pulling. To his great surprise, he saw the plastic mesh that I had used to divide the nasal cavity from the skull cavity. He hadn't gone to the trouble of calling me before the procedure to find out what had been done during this man's previous surgery.

Seeing his own error, this ENT told my patient that I had mistakenly left a "foreign body" in the wound. Seeing the danger of the situation, he also called in a neurosurgeon. This one in turn, not having any other way out, removed the whole plastic construction. The patient found himself in a situation in which the brain was hanging into the nasal cavity protected only by the scarred dura mater.

The matter went on for two years. Finally, the neurosurgeon who performed the second surgery categorically stated that my surgery had been proper and that it had been unnecessarily ruined. I was thus cleared of any blame. The patient, however, was not thrilled with the new situation. Not only did he not get the millions he had been waiting for after the trial, but he was also left in a monstrous state and undoubtedly threatened with infection through the nose. He then demanded to have another "Subczynski surgery" in that same large medical center. But they wouldn't agree to repeat the surgery that I had performed.

At his wit's end, he plotted to murder the lawyer, a Jewish man, who had convinced him to sue! I don't know how the matter ended, but I do know that the high priced lawyer was in hiding for quite a while.

One time, I was called in to Bon Secour Hospital in the middle of the night to see a twelve-year-old black child. He had a huge crushed wound on the top of the skull with a large indentation of the skull.

The procedure was very difficult. We had to remove the bone carefully with the help of a drill while also doing our best to avoid any acute bleeding from the huge venous sinus located there. Because there is zero pressure in it in a lying-down position, there is also the danger of air being sucked into the venous system, which can cause a fatal air embolism.

I finally uncovered the area of the damaged sinus, leaving the part of the bone that was blocking the bleeding. Then I uncovered the sinus above and below the injury. I cut out two semicircular pieces of the dura matter, which could be folded like an envelope around the area where the sinus was torn—so as to recreate it. When everything was ready, I removed the bone fragments in one movement. Blood spurted out, but we immediately stopped the bleeding by wrapping the sinus with the pieces of the dura matter. My assistant held them in place, and I could calmly put in the sutures. We saved the child, and he left without any deficits. I repaired the bone defect with a plastic called metylmetacrylate.

A few months went by. A police inspector came by asking to speak with me. He was leading the investigation involving that accident. He told me what had happened. A local gang of black teenagers had decided to make some money. They all lived on the same street as the victim. In the middle of winter, they kidnapped this boy and locked him up in a cold garage. Then, they went to his mother and demanded ransom. She shooed them off saying she wouldn't give them a dime! Furious, they returned to the garage and "gave it" to the kidnapped one with a hammer to the head—undoubtedly trying to kill him. They left him unconscious and bleeding and went back to their daily chore of dealing drugs on the streets. My patient regained consciousness, managed to break a windowpane in the garage, got outside, and, awfully soaked in blood, tried to get to the street until a passerby found him, and that's how he ended up in my hands.

The whole gang had been identified. Some members were found sitting in a trial taking place in the criminal court. The prosecutor was asking for my testimony as to a very essential matter—was this beating meant to inflict bodily harm, or was it attempted murder? There was a huge difference.

The inspector arranged to come get me in his police car for my own protection. My testimony was rather weighty, and I could end up being threatened by a gang member, for it wasn't certain how many members were still loose on the streets. We went into the courthouse through the back doors, and the inspector didn't leave my side for a second. He was armed. In the courtroom, I saw a whole bench filled with the accused, and all the eyes were fixed on me. I clearly testified in response to the prosecutor's question that I didn't have the least bit of doubt that this was attempted murder. The prosecutor thanked me, and the defense had no questions for me. We left through the same back doors, and the same police car took me back to the hospital. The inspector warned me that I might be in danger, but nothing happened.

A few months later, when I was doing some shopping in a large mall, a large black woman suddenly started yelling and pointing at me, "That's him! That's him!" A group of black teenagers surrounded me. I felt a little uneasy, immediately remembering my testimony in court. Fortunately this black woman was yelling in my direction for another reason. She wanted her children to see the man who had saved the life of their brother—a matter that was totally unrelated to the other one. Still, I did have a moment of apprehension.

Indeed, the tracks of human fate roll along very strange and twisted ways. A fifty-year-old black man was admitted in the emergency room of St. John's Hospital in a very serious state. He had a brain aneurism that suddenly started bleeding, resulting in a subarachnoid hemorrhage. Fortunately, after the first bleeding, as it often happens, the aneurism clotted, and the bleeding temporarily stopped. If this had not happened, the man would have died on the spot. I admitted him into the ICU. He received the appropriate medication there to lower his intracranial pressure and to maintain adequate perfusion of the brain. The arteriogram showed that the cause of this misfortune was a big aneurism situated at the base of the brain at the junction between the left and right anterior brain arteries. I had to operate.

Working very carefully under the microscope, I reached the aneurism, when to my dismay I saw that the distant portions of the anterior cerebral arteries were coming straight out from the aneurism—in other words the aneurism was an intrinsic part of the arterial system in this area. During my examination of the aneurism, the blood clot came loose, causing severe deep arterial bleeding. Because of its location at the base of the brain this type of bleeding is usually catastrophic. I didn't have a second to lose. Blindly, in a wave of flowing blood, I put on two clips. The bleeding stopped immediately, and the aneurism had been eliminated from circulation. At the same time, the perfusion to the subfrontal area of the brain was cut off! I couldn't do anything about this, though, as there was no way of changing the position of the clips. Disheartened, I closed up the skull.

Meanwhile, my patient was doing well. When I called the nurse in the afternoon and asked how he was feeling, she said that he was fine, with the one thing being that she had found him in another patient's bed. After a week, he went home in an excellent state. I waited in anxiety to see what would happen next. After all, he had for all practical reasons had a frontal lobotomy, which in its time was very "fashionable" for psychiatric problems. After a few months, I got a phone call from "his lady." My patient had never previously distinguished himself with a great deal of talent or motivation to work. He drank, beat her, and dragged about.

And then, I heard in the receiver, "Doctor, you are a miracle worker! He doesn't hit me anymore. He stopped drinking. He is even thinking of looking for some kind of a job! I won't forget you 'til the day I die!"

I was very happy that my unplanned lobotomy had such blessed results. This wasn't the end of the saga. After some time, I received a showy silver and gold invitation for that couple's wedding! God really does work in mysterious ways.

A surgery that I had scheduled was delayed. The operating room was occupied, as the previous surgeon had some difficulties, and the procedure ran longer than expected. I had to wait. You could drink coffee and eat some donuts in the physicians' lounge. I went there. I saw Doctor "L," a psychiatrist, there with a cup of coffee in his hand. We knew each other well. We were alone.

"You know, Janusz, I want to tell you about a very difficult issue that is, finally, thank God, coming to a close. I see a lot of drug addicts in my practice. A police inspector came to see me to warn me that he had found out from his informants that there was a contract out on me, meaning a paid hit! This contract came out of a ring of drug dealers. They concluded that I had learned too much about them from my patients. My life became one big hell. The kids have to go to school, my wife is at home. When getting into the car, she doesn't know if there will be an explosion after turning the key."

He had been living with this threat for an entire year. About a week ago, he finally felt some relief. The police inspector told him that apparently they had decided to leave him alone, that the contract had been annulled.

I stayed there until it was time for my surgery, and Dr. "L" went to his other hospitals to make rounds. Two weeks later, I found out that he was killed in a car accident at the intersection of two streets in front of one of the hospitals. He drove a small Corvette sport car, and he had been hit by a Lincoln Town Car. He died instantly. The verdict in this case was involuntary manslaughter. To this day, I don't know if the accident was a coincidence or an intentional hit.

"I can't stand the sight of blood! It clearly makes no difference to you, because you're a neurosurgeon," I heard from the lipstick-painted mouth of a certain lady. She said this authoritatively, with a light dose of contempt. But she is, after all, a subtle being, not lowering herself to the level of a person whose business is cutting people up.

"Fine," I said. "Apart from the objective fact that surgeons are essential, have you ever once thought about how someone becomes such a 'butcher' and what he has to go through, how he has to shape his personality?"

"It doesn't really concern me," she said. "That's his problem."

Indeed, it is a problem that everyone has to deal with individually. I lived through years in this profession. My colleagues were surgeons in various specialties. They were people from varied backgrounds and ethnicities, usually cultured, somewhat egotistical, but all engaged in their work. Still, all of them, apart from a few psychopaths (because there were some of those, too), distinguished themselves with a common attribute. They tried to do their work in the best possible way, putting a lot of effort into it and not caring much about their own health.

When I was a young surgeon just starting out, one of my older colleagues told me the following maxim for my benefit: "You will find yourself in a situation when you will encounter trouble, when, for example, the bleeding will cover your operative field, when you'll be tired, when you'll have had enough—at the same time endangering the life of the patient. These are moments known very well to all of us. What do you do? First and foremost, you can't give up! You can't break down. You have to slow down and decrease the bleeding, get through your own fatigue, and say to yourself, 'It wasn't until this very moment that I began to perform a real surgery!'"

How apt his words were!

The following incident could be an illustration of such a situation. A middle-aged woman was admitted to the hospital with the recurrence of an acoustic neuroma. She had been previously operated through the acoustic labyrinth, but the tumor had been only partially removed. The recurrent tumor covered the whole left side of the posterior fossa. All the existing nerves and blood vessels were drowning in the tumor mass. I began the surgery at 7:30 in the morning, and I finished at midnight! I operated in a sitting position with special rests under my forearms so as to minimize any shaking of my hands. I operated using a microscope. I took several breaks during the procedure to empty my bladder and drink some orange juice.

In this very case, in which I achieved what I had wanted, namely complete removal of the tumor without worsening the patient's neurological state, that maxim of my older colleague was so right. Often no one, or at least not many people, including patients, realize what difficult work surgery can be. After all, it doesn't even end with the surgery. After getting home, you have to call the ICU to ask about the patient's state, eventually giving new orders. And it wasn't only the one patient in my care. When I finally fell into bed, I had the feeling that I was still stuck on the seat of that surgical chair, with the only difference being that my back was touching the bed.

While still in Poland, working in the neurosurgery department of the Medical Academy, I was on-call on Christmas Eve. A patient was brought in with a brain tumor that required immediate surgery. Celebrating Christmas Eve with my family became obviously impossible. I barely finished the procedure when another patient was brought in the middle of the night who also had a brain tumor and was in a similarly serious state. I operated on this one as well. It was ten o'clock in the morning of Christmas Day when yet another patient with a brain tumor was brought in. When I finished the third surgery, it was dusk, and the holidays had already passed! Leaving the hospital in the late afternoon, exhausted beyond belief, I felt as though I were being purposefully hurt, which, of course, didn't matter to anyone and no one was to blame for it; it was, after all, just a part of my professional life!

Having a private practice in Detroit, on my own and not belonging to a group, I was on home call twenty-four hours a day, on ordinary days and all the holidays. I knew that at any time, day or night, I could be called to an emergency case. So many times, during a recording session of a POMOST broadcast, I had to leave my coworkers and transform, or rather return, from being a "political activist" to my fundamental profession.

I would like to respond to that woman now who couldn't stand the sight of blood, now that distance and time separate us. I also don't like the sight of blood, and it incomparably irritates me even more, because it makes a precise surgery all that much more difficult. What differs between us may be only this, that I had to get over not only the aesthetic unpleasantness of it, but also actively control the bleeding during surgery, keeping in mind the constant threat to the patient's life.

And is there some kind of prize? There are huge and invaluable ones, like the sight of a smiling patient, who sometimes has been torn from the clutches of death.

I was going home after a full day's work. As I opened the door, I heard the phone ringing inside the house. I got to it in time. I heard the familiar voice of a pediatrician I knew well.

"Janusz, it's good that I caught you! I was with Dr. 'S.' His daughter was on a concrete slide in the park and slid down so unfortunately that she hit her head. We took her to St. John's. She's in the emergency room with her father."

"Is she conscious?" I interrupted.

"Unfortunately, no!"

He wanted to add something more, but I wasn't listening. I immediately got in the car and rushed to the hospital. This nine-year-old girl, the daughter of my good friend, was in a serious state. She didn't react to pain, and her left pupil was significantly dilated—a certain sign of an epidural hematoma that was growing quickly, as a result of arterial bleeding. We took her to the operating room immediately. I opened the skull instantly. Indeed, there was arterial bleeding from the middle meningeal artery. I stopped it without difficulty and removed the hematoma. The surgery was finished. One dilemma remained—had the hematoma's compression of the brain stem caused some permanent damage? Fortunately, that didn't happen. The child quickly regained consciousness. For some time, she had some difficulty with balance and some trouble swallowing. These signs confirmed the severity of the situation—how little more was needed to cause a tragedy, how critical were those few minutes prior to her surgery.

She and her parents were incredibly grateful to me. Many years went by since those moments. I lost touch with Dr. "S." And then, one day, he called me with best wishes from his daughter, saying that she really wanted to tell me something. They both wanted to visit me. I opened the door and saw a beautiful young woman with dark hair and large, almond shaped, black eyes. My now much older friend "S" stood with her. First, she handed me a silver hand-crafted Egyptian tray (they were Egyptian), then told me that she had something very important to say to me.

We sat down in some comfortable chairs.

"I'm listening," I began politely.

"You saved my life. I will never forget that. I think that it is my obligation to pay back for this, for what you did for me. I will repay by going to medical school; I will devote my whole life to the saving of others. I wanted you to know this."

A tear welled up in my eye. These were not empty words, for I could see her determination when she spoke them. Indeed, she completed medical school, though I don't know where she is working or in what specialty. I am sure, though, that she is a doctor who has found her real calling in life, benefiting many, many others. She can stand the sight of blood with fortitude and gives all that she can of herself to help others.

One of my patients was a judge, an older, cultured man with advanced degenerative changes in the spine. He needed surgery. Using the models I had, I explained to him what the situation looked like and what should be done. In the presence of my secretary, who was making note of the conversation, I told him about the expected postoperative results and possible complications. He listened calmly, asking questions here and there. He agreed to have surgery and asked when it would be. I called the operating room to set up a time. In the meantime, he looked around my office. Seeing numerous diplomas on the wall, a small bookshelf with books, and a model of a brain, he said, "Here I'm in your courtroom where the verdicts that fall are higher and more difficult than the ones in my courtroom."

I was surprised by this comparison. I had never looked at my work from that point of view. But, he was right! Here, in my office, such decisions were very often made—verdicts of utmost importance. Hanging in the balance was the greatest treasure of a person's life—his very fate.

I had been called on a consultation on a twenty-year-old woman in Holy Cross. She had an acute attack of sciatica with all the symptoms of pressure on nerve root L5 on the left side. The radiological examination revealed destruction of the fifth lumbar vertebrae by a tumor. It had all the characteristics of malignancy. There was no alternative but to operate. I knew that I wouldn't be able to remove the whole tumor. I could relieve the pressure from the compressed nerves and be able to provide histological diagnosis on the basis of a biopsy of the tumor tissue.

After the surgery, her symptoms went away, and she felt good. The histological tests didn't offer any illusions; it was giant cell sarcoma. A rather rare tumor, locally malignant and in the initial phase not spreading to the distal locations. It could often be cured with radical excision and a large dose of radiation.

I didn't have much experience then with this type of tumor. I got in touch with the larger neurosurgery centers in the States. Almost all the people consulting me said that the patient had a bad prognosis if I didn't do a complete resection followed by radiation therapy. After discussing the problem with an orthopedic surgeon, we decided that we could remove the tumor in two phases and then stabilize the spine with bone grafts.

Our patient understood her situation very well. She asked us to do all that was in our power with full knowledge that she might come out of it with paresis.

In the first phase, I removed the large mass of the tumor and a big piece of the body of the fifth lumbar vertebrae. Then, the orthopedist and I stiffened that part of the spine with bone grafts from the pelvic bone. She went through the surgery well with fairly limited blood loss.

After a week, we went through the second phase with the participation of a general surgeon. After opening the abdomen and moving her organs aside from the body of the fifth lumbar vertebrae, we removed the rest of it, replacing the space between the sacral bone and the fourth lumbar vertebrae with a piece of fibula from the leg.

Her postoperative course was faultless. After less than a week, she started walking, had no problems urinating or having a bowel movement, nor did she have any sensory disturbances or paresis. Everyone, including the patient, was very happy. Weeks later, when the bone grafts were accepted and stabilized, we sent her for radiation therapy. She handled it well, and her condition was improving quickly. We did the last operation in July.

Then, near the end of October, my patient called me sobbing, "Doctor! Doctor! Oh, it's awful!"

"What happened?" I asked, thinking about all the possible complications that could have arisen.

"I'm pregnant!"

Well, I was really surprised. I knew that sexual intercourse must have been quite painful for her. Still, she was pregnant, and I stood before a serious dilemma. Keeping the baby could have fatal results, for the very change in the spine adapting to pregnancy could be enough to break down the bone grafts, on which—truly—the entire spine was resting. Not to mention that during the first three months of her pregnancy, she had received six thousand rads. The chances that the fetus had not been damaged were close to zero.

I am against abortion with one exception—when the life of the mother is at risk. I also cannot agree with the Catholic Church's position forbidding the use of contraception in marriage. This position has caused many family tragedies.

Debbie—my patient—came to me crying. I explained the situation to her as well as I could. And she wanted to know my opinion, if she should abort the baby. I shied away from a definitive answer. The decision was hers to make—I made this clear. My obligation was only to present her with the facts. She decided to have an abortion. It was not done at the hospitals where I worked. Catholic hospitals did not do abortions.

I think that she made the right decision. I know that there are people who would condemn me and my patient for this.

Twenty years have passed since these events. Debbie didn't get married. She works, often having pains in the lumbar spine area because of degenerative changes. But, she's alive. And she's grateful to me.

A few years later, I received an invitation from the then archbishop, Cardinal Szoka, to participate in a committee meeting in the Detroit archdiocese concerning medical ethics. My close Italian colleague, DeLisio, received a similar invitation. We were invited for dinner to the archbishop's residence. He welcomed us warmly. A committee had been put together in the archdiocese with specially trained priests—a theologian, a philosopher, and an ethicist. We were to be added to this team as the medical experts—I for matters of brain function and DeLisio as an expert on intensive care.

The discussion topic to be resolved was what to do in cases in which tests done during pregnancy revealed an anencephalic fetus. This is a situation (a state) in which the fetus develops only the neural center of the brain stem, while the development of the cerebral hemisphere does not occur. The delivered creature can breathe for a time but will die after a few days. It is incapable of independent living.

The question to be explored by the committee was a significant one—can you and should you remove such a fetus, or should the mother carry it to term knowing about the inevitable finale? The position of the Church then was unanimous—don't remove it! The Church took the position of not touching any life that had already begun.

The argument for interrupting this pathological pregnancy was the fact that there was no viable baby to be had. Death would inevitably occur within a few days of delivery. It was pointless to keep it.

The psychological trauma for the mother, living with the knowledge she is carrying in her womb a being incapable of living outside her uterus must be overwhelming. The theologian and the Catholic ethicist took the position that there is no other alternative but to carry to term in this unfortunate scenario. I couldn't agree with this. I used the following argument—such a being cannot think and cannot function, but it is capable of the most primitive sensation, which is pain.

We looked over the literature on the subject. I was undoubtedly right. Everyone who tries to live in agreement with moral principles does not want to expose or inflict pain on anyone. After long debates, we worked up a joint protocol under which we all signed our names. In accordance with it, an anencephalic fetus could be seen as the one case—not conflicting with Catholic doctrine—to abort the pregnancy.

The protocol was presented at a conference of American bishops, but our recommendation was not accepted.

I still couldn't agree with this—my conscience simply wouldn't let me. I explained to the chairman the committee that I couldn't work with conviction at the conferences, because I couldn't agree with the position of the American bishops. He understood my position quite well.

Soon after I was called on a consultation in the neonatal ward in St. John's Hospital. A baby had been born not only with hydrocephalus but also with severe maldevelopment of the cerebral cortex. Practically speaking, there was very little brain tissue of the hemispheres, only a brain stem was fully developed. In its place was a large sac of cerebro-spinal fluid without the shield of the cortex. I was called to put in a shunt—draining that fluid through a valve, which controlled the intracranial pressure, into the abdominal cavity. This surgical procedure could maintain the life of this being that did not have any chance of even primitive further development.

I had a conversation with the parents. I explained exactly what they could expect, namely the prolonging of life without any hope for further development, because sooner or later, this being would die of inevitable causes. I advised them against this surgery as an act of cruelty prolonging suffering. I stressed to them that this creature, incapable of any reasonable living, still could feel pain. Implanting and changing shunts would be not only senseless but also cruel.

The following day, I found out that the pediatrics chief had sent that newborn to Children's Hospital. And so, my contact with this child ended. Two years went by. I was home. The telephone rang. I heard a desperate sobbing voice, "Doctor! I'm calling you so that you know that you were right then. My husband and I regret with all our hearts that we didn't listen to you. That shunt was put in at Children's Hospital. The child is still alive, having no contact with the environment, no possibility of even turning on its side. This is awful! It's horrible! Why do doctors let these kinds of situations arise? You were the only one who presented the situation to us honestly and openly!"

And again, some time went by. I got a phone call, strangely enough from a national television channel. "Is this Dr. Subczynski?"

"Yes," I replied.

"This is Editor "M." I'm working on a story about hopeless cases of undeveloped fetuses. I got in touch with several families who have experienced such cases. I also spoke with the mother of a child whom you consulted and then refused to perform a procedure to relieve the pressure of the hydrocephalus. I would like to have a TV interview with you. It will be on our show in a week."

Indeed, a whole television crew showed up, armed with the essential equipment for recording, with the woman to whom I had spoken. She began with questions about the initial state of the child, if there were indications to relieve the pressure of the hydrocephalus—and why I had refused to perform this operation. At a certain moment, I figured out that I was dealing with a representative of a fanatical group that took the position of maintaining life at any cost, not recognizing any other circumstances. I had been chosen as a representative of the barbarism evident in all of America! I was perfect for such a role. First of all, I was a foreigner, and beyond this, I held a position that was decidedly against the one being propagated. If I allowed her to keep me in this role in front of millions of viewers, I would have been ruined! And that's what was intended.

I knew the measure of the threat, and I decided to defend myself. I interrupted the flow of her questions and asked her, "Does a child in such a state feel pain?"

"I'm not sure, but I think it does," she said, clearly surprised.

I asked another question, "How many 'corrections' of the shunt have been performed?"

I was speaking in reference to that same child. It turned out that the original shunt didn't function properly and that surgery had to be repeated several times.

"Did this child, shut off from any contact with the world, feel pain then?"

"I think so," she admitted.

"Then, what kind of law or right allows for the torture of a being that is incapable of having any kind of life? Is it only because life should always be preserved and nature should not be allowed to run its course? Because leaving this being alone would have led to its death. And so, in your opinion, is this a moral and ethical position, or is it simply cruelty?"

My interview ended on this note. The spotlights went off. The program did air, but without me, my name, or my questions. It seems that my words didn't fit with the a priori themes of the program.

It was a day like any other in my practice. I came to my office in the afternoon after having spent the whole morning working at the operating table and rounding on patients. The waiting room was full of patients. I saw them with the appropriate care, listened to their complaints, calmed their fears, and explained and designated exact treatments and surgeries. I dictated a lot—documents of illnesses, reports to the insurance companies, and finally expert opinions for workers compensation when they were requested.

It is in the nature of neurosurgical work to often run into legal problems—either in relation to a car accident, murder, attempted murder, or a serious bodily injury. The prosecution often requested my testimony under oath. That particular day, I was called to this role again. The incident was rather interesting, because it wasn't typical. A nine-year-old boy had been walking down the school stairs when he slipped on an iced-over step, hit his head, and lost consciousness. He was taken to Holy Cross. He soon regained consciousness, and the EEG tests revealed changes consistent with a brain concussion. He continued going to school and developed normally. A follow up EEG was normal.

Meanwhile, when he was fifteen, he had his first epileptic seizure. He received the proper treatment, and the seizures did not recur. The parents, however, were suing the school for "negligence"—citing that iced-over step as the real cause of his epilepsy.

I had the last EEG test in front of me, and it showed classic centrencephalic epilepsy. This type of epilepsy manifests most often during the teenage years and doesn't have anything to do with previous injuries.

Joann, my Italian secretary, informed me that the lawyers of both sides were waiting for me along with a court reporter. I invited them all into my office. The lawyer defending the school was an older gray-haired man with a sad look on his face, a glance full of resignation. The lawyer for the plaintiff was a full-figured woman, somewhere in her late forties or early fifties. Her hair was dyed a striking black, and she had similarly striking eye makeup and purple lips, with poorly concealed crow's feet around her eyes, a hefty double chin, and a characteristically Semitic nose. She carried herself in the manner of a haughty young woman. She had a thick volume tucked under her arm, *Mechanics of the Head Injury*, written by one of the professors at Ann Arbor University. Her big bust covered up most of the volume, though it was still displayed ostentatiously.

This presentation amused me a little, but I maintained composure for the situation. Then, I was formally placed under oath, after which the female lawyer began to question me. What were my qualifications? Could I present my CV? Several more banal and routine questions followed that were always repeated in these situations. Had that boy been my patient? What symptoms did he have? What did the EEG tests show? I replied to these questions calmly and truthfully. I could see, however, that all of this wasn't enough, that she was going to try to demonstrate to the people in the jury that the previous injury caused the boy's current epilepsy. She threw me a rather unexpected question—"Do you know what the mechanism of a head injury is?"

I replied that I had some knowledge on this subject. Then, she triumphantly took the book out from under her arm, or rather her bust, about the aforementioned injuries.

"In your opinion," she asked accusingly, "shouldn't head injuries be taken care of by biomechanics rather than neurosurgeons?"

I replied that maybe the lawyer lady was right, but until now, neurosurgeons, not biomechanics, handled head injuries all over the world. This stunned her a bit but not for long.

"You don't have the least bit of doubt that the injury on the school stairs was the cause of the current epileptic attacks, right?"

"No", I answer, "I have a lot of doubts."

She was not intelligent enough to stop at this point. "Please, explain it," she said.

I didn't need to be asked twice. I began, "The EEG tests that were done after the cerebral concussion showed completely normal behavior. The current record is not characteristic of post-traumatic epilepsy but is of its own entity, classic centrencephalic-epilepsy. In my opinion, the previous injury was not the cause of the current illness."

The sad-looking school lawyer, who had been resigned and passive until that moment, suddenly livened up. His eyes got brighter. He understood that I was demolishing the whole prosecution.

Full of surefire charm, the lawyer lady asked me a series of further questions. My replies increasingly ruined the prosecution's plan, because it became clear from the given tests that it was unfounded.

"I don't have any more questions," she said passionately. "This ends our period of questioning."

Then the lawyer for the defense asked me a few questions, trying to confirm my previous testimony. The questioning finally came to an end. The lawyer lady got up quickly from her chair, stuck the volume under her arm, and turned towards the door. And I had time to add politely, "That's an excellent book," I pointed to the volume. "Please, familiarize yourself with the last chapter. It'll clear everything up for you."

She didn't respond. She slammed the door. The older man stayed where he was, looking at me with his blue, lightly faded eyes.

"God!" he said. "You look like a calm, harmless person. But, I can attest to the fact that you just stuck a knife in her belly and then twisted it!"

An Italian man showed up at Holy Cross with a crushed skull. He was still conscious and didn't have any neurological damage. Fortunately, the skull bone took the full force of the hit, and the brain was left untouched. I had to operate so as to clean the wound from bone fragments and reconstruct the skull with plastic. He left the hospital in his former state. After a week, he came to my office for a follow-up visit. He felt good, and coarse black hair had begun to cover his skull. I asked him about the circumstances surrounding the incident. I learned that he ran a small pizzeria with his brother. A biker gang showed up. One of the thugs beat him with an iron chain. I asked if he knew who it had been and if he had told the police.

"Of course I know, but I don't intend to get the police involved."

It was a rather strange answer, but I left it at that. Two months later, he came for another follow-up visit. He felt great, and the EEG tests were normal. He thanked me for my care and then added, "By the way, I wanted to tell you that the one who did this to me is no longer with us."

I thought it better not to ask about the details.

It has been said about doctors, and especially about surgeons, who are constantly living in an atmosphere of pain and suffering, that they are able to numb themselves to such a degree that others' suffering doesn't touch them emotionally, doesn't cast a shadow on their lives. Maybe it's the case for some, but fortunately, there aren't many like that. Most of us live everyday surrounded by our patients' pain and suffering, their fears and feelings of hopelessness and despair, and we cannot free ourselves totally of this burden.

From this, I would like to go to four teenagers who were brought in to the emergency room at St. John's after a car accident. They were all in a very serious state. Tousled light hair, tanned faces, strong developed arms and biceps—they were pictures of health, youth, and vitality. There were light blue eyes looking at me with a dumbfounded expression, totally unaware of the horror of the situation. One of them had a cervical fracture with irreversible damage to the cervical cord. This meant that he was, literally, a living head on an immobile, numb body, with minimal movement of his fingers.

His friend also had a broken back in the thoracic area; he was in a much "better" state and situation, because he still had movement of his hands and arms but was paralyzed from the nipples down. The third had a similar neurological situation with full paralysis of his legs, numb from the waist down. The last one, the "luckiest," had partial paralysis of his legs with permanent paralysis of the bladder and rectum.

These neurological changes were irreversible. The first three had severed, or rather crushed, spinal cords in various places. The fourth one also had irreversible damage to the end of the spinal cord.

The emergency room doctor on-call told me what had happened. It was Saturday. One of the boys asked his father to let him take the car—he had a driver's license already. He wanted to go for a "ride" with his school friends. They hit the road looking for adventure, for speed. They quickly came to the conclusion that, even though it was illegal while driving, they should buy some beer. The radio blared in the silence of the night with macabre rock music, the beer started disappearing, and their laughter got louder and louder. The wheels were screeching on sharply taken turns to the honking and yells of normally moving "old fogies." It turned out, however, that the father's car didn't have enough power to really speed through the streets. One of the boys remembered that his neighbor had a sports car in the garage. They drove up to the house and opened the garage—the door wasn't locked. They hot-wired the car to start the engine. They revved the engine and hit the road. They drove onto the highway on the periphery of the city to try out the real speed of the car.

Then, they heard a siren and saw the flashing lights of a police car behind them. They fell into a panic; they were driving a stolen car, and what's worse, they were three sheets to the wind. I have to add here that they had no intention of stealing that car; they just wanted to take it for a ride and then return it to the owner.

The only idea they had was to race away. They started going insanely fast. The drunk driver lost control of the steering wheel. They drove into a tree at full speed.

Let's leave aside any kind of moralizing. They undoubtedly acted wrongly, even criminally. They undoubtedly deserved severe punishment. But such horror, the worst possible, to live the rest of their lives as immobile shells?

I wrote my orders, dictated the patient histories, referred them for further tests, and called in consults from a urologist and an orthopedic surgeon. I couldn't change anything as a neurosurgeon. My task was to keep them alive and try to prevent any further complications. I looked hopelessly at their speechless, questioning eyes that shifted from me to the nurses hooking up IV's or putting catheters in their bladders. They didn't feel pain. They still weren't aware of the severity of their fates. That would come later. They would undoubtedly get some religious support from an intelligent man or woman who would explain to them that life in a wheelchair wasn't so bad. But it would be a life without hands or working legs, without movement, and without family, without sex. The religious person would explain to them that suffering makes you noble and leads to the path of glory. They would hear all of this, presented to them professionally.

The parents were already waiting in the waiting room—a small crowd of horrified people still unaware of what had really happened. They were ordinary, upstanding people who were hardworking, raising their children as best as they could, people who were like millions of others. It was my dismal responsibility to present them with the whole truth of the matter. They looked at me with eyes full of fear when I threw words at them that were as heavy as boulders. And maybe they didn't even understand it all yet, maybe it really wasn't hitting home yet? The verdict was unanimous—paralysis for the rest of their lives, incontinence of urinary and bowel systems, complete numbness, the possibility of complications, and the need for constant care for the rest of their lives.

The boys ended up in clean, white beds, and the only sign of life and recognition was their eyes—following the movements of the nurses and doctors around them.

The appropriate police report was put together, and the owner of the demolished car filled out the necessary forms so that the insurance would cover at least most of his losses. I can't leave out that he later looked for full compensation for the damages by suing the parents of those boys.

It was almost dawn when I went home. The whole time, the image of those teenagers stood before me. I had to try to get away from that image so as not to have an accident myself. But one thought throbbed in my head like a pounding sledgehammer— why? Why such a horrible punishment for an incredibly careless move? Why? I couldn't find an answer. I fell asleep with this question in my mind. To this day, I still can't answer it.

I was performing a standard surgery to fuse the broken cervical spine for a patient who was left completely paralyzed with the exception of some minimal movement of his hands. Surgery had to be performed, because this segment of the spine was unstable and any attempts at rehabilitation and adaptation would have been impossible. I did the fusion using a bone graft from the hip. The procedure went smoothly, without any particular complications and with minimal bleeding. The patient was taken to the ward in good condition. He healed quickly and soon left St. John's Hospital to spend six weeks in a university rehabilitation center. I lost sight of him. The insurance paid me for the surgery, his chart made its way to the archives, and his dramatic story started to fade from my memory. After all, he was one of many who came through my hands.

Many years went by. I was called in for a consultation. The patient's name seemed familiar to me. The ghost of a person lay on the bed. Yes, this was the same patient. As a result of the previous injury, he had experienced a horrifying degree of muscle atrophy;

he was a human skeleton with a living and, unfortunately, thinking head. He was admitted for the umpteenth time because of one of the most common complications—a urinary tract infection with secondary septicemia. I determined that my fusion of the spine was intact. Though a longtime veteran of these scenes, I was overcome by fear at the sight of this unfortunate soul, followed shortly thereafter by a feeling of blame, however undeserved. It was I who caused him to live all those years in anguish, in suffering, with fused and stable surgical spine.

This feeling of helplessness is the worst feeling for a surgeon, for he is the one responsible for his actions before people and before God.

I spent similar moments next to the bed of a young woman who, after the successful clipping of an aneurism, was slowly dying from a secondary spasm of the arteries. And I spent moments by the bed of another patient, for whom I had successfully removed, though only partially, a malignant tumor of the spinal cord. After the surgery, she enjoyed her newfound strength of movement and her newfound life—and now was dying with no hope or possible help.

Still, these awful cases are compensated by triumphs. Saving a child's life is always one of them, as is bringing the one provider of the family back to work, or the joyful and grateful smile of a patient coming for a follow-up visit with his surgeon.

Now, when I am already "in a state of rest," retired, and my hands operate with only a pen or pruning shears in the yard, I recently heard the greatest and most valued compliment of my life.

Five years ago, I operated on a man who was about sixty years old with a malignant brain tumor in the right parietal area. The surgery wasn't complicated. The patient didn't experience any functional problems and went back to work—and he worked hard. Though he was the owner of a large company that handled asphalting the roads, he often went to do the physical work with his employees. He had a wife and daughter. They were of Dutch descent. After the surgery, he received a round of chemotherapy.

He, his wife, and daughter were informed that the recurrence of the tumor was only a matter of time.

Even now, I feel his wife's glance, staring at me with the question—is that fatal moment upon us now? A few years went by. The tumor recurred, but I could still operate and radically remove most of it. My patient maintained the same lifestyle. His wife came with him for the follow-up visits and could never hold back her tears, which depressed us both.

And so, I found myself retired, having referred the patient to the partner who took over my practice. Years later, as I was wandering around the lake in Grosse Pointe where I lived, I suddenly ran into the mother and daughter. My first question was to ask politely how my former patient was feeling. I learned that, despite the malignancy of the tumor, he was feeling fine, and it had now been five years since that first surgery. During this conversation with his wife, she started crying in her usual way. Looking up at me with tear-filled eyes, she said, "I can't understand why I can't hold back my tears when I talk to you. This never happens when I see the doctor who took over your practice!"

Well then, she felt in her heart the same thing that I did as a doctor, namely compassion, a bond to that large and massive build and strong character. I felt that compassion for the wife and daughter as well.

I encountered people of various races, nationalities, ethnic backgrounds, and social positions. You might think that their reaction to the stress caused by illness, pain, or surgical intervention might be varied. Such a variance doesn't exist. They sometimes differ in the way they express their emotions, but the stress itself is always the same.

Another observation I made grew out of my belief that most people are honest and good in the traditional sense of those words. Rude, aggressive, and even threatening behavior is most often the result of fear and hesitation that arise from the extreme situations in which they find themselves. They remain good, however, in the depth of their being. This overall optimistic outlook isn't ruined by the rare times when individuals who are inherently bad cross your path. Such people can completely change the way you perceive the categories of good and evil.

This following is an example of this.

In the late '70s, the parents of a sixteen-year-old girl came to see me; they were wealthy, cultured, and kind. The daughter was suffering from severe headaches that had been troubling her for about six months. Acute pains were devastating the pretty, healthy young woman. From the moment they walked into the office, I was struck by the daughter's behavior; she seemed full of fear and rather stiff. She didn't say anything and didn't look up, clearly avoiding any eye contact. While her mother was describing her symptoms, she didn't react at all, as if it didn't concern her. She answered my questions with a brief "yes" or "no." Yes, she had headaches. Yes, it was hard for her to sit through an entire class at school. No, she wasn't vomiting. No, she didn't have dizzy spells. Her periods were regular.

I didn't find a single abnormality in the neurological examination which might suggest an organic disease. I sent her to have several further tests. All the results were in the normal range. She still maintained that she had severe headaches and that it was hard for her to last through an hour-long class. She got good grades, but they had clearly gotten worse in the last few months.

Not having a clear explanation, I figured that she had migraines, and severe ones at that. In those years, I had gotten rather good results by treating this condition with an IV infusion of Novocain and then treatment with dihydroergotamine. I admitted the young woman to Bon Secour Hospital, where I was on staff.

I was still very bothered by her behavior. I called in a psychiatrist, considering the possibility of early-stage schizophrenia. My friend couldn't make a definite diagnosis after the first examination, but he gathered enough to know that the cause was most likely a fear of someone or something. After several sessions, he uncovered the cause. She broke down and, sobbing, told him about her tragedy.

She was a student in a high school in Grosse Pointe. One of the teenagers in the class was a drug dealer who sold heroin, cocaine, or a mix. With his help, the youth of the so-called better homes started on a path to nowhere. Parents didn't know anything about this. The young woman's misfortune was that she had witnessed one of his transactions. The young delinquent threatened that he didn't need any witnesses and that she had better keep quiet. If she didn't, he would kill her! He made her completely neurotic. She was afraid to open her mouth and afraid to confide in her parents.

Of course, she didn't need any medical treatment, as the solution lay in resolving the blackmail situation. The school couldn't do anything, because she didn't have concrete evidence other than her testimony. The police to whom we turned were also powerless because of a "lack of criminal evidence." The dealer knew that the ring of those who knew his secret was getting bigger. Her safety was really in question. The powerlessness that enveloped her parents, the psychiatrist, the police force, and me drove us mad. There was no clear way to free her from the torment of this dealer.

A few weeks later, her father came to my office to inform me that, for the good of his daughter, he was going to leave a rather lucrative job in Detroit, sell the house, and move to the other end of America.

And the criminal stayed free, with the only difference being that he was now more careful than before.

I don't remember what exactly brought the young, pretty twenty-year-old young girl to my office. I was struck by her apathy, her absence of expression indicating any kind of feeling; it was as though she completely lacked any contact with the person to whom she was speaking. Despite her young age, she gave the impression of someone who had already experienced everything and was only waiting for death. The story of her life was unfortunately rather typical of the thousands of youths like her.

And so, she began to be sexually active at age thirteen, which led to a state of "frigidity." She was no longer capable of orgasm. At this point she reached for cocaine to regain her sexuality. She quickly had to increase the dose she was using. Sex became completely unnecessary—only the drug remained. But even this became weak, so she started using heroin. From the point of view of a drug addict, the satanic nature of drugs lies in the state of indescribable ecstasy that you reach during the first try. As one drug addict described it to me once, it goes beyond having a thousand orgasms—that can never again be attained! The following increasingly strong doses don't lead to that same euphoric state. The sensation never returns in its original intensity.

I looked at this young woman—at her total indifference, lack of any interests—and suddenly came to a paradoxical conclusion. Namely that I, already an older man was incomparably younger than she was. I had ambitions and plans; I was working towards some kind of goal, while she wasn't wishing for anything.

I once looked into the statistics of drug addiction. The average lifespan of a drug addict from the moment he begins using heroin is just about two years. This confirmed my conclusion that the young woman was, literally, a few steps from the grave.

Heroin, that satanic (with no exaggeration) drug, does not always win. I was once called in for a consultation on a thirty-year-old patient with a subarachnoid hemorrhage. He was in a serious state, half-conscious. The veins on his forearm were blackened from countless needle sticks. The cardiologist determined bacterial endocarditis caused by dirty needles. The arteriogram of the brain showed that the hemorrhage had been caused by an aneurism in the peripheral part of the middle cerebral artery. This type of aneurism, as opposed to those most commonly seen, was caused by an infected blood clot from the heart and secondary infection of the arterial wall.

After achieving the therapeutic level of antibiotics in his blood and stabilizing his heartbeat, I performed surgery. The surgery was easy, because I had good access to the aneurism. After the surgery, he quickly began to recover and went home on high doses of antibiotics that he was to take for an extended period of time. His treatment was being monitored by an infectious-disease specialist as well as a cardiologist.

I remember him well—exhausted, emaciated, dirty, wearing old rags. After discharging him from the hospital, I lost touch with him. After a few years, he showed up in my office, slightly gray-haired, well-dressed, shaved, nicely put together. This was the same drug addict! He just came to tell me that, being near death, he finally understood that his life was going downhill fast. He decided to fight. He declared war against the devil in that dirty syringe with all his willpower. He won. He went back to his family and to work; he was reborn. I learned that he had previously been a well-educated and cultured person. It had been heroin that pushed him down to the gutter.

Unfortunately, this patient was the only case in all the years of my professional career that experienced such a comeback from heroin to normal life. Isn't that awful? One case over decades of work!

13

Continuing the Fight for Poland

URING THE FIRST few years of my time in the United
States, I discovered to my surprise how many people,
who were often well- educated, held Marxist views. One
such nest of Marxist utopia, hidden in the guise of liberalism,
was the university in Ann Arbor, located some twenty or thirty
miles outside Detroit. Knowing communism first hand, which
was a painful thorn in my consciousness, I couldn't understand
the communist inclinations of these people. It really upset me and
made me feel sorry for them when I heard some highly positioned
people say that communism was a pure and beautiful idea ruined
in the Soviet Union. Some of them also held that Christ was the
first communist.

U.S. politics were based on the principle of dividing the world
into spheres of influence, with full approval of Soviet Occupation
in the defeated countries of Eastern Europe. I also found out that
General Patton, who reached as far as Prague with his tank divisions in the last phase of the war, was ordered to retreat from there,
obviously for political reasons. Later on he died in a "car accident."
During the Korean conflict, when victory seemed to be favoring
the American side, a treaty was drawn up ending the war despite

the protests of General MacArthur, who had been the chief general of American forces and a war hero in the Pacific theater during World War II.

There were also strange things going on among Polish-American people. Chairman Mazewski didn't take any concrete position, and most of them maintained complete indifference towards the occupying regime in Poland for completely prosaic reasons—they wanted to have access to the "old country" so they could go there to show off their wallets full of dollars, their wealth.

One of the advisors in the White House was Heinrich Sonnenfeld, the same Jewish man who, in his time, had said that joining Poland to the Soviet Union and destroying its national identity could ensure peace and balance in Europe. This doctrine nearly became an official policy, closely upheld in international U.S. politics.

I also found out that there were other political forces in the United States that felt and thought similarly to the way that I did, who confirmed the Satanism of communism and treated Soviet Russia as a dangerous, ruthless opponent and enemy. These people didn't approve of the Yalta Agreement and stood as an active force of resistance against the red plague that was spreading over the world and the United States. These people were gathered in the Republican Party, mostly in its conservative wing. I received letters from both parties, Democrat and Republican, with proposals to make donations to their electoral campaigns. I quickly decided that I would only support the Republicans, because the party held a similar position to mine against the criminal Soviet system, which Reagan later dubbed "The Evil Empire."

Polish-Americans did not play a significant political role. They were quite numerous, especially in Chicago, New York, and Detroit, but they always tended to vote for Democrats, those who supported the Yalta Agreement.

I came to the conclusion that I should enlarge the group of representatives from subjugated countries, such as Poles, Ukrainians, Lithuanians, Latvians, Estonians, Hungarians, Romanians, and

Bulgarians, in the framework of the Republican party so that we could stand together as one political block. Through sheer numbers and the permeation of influences into these diaspora, they would have a significant influence on the direction of American politics.

I met one of the leaders of Ukrainian emigration, Dr. Paul Dzul, as well as the leader of Belorussians, Dr. Sezak, an anesthesiologist in St. John's Hospital who often worked with me on the medical level. We arranged to have a meeting in my house. They agreed with me to work together politically right away. Soon, a Lithuanian organization as well as a Latvian and Estonian organization joined with us. The chairman of the Ukrainian Congress also gave his approval for such a cooperative initiative, with the condition that it would also be supported by the Polish-American Congress. I then tried to get the support of the PAC. Unfortunately, I didn't get anywhere. Chairman Mazewski was being influenced by Jan Nowak Jezioranski, who was rumored to have been paid by David Rockefeller.[3] The direction of PAC politics was allegedly dictated by J. Nowak Jezioranski, according to the directives of David Rockefeller.

That's how the ring of political activism was thus defined and closed—with full acceptance of the Soviet Occupation in Poland. There was nothing to look or wait for in terms of help from that PAC organization.

Pope Paul VI died on August 6, 1978. His successor to the Vatican was John Paul I, the pious cardinal from Milan. He was not the pope for long. He decided to publish an encyclical in which he would define communism and masonry as satanic cults. He was also close to releasing the list of names of the cardinals from the Vatican who were involved in masonry. He prepared a list of changes, and he was to present it the following day. And on that

---

3. In the year 2001, when false accusations were appearing everywhere against Poles from Jedwabne, J. Nowak Jezioranski joined this anti-Polish movement. In response, the **PAC** chairman, Edward Moskal, pointed out that Jezioranski had collaborated with Hitlerists, a fact that had been revealed already in 1995 through an RFE worker, Kazimir Zamorski, in the book, *Under the Antenna of Radio Free Europe* (Wers 1995).

particular night, he died, and the list was never revealed. I read a rather detailed documented description of the events surrounding the pope's death. In truth, there was no concrete evidence of mur-der, but the circumstances surrounding his death and the treat-ment of the autopsy, which was delayed by several days and done by a Vatican doctor, decidedly suggest a premeditated murder.

It came time for the next conclave. And then, one day while I was working in the operating room, one of the doctors came in and said, "Janusz! You've got a pope! Your fellow countryman is the pope!"

Cardinal K. Wojtyla took the name John Paul II—an obvious continuation of that which John Paul I began. The Soviets were really mistaken in foreseeing the politics of this pope. In Poland, he had an opinion among Soviet followers as a pacifist, rather a philosopher and thinker who was inclined to compromise. But his first decision and presentation dispelled their illusions. I am completely convinced that that's why Andropow recommended removing this "obstacle" two years later. This attempt, however, didn't work out.

John Paul II visited Poland the following year. His visit had a colossal and still underappreciated significance in bringing down communism. It showed Poles that, when united, they represented a significant force in the world. It reminded the world that Poland was a country that had been occupied because of betrayal by the Allies. I am sure that the uprising of "Solidarnosc" and the erosion of the "people's government" were the result of this pilgrimage. We were all euphoric, listening attentively to news from Poland. They were joyful, promising great things for the future, foreseeing great changes, and some significant turn in the situation of Poland and the whole "socialist camp." Yet we were also afraid of Soviet intervention, recalling what had happened in the springtime in Prague.

On the thirteenth of December, 1981, W. Jaruzelski declared a state of war. All of the prominent Solidarnosc activists were imprisoned. Jaruzelski faithfully fulfilled the mission he had been assigned by the communist tyrants to the end. I will remind people here, and it's worth mentioning, because not many Polish Americans know or remember that Jaruzelski personally awarded the medal of the Polish Committee of National Independence to the most horrible executioner of tens of thousands of Polish people who had been nominated by Stalin in occupied Poland—the notorious Jakub Berman!

From a Poland that found itself in a state of "Polish-Jaruzelski" war, terrible news crossed the ocean about thousands being arrested, about factories surrounded by tanks and gangs of the ZOMO (the mobilized camp of the citizens' militia). Still, there was a lot of news that wasn't true, like that people were being held in stadiums in the freezing cold. It was certain, however, that traitorous Jaruzelski's military government was obeying orders from Moscow. The Soviets didn't want to intervene with their own military. It accepted the solution put forth by the hands of the local traitors—agents of the KGB and GRU. Jaruzelski, to this day, wears the feathers that he was the saving grace of Poland—that he saved it from the coming of Soviet armies. How far this was from the truth! Overwhelming evidence lies in the KGB documents revealed by Christopher Andrew. These documents proved irrefutably that Jaruzelski played a zealous role; he was the most zealous Soviet puppet who cynically threw in all his military-police forces to stifle the independence movement. And who even asked the Soviet Politburo for armed intervention by Soviet and East German armies but was refused.

We knew even before the state of war of the small probability of direct Soviet intervention. American observers came to the conclusion—undoubtedly based on data from intelligence—that Russia couldn't allow for such an immeasurable armed brawl. They would have had to hold Poland in military restraints, which would cost them equally twofold—materially and politically. The West would block all credit for the Soviets, as well as block some areas of international trade, mainly that of Soviet petroleum.

Polish-Americans finally woke up! People appeared from outside our ring who finally recognized that there should be concrete action taken to expose the Soviet crimes that had been committed, specifically committed against the Polish nation—that we should put together an international resistance and fight with brutal force.

I was a member of the Polish American Congress in the Detroit division. Someone called for an unusual meeting of the section dealing with Polish affairs in which I participated. The leader of this section was Professor Chrypinski. A lot of people gathered, and the room began to fill with disgruntled words as well as proposals for concrete actions, such as intervention by the Congress exposing wrongs done to Poles in the media and putting together protests to the American and international authorities. Professor Chrypinski was sitting behind the conference room table and listened to these loud voices.

Finally, someone called out impatiently, "Professor, shouldn't we keep minutes of this meeting so that we can then deduce the appropriate conclusions?"

The professor got embarrassed. He found an excuse, "I don't have any paper. I have to go find some."

After a while, he returned with a piece of paper on which he made some notes. The meeting was ending, and people were leaving to go home. I was one of the last to leave. I saw the professor crumple up this piece of paper and throw it in the trash.

This gesture unraveled all our hopes that we could count on effective action from the Polish American Congress. It was not politically independent. Sure, they eventually did hold official protests, but against the background of the unfolding drama, they were simply inconsequential and worthless.

1985 stands as a memorable year in my life. I had professional stability, had my hands full of work, and was increasingly well-renowned among colleagues and patients. The POMOST radio programs offered a doubtless antidote to the venomous regime propaganda. I had a large ring of listeners who waited impatiently for the next program.

The situation of the radio station, WPON, of which I was the chairman, was getting better step-by-step despite all the obstacles thrown under my feet. POMOST was a strong and resilient organization with divisions in all the larger cities of the United States and analogous cells growing in other countries, mainly European. The POMOST programs, which were powerful, unyielding, and unmasked the ugliness and crime of the communist system and Soviet Occupation, were heard not only in Detroit but also in Chicago and Arizona.

During that year, I also got word that things were going badly in Chicago. A dissenting faction of POMOST arose that wanted to oust Krzystof Rac, the founder of the organization, and that took a very compromising position towards the regime. This faction put out a competing newsletter entitled "POMOST" that put forth different ideologies and tendencies. It soon became clear that Andrzej Czuma, the same man who I thought was a pillar of patriotism during our conference in Washington, was leading the divisive work. He and the other dissenting leaders had strong regime connections in Poland. They were simply ordered by the Soviet-imposed regime in Poland to destroy our uncompromising organization by infiltrating it.

More and more disturbing news reached me from Chicago about libel that was spreading and about attempts to destroy the members' good names. A special meeting was organized. I went. The aim of the meeting was to get rid of Krzystof Rac and to shift power. My presence made the agents somewhat uncomfortable. I surprised them by insisting on leading the meeting. Because the Chicago organization was divided into two camps, I was supposed to lead the meeting as a person from the outside. And that's what I did, despite the grumbling in the room. No one made the effort, however, to vocalize his protest. The meeting progressed stormily, but I did manage to ensure that Krzystof Rac retained his position as the coordinator of POMOST and that the ideological differences would be resolved in discussions. Still, nothing came of it. Andrzej Czuma and those leftover still did their dissenting work.

RECORDING ONE OF HUNDREDS OF
BROADCASTS OF POMOST

14

Tecum Sum Semper
(I Am With You Always)

MY MOTHER WAS always slim and petite, active and full of life. Yet her health started slowly to decline. Her pulse quickened, and she easily felt fatigued. Often, she would rest in her room during the day in the company of our dog, Lili, who was black as tar with beautiful shiny fur that looked like it had been styled. She was a cocker spaniel.

I pleaded with my mother to agree to see a doctor and have some tests—in vain. She claimed that she was getting older, that it was all normal, and that tests wouldn't do anything. One afternoon when I got home, I saw her in a visibly bad state. She had dark circles under her eyes, was breathing with difficulty, and had trouble moving around. Despite her rather weak protests, I took her for some X-rays. I waited with anxiety as the images slowly emerged from the dryer. When I took them in my hand and looked under the light, my heart stopped. You could clearly see a tumor the size of a fist with exudates to the pleura in the right lung. She was immediately admitted to St. John's Hospital. She breathed somewhat more easily with oxygen. My colleague, a thoracic surgeon named Jacques Bodouin, drained the fluid and

186

removed a large amount of the exudates. She felt some immediate relief with breathing. The histological tests of the tumor revealed that it was lymphoma. Then there was a discussion—what should we do? That type of a tumor is part of a larger disease that is spread through the whole system, but it is also sensitive to radiation therapy. Jacques couldn't tell if she also had lung cancer apart from the lymphatic infiltrate. He was in favor of doing a thoracotomy to see exactly what was going on there.

The day of surgery came. Wearing a gray-green scrubs, I stood by the door of the room where Jacques was operating on my mother. I waited a long time. Finally, the operating room doors opened. My colleague still had the surgical mask on his face, and his surgical apron and gloves were spattered with my mother's blood.

"I didn't find any cancer. There's no doubt that it's lymphoma."

A PORTRAIT BY MY OWN HAND OF MY MOTHER.

The prognosis in these tumors tends to be somewhat better, for a longer life.

After a moment, my mother was wheeled out. She was still under anesthesia. I stayed sitting next to her the whole time, and I was there when she regained consciousness. Night fell. She was placed in one of the ICU rooms. We stayed there together. I tried to relieve her suffering by helping her to turn and giving her sips of water. In the morning, I slept for a few hours on a doctor's cot and went to work.

My mother recovered quickly. After a week, I took her home. Then, we went regularly for radiation therapy. The tumor melted before our eyes, and her frame of mind was improving.

She got better enough so as to go back to the greatest love of her life—music. She was never a concert pianist, but she played much better than many others. She easily played all the difficult movements of Chopin's etudes and the finesse of Scarlatti's sonatas. The sounds that came from beneath her fingers worked like a soothing balm on my soul. I lived with the illusion that everything was fine and back to the way it had been, that our life was rolling along well-worn tracks. . . .

Other than music, an essential stimulus for my mother was the political activism of POMOST. She came from a patriotic family, hated communism, and was overjoyed that her son could openly fight against its evil. She carefully listened to our broadcasts, not hesitating to give me critical advice. Indeed, because we did the programs "live," there were a lot of transgressions and mistakes. This upset her terribly, but she was thrilled with the well-done programs, especially when we received phone calls from grateful listeners.

I can still see her sitting next to me in the dining room—petite, thin, with a smile on her face, a look of kindness for all the members attending her feast after a successful POMOST broadcast. She told me that she didn't long so terribly for her country anymore, that she had found her home here, and that life was full and rich, because she was participating in actions that were for the good of Poland. She often pored over the material for upcoming broadcasts, choosing what was the best.

After a year, my mother's health quickly started to worsen. She had coughing fits even with the most minimal exertion. This was a sure sign for me that the illness was back, that her body's immune system had broken down, and that the lymphoma was spreading like wildfire. Chemotherapy was the only available choice. She suffered through each round of chemo, as they were much like doses of poison. A tank of oxygen with all its accessories became a permanent part of her life. There were some days of illusory improvement when she felt like herself for a short time. At those times, hope would cloud over my clear vision of the situation. The disease's progress, however, was unmistakable.

I lived somewhat in madness. I had to work, operate, and record radio programs, for the fight against Soviet communism formed the core of my life apart from my profession. At the same time, I had to become a nurse for my mother.

Despite the illness, she was still interested in everything. She knew that she was slowly leaving this world. She was surprised that it was already happening. Still, she didn't shed a single tear for herself. Our dog, Lili, who also wasn't feeling well, never left my mother's side. Lili couldn't climb the stairs anymore, so I had to carry her. The veterinarian didn't know what was wrong with her.

One image stayed in my memory forever. My mother was sitting in a chair in the dining room. The life-giving tank of oxygen was next to her. The sun's rays fell through the curtains on her dark hair, drawing attention to the dark circles under her eyes. The eyes were the same as always—good, full of understanding. I considered what was most important now for me and for her. I knew with certainty that it wasn't political activism, nor was it my work. The most important thing was her suffering. I rearranged my life, time, and energy to accommodate it. I drastically reduced my professional obligations. I recorded radio programs at home. I was almost always nearby.

One day our dog got sick. She was vomiting and became very

weak. I found her at my mother's bed—dead—an immobile ball of black shiny fur. She died of a heart attack. I took her death as a prelude of what was to come on an entirely larger scale. At night, crying, I dug a hole in the yard, where the remains of her predecessor, Darus, also lay, and buried her wrapped in some stiff canvas. Two days later, I bought a puppy schnauzer so as to relieve the hurt at least partly. Now, writing these words, I see our last picture from Christmas of 1985 on the right side on the wall. My mother sat in a armchair by the tree with black Lili, her eyes like two glowing buttons. My mother is looking at me. I feel almost a physical presence—even though many years now divide us.

I was left alone. And again, there was a coffin. The owner of the funeral home remembered me from the time I had been choosing a coffin for my father. I took care of all the formalities. We agreed that the body would be viewed the following day at three o'clock in the afternoon. The rosary would be said the next evening. The funeral would be the day after that at nine o'clock in the morning in St. Paul's church.

I went home. It seemed awfully empty to me. It looked out from black depths of the windows, still mired in sadness, strange, somehow different. The sounds of the bustling housekeeper reached me from the kitchen; with all her gruffness, she had been able to show real sympathy to my mother and now only to me. I went into my mother's room. There were no bed linens left, and the room had been cleaned. I looked in the closet—the dresses and coats that were so familiar to me lay still, inert, doubly dead.

Inhumanly exhausted, I threw myself on the bed. I fell asleep. Over the last months, I had not slept through most of any night, only napped a bit in the afternoons.

The following day, feeling rested though inwardly torn apart, I went to the barber, even surprised myself a bit with this decision. I had a lot of stubble. While there, I talked about the weather, described how I wanted to have my hair cut, and the barber started discussing politics, performing his routine scheme of engaging a client. I bought a black suit nearby.

I went home. And again it seemed dead, almost repulsive in its double emptiness. I went from room to room, and Chitah (the puppy schnauzer) circled around my legs. I wasn't able to accept the irreversibility of the situation.

In the funeral home, the coffin in which my mother lay was in the middle of a large room. How different she looked. My mother, to whom I had been so close, was now separated from me by the infinite and irreversible divide. She was surrounded by a colorful sea of flowers. My closest colleagues and friends really showered that big room with flowers—symbols of life, springtime, birth, and also helplessness against that which waits for each of us in his time in a scene similar to this one. They came up to me in turn, offering their condolences in quiet voices. Some of them kneeled on the kneeler. I responded mechanically and exchanged polite words, incapable of sensible thought and reaction.

I remember the closing of the coffin, my last glance at my mother's face, and then only the lid of the coffin. The Holy Mass. The homilies of two chaplains—in English and in Polish. I remember the themes of these farewells—a polish woman, living with the hope of reclaiming her fatherland, unbreakable in her convictions.

I stood at the cemetery pierced by a cold April wind. Mr. Borowiec, a veteran of the Home Army, tried to cover the coffin in a Polish white and red flag. The gales of wind blew the flag around, as if wanting to lengthen my mother's earthly presence.

Then, there was dinner in the company of my closest friends and extended family—the faces of people who were so well-known to me. I was sitting at the place in which my mother used to sit. Now, I was the host, the only and last one.

I went back to work, to a somewhat normal life. My mother had been a great support for me, a soothing balm. Oddly enough, I now felt the most relaxed while performing surgery—I had to shut off, get out of my psychological rut, and focus on what I was doing. I literally threw myself into the whirlwind of work. I was doing six or seven difficult surgeries a week. I started making a lot of money without even trying. My approach to patients changed. I saw them in a different light, in another perspective—the ultimate, eschatological.

Nighttime was the most difficult when I was completely alone—I only recorded radio programs twice a week. They filled partially the emptiness of those nights.

My older colleague, Dr. Haddad—whose passion was music but who never had the opportunity to learn how to play well being a surgeon—suggested that I go back to music and start lessons from the beginning. This idea appealed to me. I would be close to my mother through music.

Two weeks after her death, I had to go to a neurosurgery conference in Toronto. At night, I went down to the hotel restaurant for a late dinner. The huge hotel block contained a four-cornered space covered in a glass roof under which trees and green shrubs grew all year round. A concert piano stood there as if in open space. I didn't notice when a modest-looking woman went up to it. My pondering was suddenly interrupted by the sounds of Schubert's Impromptu, the same one that my mother had played so often! This shocked me. How can it be, after all she's dead, I was at her funeral, but here she is playing, in this unknown hotel in far off Toronto! After a moment, I regained my senses, but the pearly melodies of Schubert stayed with me forever, linked to that moment of surprise.

And now, in this atmosphere of eternal separations, I give voice to my dear dog, Chitah. She really deserves such a farewell memory.

My first sensation was the warmth of my mother, her scent, the taste of the milk from her nipples, and the intense fight with my brothers to get to them. My world was made up of smells and touches, because I couldn't see anything. I only wished to calm my hunger. I slept a lot, safely snuggled into my mother and siblings.

One day, my eyes opened. I saw the world, shadows and rays of sunlight, people leaning over our basket. They took us up in their arms. I saw a huge face, heard unfamiliar voices. I didn't feel that these human creatures intended to hurt me. I wagged my tail and tried to be polite. Then came the day when I was first made to feel pain; my tail and ears were trimmed. Bandages were put over them. I tried to rip them off so as to lick the wounds. After a few days, I felt better and started going out from our nest to visit this wondrous world.

This didn't last long. Some unknown people showed up who smelled unfamiliar. I was put in a cage, and the cage was thrown onto a truck. It was awful! I found myself alone, without my mother, without my siblings. I heard the doors slam and then darkness fell. Something rumbled, a stinky smell reached my nose, and suddenly the darkness and I moved at a speed unknown to me until then. This noise and swaying started to make me sleepy, and every once in a while I would wake up and then fall asleep again. After a few turns, the monster carrying me started to slow down. Again, I saw the light of day.

Some people showed up and took me in my cage to a place filled with the desperate complaints of other dogs. I was soon given something to drink and something to eat that wasn't at all reminiscent of my mother's milk. And again, I was thrown in a cage, where there were other similarly poor dogs. The cage floor was covered in a layer of cut up newspapers, and the smell of urine and excrement rose up from them. We were all dumbfounded, and everyone was bigger than me. They stepped all over me, and I couldn't get to the bowl we were supposed to share that was placed in the corner of the cage. I saw people coming and going; a lot of them came with children. Every once in a while, one of my unknown brothers was pulled out of the cage, and then people looked at him, petted him, and most often put him back in the cage. I was also taken out a few times, cuddled up to a face and let loose in a separate small pen.

Then, a different person showed up. He stood in front

of our cage for a long time, looking at how the larger and stronger dogs were constantly stepping on me and knocking me over. He said something to the woman who minded our imprisonment, and I was taken out of the cage. He took me in his arms. I felt warmth radiating from him, felt his scent and something else, as though he understood my misery, as if he felt compassionate.

They let me out in the pen. I tried to show off all that I knew how to do. I wagged the remains of my tail, lightly bit his finger. And then a moment later, I was in his arms, and we were alone. We were in the front seat of a car with me sitting next to him. We moved. Surprised, I peed. It leaked from the carrier onto the seat.

We pulled into a dark garage, and he carried me into a large house from there. New smells, new space. The moment he put me on the floor, I started running from corner to corner, looking for a way out, familiarizing myself with the terrain.

A thin, petite woman sat in the corner of the dining room. A large tank connected to a thin tube stood next to her. The tube divided into two smaller tubes that were fastened with tape to her nose. She had a soft, warm voice, her hands were delicate, and I immediately liked her. She took me on her knees. I felt like I was with my mother again. I understood that she was very sick and weak, so my responsibility would be to show her affection and sympathy. During that time, I was biting everyone and everything, but only for fun, not too strongly. I understood that I couldn't bite this woman's hands even the most mildly.

At first, they put me in the kitchen behind a gate. I protested loudly that I wanted to run, to be near my master, and to sit on the knees of that woman who spoke to me in a mild, sad voice. Soon, I understood that I was supposed to relieve myself in the yard. My master taught me this. After eating or taking a longer nap, he took me out there and said something, and I began to understand what was going on.

After I learned that, I was allowed to run around the whole house. There was also another woman in the house, who was tall and smelled of tobacco. She also held me in her arms, carried me like her own child. Turning towards me, my master said the word, "Chitah." I came to understand that as my name.

Winter came. The woman in the chair was getting weaker and weaker. She mostly lay on the sofa in the living room, as her breathing was getting more and more difficult, and her hands were getting more and more weak and delicate. My master would leave the house, and upon his return would feed me and do something in the kitchen; I often saw him with tears in his eyes. At that time, I slept upstairs, between my master's bedroom and his mother's bedroom. I heard him get up in the middle of the night. I saw him turn on the light, help his mother go to the bathroom, and give her something to drink.

I was still very young, but I already felt that, besides the people living here, there was someone else in this house, some kind of implacable force, who was going to take away the woman's figure on some invisible wings.

The first snow fell. This wintry powder amused me greatly; I ran around on it, rolled through it, and went home completely wet. Such an excursion ended with a thorough drying of my paws, sometimes even washing. I spent most of the day on the woman's knees. I knew that she needed to have my warmth and presence within reach.

The winter was frosty with many blizzards, and it passed by slowly. The icicles dripping from the windows finally fell off. I saw the shaggy buds of the first crocuses in the yard.

The woman didn't come downstairs anymore. She lay in her room. She had dark circles under her eyes. My master often sat in a chair in the living room. I saw and felt how sad he was. I tried to show him some affection. I jumped up onto his knees, licked his face. He petted me and cuddled me, said something I didn't understand. I knew, though, that he was suffering, and that he was sharing his suffering with me and that he was grateful for my sympathy.

The awful day finally came when that sad woman's breathing stopped. It happened suddenly, almost imperceptibly. And then she wasn't there anymore! Only a thinned-out, tormented shadow of a person remained, so different from the figure I had seen for the first time. She was there, and yet she wasn't there at all. She didn't move. No one's words, nor my cries, reached her.

My master was left with an awful feeling of emptiness and me, the one being closest to him. Strangers took the woman's remains away. Then, even more people came, and I didn't see my master much. Finally, this all came to an end, quieted down; no one came and left anymore. We were left alone with just the housekeeper, a plump woman with a deep voice and rough demeanor. I wasn't afraid of her. I had known for a long time that a good person was hidden behind it all.

And now, something about myself. I'm a schnauzer, one of the smaller ones. The tradition of my breed is never to be afraid of anyone or anything (except storms and thunder). No other dog scares me. I throw myself on even the largest dogs with full force. Smaller ones are afraid of me. The larger ones tolerate me, which makes me even madder.

My breed has rules. We recognize and listen only to our masters; we only tolerate other people. You can even get close to some of them, as I did with Kazik, but the bond is different from my master's trust.

And so, we were left alone. Soon, a tall, somewhat hunched over woman came by who had kind and good eyes and large hands. She tried to win me over. I liked her, and she became a part of my life, feeding me when my master wasn't around and taking me for walks. These excursions were always so exciting—so many scents, so much information from other four-legged creatures, and so much movement!

Walking with my master, I quickly came to understand the word "Go!" I loved to play, especially with a ball and rubber toys. My master didn't appreciate the pleasures of such excursions. He played for a moment, and then, just when things were getting good, he turned around and walked to the other side of the yard.

I saw that he was still sad. He missed that woman whose knees had held me in my early youth. He often came home with rings under his eyes, and the lines on his forehead and face were getting deeper. This happened because he was tired from work. Sometimes, he would fall into the chair in the living room. He would look off into the distance, sad and silent. I saw that he needed help, but I didn't know what to do. I jumped up on his knees. I gently licked his face. I wanted to tell him that he wasn't alone, that he was with me and that I loved him. Sometimes, I was able to revive him and bring him out of that dull stare. He would go to the piano. He tried to play. I would lie down next to him then, and we felt good. Or, maybe it was just me that felt good.

When I was about seven months old, I noticed that something strange was happening with my vision. The world seemed clouded over. My master noticed this. He looked at my eyes. He looked very worried. We went in the car. As usual, I sat on his knees so as to look out the window. We came to a place where I immediately sensed the scent of many dogs and still other, sad and sharp, smells. I was afraid and started trembling. Some person in a white coat looked into my eyes, momentarily blinding me with a bright light, and then said something at length to my master.

A few days later, we made the same trip to the same place. My master, who looked very worried, placed me in the arms of some woman. And again, I found myself in a strange cage, horrified and missing my master. They injected me with a needle, and I got sleepy. And then, I don't remember anything after that. I woke up in the same cage. My right eye hurt, and I couldn't see anything out of it. I cried in pain and loneliness. Even my master had abandoned me! Luckily, he soon returned. He snuggled me to him, and we left that awful place together.

I didn't feel well at home, and my eye hurt. My master explained something to me lengthily and calmly, then put drops into my eyes that burned and stung. I knew that it was for my own good and that I had to allow for it. We sat together during the whole night, I in the chair on a cushion, moaning pitifully, my master next to me on the rug.

After a few days, light returned to that eye, and I began to see a little better each day. I could run around freely without hitting that side of my head against the furniture. My master still tormented me with those drops, this time putting them into my left eye. It pussed and hurt, but I still couldn't see anything; that's how it remained. I could only see out of the right eye.

This handicap not really limited me. I had a terrific sense of smell and good hearing, and my right eye got used to the new situation. I could see as if with two. I could run after squirrels again and catch balls and pinecones that were thrown to me.

There were days when various people would come by the house. They behaved loudly and laughed and talked. I met them and liked them. There was Kazik; he would lie on the floor and let me pull his graying hair. There was also Adam, but he didn't really know how to act around me. They all went to the basement with my master. I was afraid to go down there, because the stairs were very steep. They stayed down there a long time, and I would hear voices and music. Sometimes, I would stand at the top of the stairs and plead for them with a loud bark to come back up. My master sometimes took me under his arm and carried me down. There was nothing interesting down there, just an old couch, a rug, and some equipment. He would stay there for hours. His guests would talk for a long time in the area behind the glass.

These meetings usually ended with a dinner. I enjoyed this, because I always got a piece of cake, which I loved. This weakness for cake made me more and more chubby.

My master slept on his bed, and I slept on a chair in the other room. The door between us was open. I could hear everything, every breath. And that's how we lived.

I became very close with Maria—that was the name of the tall woman.

I was very happy when it snowed. On cold days, I would go outside in a sweater. I always thought that this was superfluous armor and really just ridiculous. On rainy days, my master put a raincoat on me with a hood, which was even funnier. And that's how we paraded around in the fall, gray days, mainly so that I could relieve myself outside the house and beyond the yard. In the summer, we spent a lot of time in the yard and taking long walks. We didn't always agree about this. In my opinion, such promenades were meant to familiarize me with the mass of scents around me—like what direction a squirrel ran by, whether other dogs were male or female and what they wrote in their "letters" to me.

The worst two-legged enemy I had was the mailman, so I had to figure out his route. My master was not at all interested in this jungle of scents; he only wanted to get further along as fast as possible. He never wanted to listen to me when I tried to make him aware that his type of walking made no sense.

Why did I consider the mailman my worst enemy? I felt completely legitimate in treating him as my enemy. Obviously, when someone bangs forcefully on the front door, he must be an enemy of the house. Only my master could decide if he should open the door and welcome him. My responsibility was to inform my master that someone was there and to warn that person that if he were to come in uninvited, I would tear him to shreds. It never came to this. My master always greeted that guy politely, so I also changed my demeanor. But neither my master nor Maria let the mailman in, and he banged on the door everyday! It was clear that he was an enemy, and a dangerous one. He would come in a small, white car. When I heard it and saw him, I sounded the alarm and threw a tantrum at the entranceway.

Winters went by that were snowy and frosty. They passed by with a warm wind and the strong rays of the early spring sun. Thick icicles again began dripping from the corners of the roof. Crocuses peeked through the snow, then hyacinths and tulips. The snow disappeared. The ground radiated with new life. Young leaves began to decorate the until-then naked tree branches. New buds were appearing on the rosebushes.

I always spent hours sitting in the yard watching while my master and Maria planted flowers. Every once in a while, I ran up to the fence to throw a tantrum for my neighbor, a small poodle. This was obviously just for show, for the small poodle didn't worry about it and jumped up merrily while I pretended to be angry.

Then the warm summer came, followed by windy autumn and its foul weather and cold hiding behind it. And again, the leafless trees were covered in a powdery layer of snow, and again the previously dark earth was hidden beneath a layer of white powder. The years went by one after another, faster and faster, more and more monotonous, almost imperceptibly.

My master sometimes disappeared for a few days. Then, I would sleep in the chair downstairs. I became the one watchman of the house. I was more observant during those times.

I have to admit to one weakness—I am very jealous of my master. So, if some stranger comes to visit, especially a woman, I do whatever I can so as to turn my master's attention from this uninvited guest to me. I know that I can't achieve this completely, but at least I can push my way onto his lap. If the intruder is a woman, I am openly threatening. Of course, I can't allow myself to bark, but I make it clear with my actions and behavior that this is my territory, my master, and that she has nothing to do with it!

My master would often leave at night. I woke up when he did. We would go downstairs. I would wait there, sometimes for hours, until he came back. And what a joy it was, what a greeting, when he finally came home, sometimes at dawn, and quickly lay down to sleep.

One day, my master left as usual in the morning, but he didn't come back. Maria had gone back to her own house, and another woman showed up in her place who was shorter and also very kind to me. I liked her from the first moment we met. My master still didn't come home. Kazik showed up. He talked with this new Maria for a long time. I didn't know what was going on, but I knew that they were talking about my master.

He came back after a week. He was weak, moved with difficulty, and I saw pain on his face. I immediately recognized the smell of blood. I saw a long scar on his leg. I wanted to treat it in my own way—by licking it—but unfortunately, to my surprise and even pain, my master wouldn't let me do this. He recovered quickly. Now, he had more time for me in the house and the yard. He sat there in the shade of the trees with a book in his hands. A few months went by before he felt like himself again full of energy.

The vision in my right eye started to get worse. I tripped over objects, mostly those on my left side.

We went back to that terrible place I had almost forgotten about. I heard the lamentations of many dogs in the distance. This one was different from the one where I had gotten my first surgery. An older man with a kind voice examined me for a long time, and I was blinded by the light. I *knew that he wanted to help me, so I let him do everything, though I was awfully afraid. I ended up in a cage again, got an injection, and lost consciousness. After waking up, I couldn't see anything. I could smell and hear noises, but the world was a black void. My master took me home. I recognized everything by its smell and was overjoyed to be home, but I was horrified by not being able to see what made up the essence of life. And then one day, light shone into my eye. Soon, I could make out the shapes of objects, directions, and obstacles in my path. Vision had never been the most important attribute for me. I was led by my sense of smell, but those days without light were awful.*

My master eventually started to move more slowly. He played the piano a lot but moved around less. His steps became slower and less springy. I also liked to take longer naps. I played with pinecones happily, but it was good to sleep after dinner on my favorite chair in the dining room, warming myself in the warm rays of the sun coming in through the window.

Many, many days went by. My master left and came back, various people came and went, and some of them stayed a few days. Maria also left our house. She was replaced by Regina. I liked her, because I knew that she understood me. It wasn't so good with Joanna, who sometimes came over to talk to my master. I never really liked her; her manner toward me was cold. When she got a bit too intimate, I bit her on the finger so that she would remember who reigned here! I told you already about my jealousy. Yes, I was jealous of everyone who captured my master's attention, but my jealousy of women was different. After all, I was the lady of the house, the lady for my master, and then these women would show up who clearly wanted to take him and my house away from me. I couldn't stand them. I didn't reveal this sentiment so as not to hurt my master, but I shuddered at the sight of them.

One winter morning, I found myself in the car with my master, Regina, and Adam. I always liked trips, looking at the moving views in the car window, but this time there was too much and I lost patience. We drove for an awfully long time. At first, the fields were covered in snow. Then, I saw some grass, then mountains and dark walls of fir trees with the mountain peaks high above them. We drove along winding roads for a very long time. Every once in a while, we would stop. After getting out of the car, I immediately tried to familiarize myself with the new place, but we would soon be on the road again. I spent the nights with my master in some strangely smelling bed, and then we would be on the road again. The views from the window were different again. There were no clouds in the sky, the sun shone brightly, and the greenery was flourishing. It became warmer, even hot. I never liked the heat and always preferred winter to summer.

We finally arrived at a strange place on a hill. I immediately recognized the smell of my master in the house that stood there! I ran around all the corners with excitement and all through the yard, because I knew that this would be our house. I got used to the new conditions soon. We were going for long walks again, though the world was very different from the one I had gotten used to over the years. The smells were different, more intoxicating. There was also the smell of salt in the air. I noticed other animals that were unknown to me. This was all intriguing. I found two sofas in the living room that were familiar to me. I chose one to sleep on. And it was like the old days again—I could hear my master's breathing through the open door.

I didn't like the new climate. I preferred to stay in the house. I often napped on the cool tile floor. In the evenings, I would sit with my master; he would look at the flashing images on the screen and listen to strange voices. I wasn't able to understand what could be interesting about this. I also couldn't stand when someone tried to take my picture. I was horribly scared of that round lens of the camera and ran as far from it as I could.

After many months, I returned to my real home after a long difficult car ride. I was very happy, ran around all the corners that were so well known to me. My neighbor behind the fence barked in joy, and I arranged a tantrum of a greeting for her as a sign that I was back and reigning once again.

Time started to get a bit confusing for me, but I know that we went to that house past the mountains and forests again. I got a piece of candy for the road that made me very sleepy, and I rode in a bag between my master's knees. I knew that we were going back, that I was again going to be in my house.

A painful node appeared under my right arm. It didn't bother me for a while, but it kept growing. I already had two such nodes on my back, but they didn't bother me. I found myself back in that awful place where the smell of many dogs and their helpless lamentations mixed with human voices. They gave me something that made me very sleepy. My master took me home immediately after I woke up. The pain after surgery wasn't that bad, and I could walk on my braces after a few hours. Still, I saw that my master was worried. He brought me some kind of capsules and tablets and made me swallow them, wrapped in some sweet treat. This fudge was my weakness, so I swallowed it even though I knew that there was something awful inside.

I got weaker. While staying in that other house, we went to see a kind woman doctor. She examined me and talked to my master. I knew that he was very worried again. I got new tablets, also given to me in candies. I felt better. The node under my arm started growing back and gradually spread through all of the nipples on the left side. I lost my appetite and most often napped. I didn't feel pain, only had trouble walking up the stairs. My life became monotonous.

I spent most of the time lying down and completely lost my appetite. I ate out of necessity so as to make my master and Regina happy.

I knew this couldn't last long. I would soon disappear, go over where others had gone, so that others could come in their place, so that some other puppy could come in my place.

I was sad, but I always tried to greet my master joyfully even when I could barely get up.

One day, my master had tears in his eyes and gave me two tablets in the candy. I swallowed them as usual. The world spun around me. I felt very sleepy, but I tried to fight against this sleepiness, though it didn't do much, and I couldn't stand up. My master took me on his lap as usual and we went to that kind woman doctor again. I don't remember a lot more. I was in a daze, almost asleep. I still felt it when they tied a rubber band around my paw. I felt a slight pinprick.

Is this all? Is this the end of my life as a dog? Nothing more?

Once, maybe once, I will again see my master. See those who showed me such kindness. Once, there, in the hazy cloud of that other and certainly better world. Because it could be no other way.

Because although material reality may vanish, real feelings, love and affection, are eternal.

15

Politics

I MET RONALD REAGAN for the first time during his election campaign in Detroit. The leader of the meeting was Michigan Governor William Milliken. Reagan was a guest at this meeting, though Milliken, who was known for his liberal opinions, didn't support the candidacy of a conservative like Reagan. Milliken behaved aggressively. Reagan reacted calmly to his disrespectful introduction and spoke to a full room. After the first few words, you could sense his ability to reach his listeners. He spoke from the heart, spontaneously and openly, and said what he thought. He didn't avoid sensitive subjects. I liked him a great deal and was captivated by his directness. I wasn't the only one. The proof was in the enthusiastic response in the room. Much later, I heard an accurate statement from the lips of one of the Democrats, "It's awfully hard to hate him!"

I had the chance to meet him a second time not only to see him and hear him but to speak with him directly during his visit to the Ukrainian Cultural Center in Detroit. He was already the President of the United States. I have a photograph with him from that meeting that I used on the cover of my book, *Na Goraco*, which was published in the year 2000 in the United States and then by RETRO in Lublin with a preface by Henryk Pajak, the owner of the publishing house and the author of many well-known political books. You can see in the photo that I look nervous and stiff with a rather stupid expression on my face as I squeeze the president's hand.

He came to the meeting in a helicopter. The president's secret service agents were very watchful so that no one unexpected would get close to him. But there were two young and not especially intelligent Polish boys who not only got close to the helicopter but, driven by incredible curiosity, climbed inside that machine! When the secret service agents saw the intruders, they threw themselves on them. They soon figured out that they were unarmed, but they had a lot of trouble speaking English. The incident did, however, delay the president's departure, because the helicopter had to be searched inch by inch for a bomb. The intruders were set free, because there was really nothing to punish them for, though the secret service agents lost their jobs.

My path crossed with that of this most prominent president of our epoch for the third time in rather unusual circumstances. He was supposed to come to Detroit. As I was then the chief of neurosurgery at St. John's Hospital, I was informed that I had been chosen to care for the president with the entire surgical team in the event of an accident or an attempt on his life. I stayed by the phone and wasn't permitted to leave the area for even a moment! I was proud of this honor and trust. The president's secret service agents chose St. John's Hospital, because it was one of the best medical center in the eastern metropolitan Detroit. They undoubtedly did background checks on all of us doctors of various specialties. I was the only Polish man among them.

My run-ins with the presidents didn't end with these incidents. George Bush was preparing for the presidency after Reagan's second term. A close colleague of mine, Dr. Bothra, who was known for his activeness in the Republican Party, organized a dinner for Bush at his house. I have to add that Bothra's family was one of the wealthiest in India and had practically a monopoly on Hindu cinematography.

Bothra called me asking if I would like to participate in this meeting. Of course, I accepted the offer gratefully.

The Bothra villa was located on woody and vast terrain. It was the middle of summer. The hot and humid air was filled with the scent of the coniferous trees that surrounded the villa. I was searched by the secret service agents, and then I parked my car and went inside. I don't know why, but Bothra didn't turn on the air-conditioning. The huge room that was glassed in on one side led out to a wooden deck overlooking the lake. The humidity was unbelievable, and it was made even heavier by the strong scent of Eastern perfumes coming from the Hindu ladies. They were dressed in traditional saris with exposed belly buttons and showed a lot of cleavage; they also wore valuable jewelry reflecting all the colors of the rainbow. Jet-black shiny hair was gathered in a large bun, complimenting black, almond-shaped eyes and carmine-colored lips; they were reminiscent of tropical butterflies with the only difference being that the abundance of their shapes hindered such a comparison.

The men wore European-style suits.

I looked around the room. I found a congressman I knew there. Like me, he felt a little lost in this exotic company. We waited for Bush to arrive. Finally, the helicopter landed, and our dignified guest was among us. You could see how incredibly fatigued he was. His face was drawn, and there were droplets of sweat on his forehead. He had to maintain composure, though—be polite, attentive, had to speak up, shake everyone's hand, and offer some pleasantry. My companion and I truly pitied him.

Bush's torture didn't end there. The host led him out to the terrace where the meal had been laid out. He sat him down at one of the tables, and the servants loaded up a huge portion of all the Hindu delicacies for Bush. If you're not familiar with Hindu cuisine, you may not know that it is very spicy and peppery! A European or American might have trouble swallowing the fiery food. Bush not only had to swallow the fire but also express his delight at this spicy, exotic fare. His situation was made worse by the fact that he was surrounded by a tight circle of Hindu women, who were nearly touching him with their busts. With the humidity, the perfume, and the heat coming from the plate, Bush had no air to breathe.

My congressman looked at me. "You know what, Janusz? If they gave me all the money in the world and all his distinction, I still would never want to be the president of the United States. In a case like this one here, I don't think I'd make it out alive!"

I completely shared his sentiment. We knew, however, that Bush had to go through such ordeals. The votes of the Indian diaspora counted a lot. He collected them to his side, like a persistent miser.

The elections were approaching in Poland. "Bolko" Walesa's term was coming to an end. The most significant candidate of the right wing was Jan Olszewski. His closest coworker in those years was Antoni Macierewicz. It was important for both of them to have some international exposure so that Olszewski could present himself as a politician having connections to the U.S. political elite. They turned to me for help. I knew Jan Lenczowski rather well from the period of protest about ending sanctions against the Jaruzelski junta. Lenczowski had organized an institute devoted to world politics called the Institute for the World Politics. Living in the main current of American politics, he knew most of the senators and congressmen, mainly in the Republican Party. I contacted him. I arranged a date for Olszewski and Macierewicz to come and have a meeting in the Senate and House of Representatives in Washington.

I waited for them in Washington. We decided that I would be the interpreter. We discussed the list of questions and issues to put forward. Peter Naimski was already in Washington. He joined us, and I hired someone to videotape our meeting.

We went to the Capitol building in the morning on a beautiful sunny day. Lenczowski came with us to lead us in and introduce us.

The meetings were fascinating. Senator Lugar was the one who had the idea—an idea that had been promoted by POMOST—to develop a campaign to renounce the Yalta Agreement as well as to expand NATO eastward so as to include Poland, Hungary, and the Czech Republic. The idea of a significant change in the U.S. political line towards the Bolsheviks was worked up at the Heritage Foundation, a conservative think tank. Senator Lugar was the first to bring the matter of expanding NATO before the Senate. In conversations with us, he claimed that such an expansion would be really imperative, but he emphasized that the opposition in the Senate led by Senator Nunn would be great.

Lugar made a rather kind impression on me. He was a modest and truthful man, who saw things clearly and who wished for good things not only for himself but also wanted to erase that dirty stain from American honor and to initiate a decidedly different U.S. political line towards countries that had been traditionally qualified as part of the "Soviet sphere of influence."

We also met with Newt Gingrich, the Speaker of the House. I had met him years ago when he came to Detroit as a congressman to help push through the Republican Party candidates. He was very polite now, too. It was evident that he wished to see Poland in NATO. He soon said that he wasn't in charge of international politics, as it was a matter for the president. However he could speak out in his own name on such important matters, and he was on our side.

Our meeting with Congressman Dornan was rather dramatic. He was the same man who led to the non-binding renouncement of the Yalta Agreement with Adam Kiernik (a POMOST member from Los Angeles). He moved me deeply when he said with open passion that the United States allies had betrayed Poland by giving her to the Soviets. He also said that it was high time to fix this mess and for Poland to become a country belonging to the Western cultural ring, to which it had been connected from the beginning of its nationhood. I have this whole speech by Congressman Dornan on videotape. It should really be seen in Poland.

After our Washington pilgrimages, we went to Chicago. POMOST in Chicago was under the leadership of Ala Dziezgowski, a strong activist in the independence movement. Ala organized a banquet for our guests. I led these celebrations as the coordinator of POMOST.

   And then, when I said a few true words about Walesa, I noticed to my great surprise that I caused obvious upset in Jan Olszewski. This shocked me doubly, taking into consideration what I had heretofore known about him. I was and still am convinced that any presidential candidate can only win the election when he gets the trust of millions of anonymous voters, and he will only get it when he is no longer a "political" candidate but a seeker of truth, as hurtful or painful as it may be. This position is what we always presented through our years in POMOST. We got bruises, reprimands, and disapproving murmurs, but through time, we convinced our listeners that the truth could be found only through us.

   A classic example of this is the Walesa affair. Was he or is he the true leader of "Solidarnosc" thanks to his civil courage, who stubbornly pushed to be the head of the organization and was awarded with the presidency? Or was it the opposite—was he a weak obedient agent in the hands of the UB who was then blackmailed by Soviet "caretakers" and surrounded by official and also Soviet "advisors?" I had evidence from many sources.

   Years ago one of our followers recognized Walesa in front of the university during the well-known student uprising as he was yelling the following words through a megaphone: "You are supposed to be learning, not demonstrating!"

   Anna Walentynowicz told me that during the coastal riots, when workers' blood was being shed, Walesa was hiding in the UB building! Soon after that, he got an apartment to live in.

   One of the main leaders of the strike in the Gdansk stockyard was Andrzej Gwiazda. When the strike was in the full swing, he went to other factories to extend the strike to a general strike. He was very successful. When he arrived back at Gdansk stockyards, to his horror, he could see workers ending their strike. When he asked why, they told that Walesa advised that the strike is over and they should go home. Only the efforts of Andrzej Gwiazda stopped this departure and resulted in continuation of the strike in Gdansk.

Walesa called off the general strike in the whole country at the moment when the Soviet puppets were preparing to flee to Moscow. Thus Walesa was responsible for prolonging the misery of the Polish people under Soviet domination.

It is clear from Soviet documents that he was fulfilling a particular role. Under the assumed name of Bolko he functioned as an informer for the Soviet special services, denouncing his co-workers. Like a Judas he served to betray his fellow workers and for a time destroyed the plans for independence.

We revealed all these facts in our radio broadcasts. It raised a storm among uninformed Polish-Americans. After all, if we wished to have a free Poland, we had to speak the truth and only the truth, because lies and half-truths dumb the masses and facilitate the endurance of the regime.

16

A Special Patient

MANY YEARS HAD already gone by when I saw Melinda for the first time. She came with her mother, a woman with big, frightened eyes that were full of pain and uncertainty and stared fixedly at me.

Melinda was really sick. She looked so young and fresh, but now she appeared slowed down, suffering from severe headaches. Despite her state, I could see that she, as a sixteen-year-old girl, was caring more for her mother than she was for herself; she was her mother's support.

Sitting at the desk in my white coat, I gathered information about her and made notes in the history and physical form—severe headaches that had grown increasingly bad over the past several months. Lately, her vision had gotten worse. She felt unsteady when she walked. She didn't have any previous serious illnesses. The form slowly filled up with information. I didn't have any doubt that Melinda was suffering from a brain tumor in the area of the frontal lobe. The intracranial pressure had to be great, because I could see papilledema in her eyes (edema of the optic nerve due to increased intracranial pressure). The CAT (Computerized Axial Tomography) scan revealed the presence of a tumor that was almost the size of a fist in the frontal skull cavity, where the frontal lobes are. The tumor had clear borders, was situated outside of the brain, but it had moved the brain tissue to a significant degree, squeezing and deforming it. It looked like a typical meningioma, a benign tumor that originates in the meninges.

We had a routine long discussion about what should be done, what the surgery was like, and what the risks were. To this day, I'm convinced that Melinda's mother didn't absorb any of what I was saying. Melinda, however, understood me well despite her suffering. They both trusted me. I felt that essential emotional connection that is well known to every surgeon—the link of trust and something more than trust that I can't describe, without which I would never perform a surgery.

After opening the skull, I saw a huge, rather hard, vascular tumor. It was easy to reach it, because the frontal lobes had been displaced. The tumor was encapsulated, and the arachnoid meninges divided it from the brain.

I cut into the tumor with an electric knife and gradually removed it, reducing its mass and simultaneously relieving the compressed brain. I sent the first fragments of the removed tumor to the pathology lab for microscopic evaluation to find out what I was dealing with. The test results indicated a malignant meningioma, a tumor that could not be completely removed and that would recur.

My one wish and responsibility was to be as radical as possible, excising the absolute maximum amount of the tumor. I had the life of a young girl in my hands, a girl who trusted me completely, lying down on the operating table. Slowly, in the most careful way possible, I removed the tumor from its capsule. Then I separated this capsule from the arachnoid meninges. I burned out the place where the tumor was growing into the bone with cauterization—literally charring the surface.

She woke up from anesthesia in a good state. She started to get better right before my eyes. The following day, she was walking around with a white turban on her head and then, after a week, she went home with a crown of hair that was re-growing after the pre-surgery shaving. She looked pretty and full of vitality, expressing gratitude towards me. Still, I had to tell her and her mother the truth about the results of the pathology tests. I emphasized, though, that I had removed the tumor as radically as I could.

The memory of Melinda and her mother coming to see me for a follow-up visit is one of the best memories I have from working as a neurosurgeon. This young woman was the picture of feminine charm and verve. The mother, who was always somewhat in the shadows, looked at me with eyes full of unspeakable gratitude.

Time passed. A year went by after the surgery. The CAT-scan didn't show any recurrence. Melinda was close to finishing high school. She studied excellently and cared for her mother, who couldn't imagine the world without her daughter in it. The husband had left her when Melinda was a child. Mother and daughter lived together and were tied to each other in good times and in bad.

Another year went by, then a third and fourth. Melinda finished high school. She had two years of college behind her. She transformed from a pretty young girl to an attractive young woman full of charm and warmth. They both felt close to me. Their visits were always a pleasant break for me. But, I always felt anxious that the tumor would grow back.

Four and a half years after the surgery, Melinda came for a visit again. When she set foot in the doorway, I knew that something was wrong. She was exhausted and suffering from severe headaches! The CAT scan showed another tumor in her head—there had been no recurrence in the original place; the new one was growing in the area of the occipital lobes!

The second surgery took place. And again the same sight—a red, lightly bluish, encapsulated tumor that was divided from the brain by the arachnoid meninges. I removed it without any difficulty. The brain expanded, and I burned out the site of the tumor with cauterization.

She felt better immediately. The next day, she felt good, the headaches had gone away, and the swelling of the optic nerves soon went away. She returned almost immediately to her active life. She got a position as the head of a team of secretaries in a large firm. She still came to me for follow-up visits with her mother or on her own. Sometimes, she would come on a bike. She told my secretary, Joanna, that she came just so that "Daddy" could take a look at her.

And again, three and half years went by. I was full of hope that I had won the battle despite the malignancy of the tumor, because there was no recurrence in the original place, and because the spread of the second tumor could be explained by the first surgery.

And after those three years, she came in not because of a headache but because of difficulty breathing! The mere walk from the waiting room to my office caused her to breathe rapidly—she gasped for air fiercely. The X-ray showed a large tumor in her lungs that had spread as far as the pericardium. I couldn't find anyone in Detroit who would operate. They felt that surgery was rather risky and didn't have much chance for success, so no one wanted to undertake such a risk. I sent her to the Mayo Clinic. She had surgery there, but the part of the tumor that permeated the pericardium could not be removed. The surgeon told her point blank that the matter was hopeless, that he had helped her somewhat, but that she would die after a while.

When she came to see me, she was sad but not completely broken down. She drew strength from knowing that she had to take care of her mother, who simply couldn't accept this terrible situation.

And again, Melinda got better after the surgery, went to work, and I saw her every once in a while at my office. The X-rays of her lungs and the CAT scan were both negative.

Two years after the surgery on her lungs, however, I was called in for a consultation in the hospital where I preformed most of my surgeries. I saw Melinda, but she looked so different! She was pale, with dark circles under her eyes. She smiled when she saw me. I don't even know what I said, for I felt a pain in my heart, and my throat was so tight that I wasn't in the state to cough up even a few words. Melinda was dying. The cancer had literally spread everywhere, from the internal organs to her spinal canal. Her resistance to the invasion of the fatal cells had been completely broken down. Her days were numbered.

And that's how she stayed in my memory and behind my eyelids forever—in that bed, ruined, in that moment of final farewell.

After decades of fighting with them, I see tumors as the incarnation of Satan, as merciless evil that is only good for destruction and torture. They stopped being organic tissue for me and became instead the embodiment of an abstract evil.

Melinda said goodbye to me. After a dose of morphine and Thorazine, she died peacefully, she fell asleep.

I went to the funeral home. Several dozen people were there, including a tall man with his back to the casket who had a cigar in his lips and was talking with a few other people who looked like him. I found out that he was Melinda's father. Melinda lay in a white dress in the middle of flowers and wreaths in the depth of the funeral hall. Her face was now free of suffering. She looked so fresh, so innocent—and so young! Only the complete stillness of her body, the stiffness of her features, revealed the presence of death. I found her mother somewhere in the corner, completely broken, with a glassy look on her face. She finally saw and recognized me. She grabbed my hand and started sobbing.

I didn't go to the funeral. Six months later, Melinda's mother came to see me, calm in the illusory calm of quiet despair. She brought me a picture of Melinda and a figure of a young girl who looked like Melinda kneeling by a unicorn.

"You liked Melinda. You really cared for her," she said hesitatingly. "I would like you to have these two little things to remember her by. I know that you will not forget Melinda, and I made this figurine myself."

Many, many years have gone by since those days. I got a lot older and had many difficult and sometimes dramatic experiences. The figurine of a young girl leaning on a white unicorn still stands on the mantle in my house. And I still have Melinda's photograph.

MY PATIENT MELINDA HAD TWO BRAIN
SURGERIES AND SEVEN YEARS OF FIGHTING
FOR HER LIFE, FINALLY IN VAIN

17

Heart Attack and More

F OR A WHILE, I had felt the need to rest after briefly walking
at a quick pace. The first such worrisome episode happened
in Boulder, Colorado, during a memorable conference in
which Kaczorowski was given approval to bestow the national
insignia of the Polish Government in Exile to Lech "Bolko" Walesa.
Walking along the mountainous terrain there, I suddenly felt an
acute tightening in my chest. Completely out of breath, I had to
stop and wait a long time for relief. Tightening in my chest slowly
subsided.

Such episodes began to happen more and more frequently.
Once, I was clipping a rather difficult and dangerous brain aneurism. In the moment when I put on the clip on its neck, solving
the problem and restoring the patient's health, I felt a strong pain
in my chest. I waited a moment, not showing that I was feeling
so awful, and then I calmly finished the surgery. I knew, however,
that I had to go see my colleague, a cardiologist. The EKG was
completely normal. The "noninvasive" tests—a stress test together
with an isotope test—was within normal limits. My cardiologist
assured me that nothing unusual was going on, but he gave me
some nitroglycerin tablets just in case the pain would recur.

I didn't have to wait long. On my way to the operating room, I again had that indescribable tightening in my chest. Dr. Ali Kafi, a cardiosurgeon, happened to be walking by. I stopped him.

"Listen, Ali, I think that you'll have to operate on me soon!"

"Don't talk nonsense!" he said. "If the results of the noninvasive tests were normal, then I don't think there'd be reason to operate."

A week later, I couldn't sleep almost the entire night. I felt awful, though it was hard for me to describe what was wrong with me. I didn't feel any pain. I stumbled out of bed in the morning. I went to the hospital. I rounded on my patients with difficulty. I still didn't feel well, and I couldn't figure out what was going on. I went home to eat something. Nothing appealed to me. I had no appetite. I had to see patients in the afternoon. I didn't feel well on the way to the office in the car, but even now, looking back in hindsight, I can't pinpoint what was bothering me.

My secretary, Joann, cried out in horror at the sight of me, "You're completely white! Deathly pale!"

I fell into the chair behind my desk. I felt like I was dying, like this was the end. I told Joann to send the patients home and to connect me to Dr. Kafi immediately. I also took some nitroglycerin. I felt a little better. Soon, I heard his voice in the receiver, "Why are you calling? What's going on?"

"Ali. I'm having a heart attack. I need immediate surgery. I'll be waiting for you in St. John's Hospital."

"Take two nitroglycerin tablets and come right away!"

That's what I did. I drove myself to the hospital. I parked the car, and then signed in as a patient. I ended up in the cardiac care unit immediately. I was given an IV of nitroglycerin and oxygen. I felt somewhat better. Ali Kafi and my cardiologist showed up. The need for surgery, and more specifically, the need for cardiac catheterization of the coronary arteries wasn't even a question. The only thing left to decide was who would do the procedure.

Ali Kafi was then using an invasive cardiologist who didn't belong to the same group as my cardiologist, who also had such a specialist at his disposal. So they had a dispute of a rather delicate nature as to who really had more of a right to perform this procedure.

I was furious.

"Enough of this talk!" I cried. "The one who can do it the earliest is the one who should do it!"

That's how I interrupted the competitive sparring. They took me to an X-ray room that was outfitted for cardiac catheterization. After the injection of dye into my coronary arteries, I developed an even more significant ischemia of the heart muscle that, fortunately, only lasted for a short time.

At one moment, I got a feeling of weightlessness; I was in a fog permeated with some kind of light. I heard a voice from far away, "Janusz, it's just for a moment. It'll be better momentarily."

Indeed, when I opened my eyes I saw the dark-skinned face of Ali Kafi, with his kind, black Persian eyes, above me.

I learned that my life had really been in danger, because the main coronary arteries were occluded to ninety-five percent of their diameter! Immediate surgery was necessary. Of course, I agreed to it, under one condition—if there would be serious complications, they should not try to resuscitate me.

I was wheeled out of the catheterization room. My two secretaries, Joann and Doris, who had recently arrived, were waiting for me in the hallway. They had been informed of my situation. I gave them some final instructions, and then I was taken into the operating room. I had been given a large dose of Valium before the catheterization, so I was in a bit of a daze. The OR doors opened—they were so familiar to me! I looked at the ceiling, at the shadowless lamps, at the shiny equipment, at the faces of all the familiar people. The gurney was wheeled next to the operating table. I heard, "Now we're going to move you onto the table."

"You don't have to; I'll get on it myself!" I propped myself up on my elbows and moved my torso onto the table.

"God!" I thought. "It's so nice and soft!"

I got comfortable and crossed my legs as I always did, and that was my last memory from before the surgery. My good friend, Dell, "turned off" my consciousness.

I woke up. I was lying on my back. I felt an intubating tube in my mouth and trachea. "I can't cough," I thought. I wanted to move my finger, but I couldn't. "Aha, I'm still paralyzed by the pavulon!" My consciousness faded out again. I woke up again; or rather, I was woken up by a horribly painful hiccup. I felt an indescribable pain with each spasm of my diaphragm. This suffering didn't last long. I was given some Thorazine intravenously and again fell into nirvana.

When I woke up after this, I had no idea how much time had gone by since the surgery. I could think somewhat more clearly now. The long scars on my chest and both of my legs, from which the venous grafts were taken to recreate coronary circulation, really hurt. My first thought was, "The surgery was a success!" Despite my poor frame of mind, the awful tightening in my chest had gone away, so everything seemed okay. That same day, I was thrown out of bed into a chair, where I sat lightly dumbfounded and awfully achy, filled with dread at the prospect of even the smallest movement. I did have some kind of soup and drank some juice.

I found myself on the cardiac care unit. I looked around at the nurses, who had become so well-known to me over the years, some who were close to me personally. Around ten o'clock, Ali Kafi came by. He looked at me with his black eyes.

"I did seven bypasses so that you could return to work." Having said this, he turned on his heel and went to see the nurses about my orders.

During that phase, the one problem was my colleagues visiting me "from the goodness of their hearts." Because they were doctors, the nurses didn't know how to throw them out. The visits lasted all day. I smiled stupidly and with difficulty, trying to maintain some dignity in that less than honorable position.

One of my close friends was Dr. Peterman, a German. As a young boy during the Second World War, he ended up in a Soviet prisoner-of-war camp. He escaped from there and by some miracle got to the West. We shared a love of music and classical literature, including the good works of the present day. He showed up at my door in the afternoon. He brought a cassette and a rather thick book.

"Janusz, I brought you a special recording of Bach. It's rather original. And this book covers a mass of information about sculpture art in the early Middle Ages."

I thanked him, smiling and at the same time frowning in pain. I was left alone with the nurse. She couldn't contain her laughter. I looked at her scoldingly.

"My God, I'm not in a state to enjoy these gifts from Dr. Peterman. I am not even ready for a Mickey Mouse comic."

The next day, I was released from the CCU to the cardiology ward. They also removed the drain from my chest and the wire from my heart that were to serve as connections to a pacemaker in the event of cardiac arrest. This drain removal from under my heart was not a pleasant experience. I had known a lot of pain in my life; for instance, during the occupation, I had a broken leg that was set with no anesthetic. But the pain and sensation associated with your insides being pulled out was something incomparably worse. I was reminded of the torture against "pagans,"–Slavic people, by the Teutonic Knights, supposedly fighting for Holy Mary, also called the Knights of the Cross. They would cut into the abdomen of the unfortunate captive, grab his intestines, and nail them to a tree, after which they would chase the victim around the tree with a hot iron until he tore out his own insides and died in suffering.

The night nurse was a good and friendly woman. I disliked pain medications because of their side effects.

But, I couldn't sleep. Despite my weak protests, she gave me some Darvon. It didn't help much. She came with another one, rearranged the bed, and said, "Goodnight."

I woke up convinced that a Soviet spy was at the foot of the bed! I wanted to cry out and warn the personnel—all for nothing. It was just a hallucination from the Darvon.

After six days, I went home. My friend Dr. Norman Bolz, with whom I had done many surgeries, was to take me. I got dressed, not forgetting my tie. I had a hard time making it look right, but it was okay in the end. The nurse came in, looked at me, and said admiringly, "You are the first person I've seen who has ever left to go home after that surgery with a tie around his neck!"

My housekeeper greeted me with open surprise, while my doggie, Chitah, almost went crazy with joy. She closely sniffed my left leg, sensing blood there.

I knew for obvious reasons that the main factor to my getting better was to move around and do physical exercises. I walked around the house as much as I could, going up and down the stairs. I could move quite freely. Instead of getting "stuck" without breath, I felt better and stronger with each exercise. My surgery had taken place on February 27, 1992, and I was seeing patients in my office again on April 15. My first day back at the office was its own kind of experience. I saw a waiting room full of my post-operative patients. They were surprised by my coming there. Someone yelled out, "Doctor, what are you doing here? For the love of God, take care of yourself!"

A week later, I was operating again. Ali Kafi had done a good job.

I still have the memory of circling in that state of weightlessness from those preoperative experiences. I was floating in that light space. It was a pleasant experience, free from pain and fear. Like everyone, I fear the suffering that precedes the departure. Still, I don't fear death itself. It's not that bad at all. It's how it was at that moment—as if a person has embarked on yet another road, freed from his burdens, weightless.

Dr. Benjamin Haddad, the oldest neurosurgeon and founder of neurosurgery at St. John's Hospital, was the chief of this section of neurological surgery. Part of the chief's responsibilities included administrative work, organization of specialist meetings, taking care of operating room equipment maintenance, and most importantly, checking up on neurosurgeons who were on the hospital staff and had the right to admit patients and operate on them. This is a difficult and thankless position, especially when you take into account the level of difficulty, problems, and dangers in neurosurgeons' work.

One day, Dr. Haddad proposed that I take over the position of chief of neurosurgery. He was tired of the additional administrative responsibilities. He was awaiting retirement in a few years, and he wished for the department's work to continue without any greater problems. We knew each other well and respected each other. I agreed and became the chief of neurosurgery at St. John's Hospital and Medical Center. During this time, St. John's hospital transformed from a first-class general hospital to an unbelievably developed medical center that had more than twenty operating rooms, each one the site of more than a thousand surgeries a year. The high quality became apparent with the number of specialists in various rare subspecialties.

I got to work. Because part of my new responsibilities included participating in conferences about the operating rooms, I could present the needs of our department and considerably improve the equipment in the ORs. I also organized a new committee called the neuroscience committee. I was its head, fulfilling this function as well as that of neurosurgery chief. Specialists in fields having to do with the nervous system participated in this committee, such as neurologists, neurosurgeons, neuroopthalmologists, neurootologists, rehabilitation specialists, anesthesiologists who had experience with neurosurgical cases, neuroradiologists, and finally the representatives of the administration for whom the committee meetings were valuable, because they set forth plans for the future. Our meetings had a twofold character. One focused solely on analysis of clinical cases, while the other had as its goal the establishment of so-called "passways"—guiding rules for management in concrete emergency cases, for example of the patients with subarachnoid hemorrhages.

Generally, it was interesting work. Everyone learned something new from someone else, as each one of us had come out of a different school of thinking with a different operating technique. We complemented each other, recognizing that cooperation expanded our common possibilities. The result of this cooperation was surgeries in which not one but two surgeons from various subspecialties would participate. This really improved surgical outcomes.

The level of medical care increased significantly. Another reason for this was specialty training for nurses, who became essential links in the surgical team. With the incredible advances in technology during those times, the operating room transformed itself from a domain of one surgeon to a place of cooperation of a neurosurgeon, physicist, radiologist or neurootologist.

At that time, I was performing many stereotactic surgeries. They require a high level of precision as well as dexterity with a computerized apparatus. I would never go into such a surgery without the assistance of a physicist with whom the course of action was determined. We were then using not only CAT scans (Computerized Axial Tomography) but also MRI (Magnetic Resonance Imaging). These two diagnostic techniques revolutionized neurosurgery. While frequently attending science conferences and reading specialty literature, I was thrilled by the method used to transform the MRI information into a three-dimensional model. This permitted not only to see the brain under different angles but also allowed performing a simulated operation before a real one.

I looked for just such a computer. In spite of the expense I convinced the administration to buy it. Initially, people acted with reserve towards this new technique, because no one understood it well. Later, it became an invaluable tool not only for neurosurgeons but also for orthopedic surgeons. During that phase of my life, feeling good once again after having had heart surgery, I threw myself into my work at full force. I did surgeries on many more difficult and complicated cases.

I remember that when I first walked through the doorway of St. John's Hospital, the chief of surgery was Dr. Joseph Grady. His partner was Dr. Farynga—the first initiator of cardiac surgery in the hospital. They were surgeons with a real vocation. After getting to know me, they treated me well. Joe Grady's right-hand man was Larry Lloyd, who was still a resident in those days and then became a full-fledged surgeon. Joe Grady depended upon him, and Larry took over the teaching of residents, which was difficult and demanding work. Meanwhile, Joe took care of the administrative side of surgery. I also participated in teaching residents, leading them through a year-long course in neurosurgical management of trauma cases. Young surgeons liked my teaching style. I didn't give dry lectures but instead held discussions, not leaving out any funny incidents. These were rather necessary when the lessons began at 7:30 in the morning and some of the residents were coming from a sleepless night on-call.

Joe decided to leave for retirement. Larry took over his responsibilities until a new chief was found. They were looking for a candidate for the chief position in surgery who would bring in a new subspecialty. We already had specialists in transplants. Now, we wanted someone with extensive knowledge of precise microscopic vascular surgery. A special committee was created to look for such a candidate. We finally found the desired treasure in Dr. "S." He had excellent references and previously worked at a medical center that was well-renowned in the United States. We waited impatiently for his arrival. One day, I went into the physicians' lounge to grab some coffee and a sweet roll (an awful amount of cholesterol!). Dr. "S" was already there. He had dark hair (of Russian-Georgian descent) and was dressed in a black suit—he seemed like your typical funeral home director.

He jumped up from his chair, ran up to me, grabbed my hand, and said, "I am thrilled to have the opportunity to meet you! I will try to the best of my ability to help in any way I can."

This extraordinary politeness made me very suspicious. I have known a lot of surgeons in my lifetime. All of the ones that were worth anything were never gushing with their emotions, nor were they known for their particular kindness.

A few weeks later, I found out that Dr. "S" didn't know how to operate! A procedure that would take another surgeon an hour took him six! We found out that he had gotten good references, because they were trying to get rid of him. The situation was complicated. He had a signed contract with the hospital for a large amount of money. The lawyers on both sides finally reached an agreement and, after getting a good amount of money, Dr. "S" left our hospital.

After that incident, the committee that had been called up to find him was reorganized, and another search began.

We were sitting in the scrub room—Larry Lloyd, Richard Jones, the head of orthopedic surgery, several surgeons of other specialties, and me. We were talking about the search for a new chief. Suddenly, I had a thought.

"Larry," I said. "You know very well what you are! A real son of a bitch." He didn't refute it. I laid out my idea:

"Why in the hell should we look for another chief who might turn out to be the same kind of genius that Dr. 'S' was? With you, none of us has any illusions! On the other hand, you run the whole department and the resident program. Why should we spend a lot of time looking? Let's have you as chief!"

Larry was surprised by my brutish motivation. The others there supported my suggestion, and Larry became the chairman of the department of surgery a week later.

His "promotion" to that position by Subczynski became a well-known anecdote in the hospital. I was right. He did and still does fulfill his responsibilities with no qualms, and the fact that he is somewhat of a prima donna doesn't seem to bother anyone anymore.

The head nurse of the operating room was Terry Cope, a German woman with a good heart and resounding voice who didn't hesitate to use it to lead her team. I liked her and respected her, though she didn't hesitate to reprimand me. She ended up having a falling out with the administration—she simply couldn't respect "authority"—and she was fired. She found an excellent job in another hospital. Karen was hired in her place. She was about forty years old and tall, with bleached blond hair and a decent figure that moved nicely. She was also difficult to work with. When I rubbed her the wrong way, she reprimanded me with sharp words. I calmly listened to her tirade, feverishly thinking of a way to resolve the situation. I opened my eyes widely and, looking at her fixedly, I said, "Karen! You look so sexy when you're angry!"

She was speechless. From that day forward, she left me alone.

Well then, if I had said something like that in the last few years, I know I would have been sued for sexual harassment! But, Karen didn't last long with us either. She didn't have a knack for administrative duties, which were an essential attribute of a chief OR nurse. Again, there was no one in command. It just so happened that Susie, a woman of Polish descent took over as chief nurse without the formal title or the chief salary.

I liked Susie for her organizational skills, her fairness, her sense of humor, and her common sense. There was a meeting of the operating room committee. All the chiefs of various surgical specialties were present there, along with representatives of the administration and Susie, as well as her closest coworkers. The meeting was boring and routine, touching on the purchase of equipment, the organization of the operating room, etc. At such a meeting, there is always someone among the surgeons who comes forward with usually unjustified complaints. It bored me and angered me slightly. I looked at Susie and, not really thinking, I raised my hand.

"Dr. Subczynski? What matter would you like to raise?" the chairman asked.

"I have an idea. I propose that Susie, who does her job as chief nurse of the operating room so well, be promoted to that position."

This proposition was really out of place, for I hadn't discussed it with the administration or talked about it with Larry, who was then the chief. It literally came out of nowhere. My idea was ignored in silence, but Susie was the chief the next day! Later on she thanked me somewhat surprised by my unorthodox method of nominating her.

* * *

From the moment I took over the chairmanship of the radio station WPON, the "Station of Nations," it became clear that the station was going bankrupt despite the newly injected money.

There were many reasons for this—the aforementioned theft

by the directors of the radio programs, complete chaos and disorder in management, and the lack of support of English-speaking people.

I lay awake many nights thinking about what I could do. I didn't care about the money I had invested in this enterprise but rather about the money that other retired Polish people had invested, who in their naiveté had trusted Mr. Rozalski, the director of "Polish variety shows," and had purchased "preferred" shares, which were supposed to yield twelve percent gain. Of course, this was pure fiction. The station's broadcasting equipment was ruined—some of it was completely useless—and the towers were threatened with catastrophe. The only thing with any real worth was the square on which the radio towers stood. Because of the urban development in that area, its value had greatly increased.

I came to the conclusion that the only solution was to sell that land. But, we would need a new place for the towers. I found a piece of land in Comers City. I sold our parcel for $900,000 and bought the new one for $200,000. I paid off our long-standing debts with the remaining money, using it for unpaid bills, an investment company who had been called in to save the station, and the bank. But, I still had to pay all the shareholders. I decided that the only solution was to buy back their shares with my own money. My lawyer nearly tore out the remains of the hair on his somewhat bald head seeing what I was doing. In his opinion, I was good-naturedly ruining myself.

During that time, I owned most of the shares of the station, so I could decide its future. My lawyer suggested that I hire his sister to manage the station. Mary, a corpulent and energetic woman who was anxious and, more importantly, honest, got to work. The station immediately stopped being in deficit! Though in truth it didn't make any money, at least it no longer operated at a loss. I could slowly pay off the old debt and buy new equipment, and the quality of the radio signal significantly improved. I felt some relief. My money was no longer going to waste. It became an investment, which after years was sufficient to ensure my financial well-being. And, I could scrupulously keep the word that I had given to the Polish-American investors; all of them were paid, with the exception of a few dozen who we couldn't locate. Recently, Mary told me that she had found several more addresses with the help of the Internet and had sent out more money.

Thus, I had become the majority owner of the radio station completely involuntarily. I still am to this day. I have received offers to sell it. My lawyer had been wrong in saying that I was committing financial suicide. Or maybe God decided to reward me for not wanting to hurt poor old people.

All the people who wanted to sustain Polish programming became the most ardent followers of the POMOST radio broadcasts. Many of them gathered in groups to listen to the broadcasts together and then discussed them. This was really moving for me, and it also reaffirmed our obligation to inform the public honestly.

I soon specialized in political commentary, and these commentaries inspired the greatest upset in the PRP servants. My programs in Detroit, Ali Dziezgowski's in Chicago, and Wiktor Zolcinski's in Phoenix, Arizona, became the antidote for the propaganda venom that was flowing over other radio stations and newspapers. It was really at that moment that I understood how deeply the Polish-American community had been infiltrated by agents of the PRP regime, how subtle that network was, and how well it functioned. Of course, we were a splinter in this network that was tearing holes through it. We were to be destroyed at any cost. They couldn't get to me financially, because I was independent. They tried to instigate malpractice suits calling my Polish patients who might have a political gripe with me. They also distributed slanderous letters about me. This action did not succeed. Those patients came to me themselves to warn me

During this time, my closest coworkers were Kazimir Weber and Adam Sygulinski. Kazik was a machinist from Stalowa Wola. He had been sentenced to exile and settled in Canada, just across the river. He used to come over to help record programs each week. He had a rich political past. He was a Solidarnosc activist, the top one in his factory. Arrested, he spent over a year in prison. He had then been given a choice—either exile or further imprisonment. He chose the former. He left without knowing the language, without having any contacts, and with only his two hands to offer for some work. We spent many hours together looking for material, researching topics, and recording programs.

The second coworker at that time was Adam Sygulinski. He also brought a rich past from Poland. The three of us did all the work. Of course, there were many people who came and went through POMOST, and I am grateful to all of them for their help in the fight against the evil that was ruling over the nation of Poland. Our method was to broadcast the truth—something that was not possible in our old fatherland.

We had a studio complete with professional equipment in the large, finished basement of my house. We interwove our commentaries and informative segments with music, mainly Chopin. Our introductory signal from the Symphony of the New World, so mighty in its sound and so tragic, went quite well with the theme of our words.

18

The Work of Sisyphus

ELECTIONS WERE TAKING place in Poland. Aleksander Kwasniewski was elected president—his real name was Stolzman, and he was the son of a high-ranking officer of the Soviet special services in the PRP, a Jewish man who was famous for breaking down post-war resistance. The independent candidate, Jan Olszewski, lost miserably. We soon learned that the "right wing" wasn't going to give up. It was creating the Movement to Reconstruct Poland, and this movement was growing, with Jan Olszewski and Antoni Macierewicz at its head. Circles of this party also appeared among Polish-Americans. It seemed that a new force was rising, a truly patriotic Polish force that was opposed to the shift from being under one occupation to being under another—this time much more evil, because it had been organized by enemies who were born and raised in Poland and who aimed to destroy national identity and subordinate Poland to a ruling clique of post-communist Jewish junta. It was said in this country that the Reconstruction Party and the Solidarnosc movement, already injured and weakened by Lech "Bolko" Walesa, accomplished the takeover of the government.

We were prematurely happy, and it was unfortunately in vain.

Like a thunderclap on a clear day, the news came that things were not going well in the Reconstruction Party, that a dissolution was near, and that two factions were developing. I knew both Olszewski and Macierewicz personally. This last one wanted to reach an agreement to join forces before the election. Meanwhile, Olszewski disagreed and refused to cooperate with Macierewicz.

I will never forget that hour-long nighttime conversation I had with Jan Olszewski. I tried to convince him that if there were already miscommunications and animosities, then they should be put aside and forgotten for the good of all—and also that the period before such important elections in Poland was not the time for personal battles.

Meanwhile, Olszewski, instead of going along with my suggestions and proposals to unify, expressed anger and upset towards Antoni Macierewicz. In the end, though, I still thought that I had convinced him of my opinion. I was wrong. The next day, long articles full of mutual accusations and clear hostility appeared in the "opposition" press. The coalition of the Right was broken. The Reconstruction Party stopped being a significant political force. For a long time, mutual accusations about dissension were meagerly presented in the opposition press. The Right was so engulfed in the mess of destruction in its ranks that it completely forgot the essence of the matter, about who really ruled in Poland and what kind of programmed consequences were going to result.

I wrote a letter to Jan Olszewski in which I clearly called for unification—all for nothing.

The breakdown of the Reconstruction Party of its own accord was undoubtedly a huge tragedy for many Poles, as well as, and maybe especially, for me, though I had lived for decades outside of Poland.

After the breakdown in the Reconstruction Party, the party didn't have an essential role in the Diet. The mutual destruction and mud slinging continued. We found out about the rise of newer and newer factions of the "Right Wing" whose main task was to discredit their political "predecessors." The opposition newspapers got busy promoting their idols. This type of promotion didn't get very far because of scanty publishers and difficulties in distribution.

I wondered what had caused such an easy and sudden breakdown of the Right. Was it a coincidence?

There was talk of infiltration by Soviet agents. Indeed, there used to be a KGB institute in Minsk that existed for the purpose of scientifically testing methods of mass population control. It is absolutely certain that in the first phase of the real existence of Solidarnosc, professionals from this institute were brought into the movement. Supposedly, such professional destructive work was being continued among Polish-Americans. A lot has been said and written about the psychological devastation of the Polish consciousness during the last fifty years because of the terrorist utopia of Marxism-Leninism. Patterns of thinking, even of the opposition, were and still are shaped by the decades of this collective brainwashing.

An argument that might explain the hopelessness of the independence and national movements is the dependence of all the foundational national and social structures, including some of the agriculture, on the Russian occupier.[4] The occupation is no longer apparent, but the structures remain—in the military, in the UB, in the intelligence and counterintelligence actions, in the administration, in the universities, in the high schools. The web, numbering hundreds of thousands of people, holding these structures together does not wish for its demise. The standard of living for these people is dependent upon the maintenance of these conditions.

When you look from a distance at the "post-war" situation in Poland, and when you compare it to that in Hungary, in the Czech Republic, and the remaining Eastern European countries, then the convergence of the systems preserved there is strikingly similar. It is post-communist mainly Jewish mafia which took over total power. Everywhere there exists a rapid plundering of national

4. The theme of discussion—all of these "elites" are presently servants of Western globalism and liberalism, though in reality, their ideological and nationalist origin has its roots in Soviet communism.

wealth in the guise of "privatization." This has been a common denominator. Economic degradation almost reached to the level of the Third World. Those in power are the sons and daughters of the tyrants sent in after the war by the Soviet communists. Their first task was to physically exterminate any remaining, surviving Polish intelligentsia. Today, they make up part of the global system of domination over nations.

Thus, you shouldn't blame only the nation for political and national ignorance, keeping in mind that though they vote in the elections one way or another, the new leaders were determined ahead of time. The strength now lies with mostly Jewish financiers in the West, mainly American, who covered Russia in the blood of brotherhood under Trotsky's command in 1917.

Will this global mafia win? The battle goes on. There are rays of hope. The resistance is gathering strength. Tens of thousands of protestors appear at the meetings of this global international mafia that are organized in various nooks and crannies of the world and transform these cities into battlegrounds.

One method of resistance is the black market, sometimes called the free market, totally out of reach of the government and being the core of economic growth and life of the country. The second source of income is influx of the dollars from all over the world from the Polish diaspora.

19

Retirement

THERE COMES A moment in the life of a surgeon, especially
one who performs difficult and dangerous surgeries, when
he can't stop thinking about the person whose life depends
on his hands during the course of a surgery. He can't focus solely
on the mechanics of the surgery, because he is constantly bothered
by the thought that the patient might come out of the procedure
impaired, that the surgery might mean only prolonged suffering
for him. This thought pierces like a splinter, making a surgeon's
work more difficult.

When this moment begins to repeat itself, you should get out
of active surgery. You should leave the operating table forever!

A young neurosurgeon in training, even the best and most
noble-minded one, sees mainly medical "cases" that need surgical "resolution." Of course, he wishes for the patient to leave alive
and experience a radical improvement in his condition. Successful
procedures please him, while the unsuccessful ones bother him.
All the same, the barrier of his youth and vitality distances him
emotionally to a certain degree from the sea of tragedy in which
he spends every day. He is also convinced that he can do every-

A MEXICAN BOY FISHING IN FLORIDA NEAR
MY HOUSE; PAINTING BY THE AUTHOR

thing or almost everything, and he feels even surer of this under
the supervision of an experienced surgeon.

There comes a moment in his life, however, that he is left alone.
He has to make the decisions alone, be responsible for them, and
operate alone. Though he has a significant team around him—an
assistant, nurses, and an anesthesiologist—he is still alone in his
decisions and actions.

I remember such a moment, when I found myself in this leadership role for the first time, like a ship captain on a stormy sea.
I didn't have anyone next to me who was more experienced who
could help me or advise me. I managed to get a grip on my fear
and uncertainty. From those first situations, I discerned the following guidelines for action—never undertake a surgery in which
you might feel uncertain, even if you know the technique very
well; always be sure that you have exhausted all the diagnostic
methods and are in this way appropriately prepared to operate;

think through all the details the day before surgery; be prepared at every moment for the worst possible complications—and if you always remember this, they can be avoided; be sure that surgery is absolutely necessary; if it is necessary, do everything to minimize injury for the patient.

These rules have been encoded and beaten into my personality as a neurosurgeon, but these rules also carry over into my behavior outside medicine. Surgery is not an easy profession, but also lucrative. It is a life whose circumstances differ from those of other people. I would call it a state of being rather than a profession.

Through my decades of work, I met many surgeons of various specialties, ethnicities, and races. Their common denominator was a specific lifestyle, in which there is not even a minute free from obligation; he doesn't have the luxury of completely cutting himself off from this sphere of work. After doing a difficult surgery and getting home, I had to stay in touch with the ICU, often answering questions for the night nurse regardless of the nighttime hour, not to mention that I had dozens of patients at the same time! An experienced surgeon knows his limitations. He also knows what he is capable of performing well and does it—later rejoicing with patients who had good results or enduring dramas of those who didn't. When it comes to the crucial moment, however, to the actual surgery, he stops thinking about the patient on the table but concentrates only on the task at hand. Still, he can't escape the moment when he becomes aware that a father of a family or a mother of small children is lying in the operative field. Then it becomes much more difficult for him to make rational decisions, because he feels great responsibility for the person undergoing surgery that may even carry over into a feeling of responsibility for this person's children! This burden weighs heavily on him.

As years passed, I garnered the respect of not only my patients but also my colleagues. My practice grew such that at least one third of new cases were referred to me by families of those on whom I had previously operated. I also saw patients of doctors who knew me, as well as nurses and their families. I got a good name among the rather numerous Italian population and, strangely enough, the

German diaspora. I operated on the German vice consul. We had a lot in common, namely a weakness for dogs! I even had a patient from Pakistan.

St. John's Hospital became one of the main medical centers in metropolitan Detroit; it grew, and as it did, I expanded my renown as the chief of the department of neurosurgery, responsible for the full functioning of that specialty. I never was and never will be a "snob," but at the same time, life itself brought me into a group of specialists with a deciding voice.

And it was right at the peak of my being in this position that I began to have those bothersome fears about the person on whom I was operating, about his fate's dependence upon me. They were like dark clouds blocking out a realistic outlook on the situation. I knew that I had to leave, though I had no concrete reasons to capitulate like this.

This was a tough decision. Surgical procedures become a crucial element in the life of a surgeon, often determining his time and energy. I was horrified by this thought of leaving. What would this mean for my practice?

I would no longer be making significant decisions.

My whole world up until this point, this whole complicated mechanism of surgical life, would be sidetracked and would eventually come to a standstill.

I would stand before the unknown, otherwise called old age, and then death.

I am convinced that every reader of this fragment of my remembrances who has crossed through this "strip of shadow," like I have, will agree that I am right and will understand the depth of this looking ahead, or rather down.

The right time to leave—and I'm not only talking about my profession—is the moment when all of those around me would be surprised, and maintain, without pretending, that my decision was too early. It was nice to hear, "Doctor, you must be kidding! You really want to stop operating? But you have a huge practice and excellent outcomes!"

Indeed, this was true, and these surprised exclamations were sincere. It is awful when people talk behind a surgeon's back—so that he won't hear or will be the last to know—saying, "It's about time for him to stop operating. He's clearly not cut out for it anymore!"

I knew very well that my retiring from the profession wouldn't be easy for many reasons. And yet, I always had and still have many other interests, which I could never satisfy while moving in the world of a prestigious specialty and function. For example, I always liked to write—this finally took expression in this present retrospective of a rather stormy life. I always had ambitions to play the piano, though never with expectations of greatness. I always liked painting, though being fully aware of my limitations. My talents obviously do not rise to the level of a Leonardo DaVinci.

I was most struck by the hidden mechanisms that determine people's fates. How did it happen that seemingly from out of nowhere events led up to the French Revolution? Is what has been written about it until now truthful, or was its eruption determined by unknown, secret culprits' efforts? Why were there two genocidal world wars that were really insane from the point of view of each of the fighting sides? Why does it happen that most of the heads of countries usually have a rather ugly past, many, so many, of which are almost criminal? Why were psychopaths like Napoleon, Hitler, Stalin, or Trotsky, able to subjugate masses of people?

Having the dramatic experiences of the Second World War, the German Occupation, and then the Soviet PRP behind me, and as a being who thought about and recognized obvious facts, could I not then ask myself questions about the genesis and goal of such events? Political activism in POMOST, of which I became the coordinator after Krzysztof Rac, empowered me even more and pulled me into the political sphere. My commentaries became well known to many people. I started writing to resistance newspapers and found a good audience there.

Still, distancing myself from the narcotic of operating—the drama of the operating table and going into a completely other world—and finally breaking off ties with patients with whom I remained often in close contact was painful, like a quiet shock, throwing me into a kind of emotional void.

I gave my practice to two young and very well-educated neurosurgeons. I gradually transferred it over several years, but the day came, and then within it the moment, when I looked at my office, at the desk, the model of the spine and brain standing on the cabinet, and the elephant with his trunk lifted (for good luck) for the last time; when I looked at the screen on which I had looked at thousands of X-rays; when I said goodbye at last to the secretaries with whom I had worked for over twenty years. And when I finally closed the door of my office, or rather no longer my office, behind me, I felt . . . aha! What does the captain of a ship feel leaving his cabin after twenty years? That's just it—emptiness. And soon afterwards, a feeling of undeserved hurt that all that I had worked towards and finally achieved, that made up the essence of my existence, was now somehow all behind me.

My departure from this profession didn't end with my closing the office door from the outside. After a few months, I was informed that the medical team at St. John's Hospital was organizing a special farewell reception for me. About 180 doctors showed up for the benefit! The crowd was unbelievable. They asked me to speak.

I said the first good thing that came to my mind:

"I feel sort of like I'm at a wake, with the only difference being that the deceased isn't lying down yet but has instead chosen a standing position."

That's exactly how I felt—a wake at which the deceased is not yet in a horizontal position. I did have the quiet satisfaction, however, that so many friends came willingly, spontaneously, to this sad affair. This was the first affair in the history of St. John's Hospital when so many openly demonstrated friendship and respect for a departing surgeon.

It was made even more pleasant knowing that the one being honored was a Polish man.

When I was still working, though at a slower pace, and my younger partners were gradually taking over the weight of my responsibilities, I went off for my first real vacation—the first since leaving Poland! I chose London. I wanted to see that city. And from there, I went to Spain. At that time, all of England had just been shaken with the death of Princess Diana. I arrived there on Thursday, and the funeral was supposed to be on Saturday. I happened to find out some interesting details concerning the Queen of England. Supposedly, she hated Diana. She found out about her death while she was at church in Scotland. She forbade informing anyone about this tragedy. The upset of her followers was so great and growing so quickly, however, that Prime Minister Blair advised the queen to offer her condolences on television. The speech wasn't made until Friday afternoon, but it did somewhat quell the atmosphere of shock.

A crowd was moving at a slow pace, silent and disciplined, before Buckingham Palace. They walked up to the tall iron fence, leaving thousands of flowers and wreaths and further on signing their names in a remembrance book. I was struck by this crowd's discipline. There were hardly any policemen around—the people knew how to behave on their own so as to make an effort to be part of that important moment. Still, this was also a demonstration against the queen! Unlike the rest of the royal family, Diana knew how to mix with the crowd and reach out to people's hearts. She was a princess of the people who had been thrown out by a disliked queen.

Spain thrilled me with its richness of sacral architecture and its huge collections of artwork. I was particularly impressed with the old Moorish abode named Alhambra, in which the fountains that are supplied by the aqueducts from the mountains are still working. I saw tall columns, characteristic double arches, mosaics of plant motifs, and a gorgeous garden surrounded by a tall wall that was designated for the harem; the palace was built on a black granite cliff with dungeons for the captive nonbelievers—truthfully the abode was now empty but still pulsed with the old exotic life. Walking on the marble floors and hearing the echo of my own footsteps, I filled these walls with my own fantasies; I could almost see the black eyes behind the wooden grate of the harem secretly looking at the outside fountain. I could see dignitaries in turbans, armed with curved swords—all of it was so different, savage, and at the same time beautiful and colorful.

Andalusia surprised me with its contrast of gray-olive groves and vast vineyards surrounded by black, sharply peaked mountains and valleys sprinkled with whitening settlements. I was captivated by the richness of temples, a gold monstrance for the host, inlaid with expensive stones so huge that they could only be carried by the hands of four men with special stretchers; the gilded appearance of countless altars; the flashing colors of stained-glass windows; the beautiful paintings of El Greco; mahogany wood that was carved and richly gilded for church dignitaries. One could also see the poverty of peasant people who served the rich landlords. So, it's not a surprise at all that the communist Bolsheviks were able to fuel the fires of revolution in this country of social contrasts, the victims of which were hundreds of thousands of people. The country stood in ruins, thousands of places of worship were destroyed and profaned, tens of thousands of clergy were murdered, and enormous supplies of Spanish gold were sent to the Bolsheviks' land.

I slept well the first night after leaving for retirement. There were no phone calls. I wasn't woken up to give orders. I wasn't responsible for those who had undergone surgery the previous day or the day before that. Still, I didn't feel well spiritually or physically. After years of exhaustive work and having had coronary bypass surgery, I started getting arrhythmia. As my cardiologist said, it didn't indicate anything serious but was bothersome.

Winter was coming. I thought that it would be better if I spent the winter in the tropical climate of southern Florida. I knew it well, because I had often visited Miami, Palm Beach, and Key Biscayne. I wasn't yet familiar with the western coast on the Gulf of Mexico. One of my friends recommended going to Marco Island, an island on the Gulf of Mexico near Naples. I went. The warm, somewhat humid air, the bright tropical sunshine, a herd of white ibises, palms, tons of flowers—these were my first impressions. I settled in a rented condominium at first, but I didn't stay there long. There was a view of the silver horizon of the Gulf of Mexico from the balcony with dolphins jumping and fish leaping out of the water for insects, but I didn't feel right there closed within four walls. Besides that, I missed having a piano, which was a tried and true method of therapy, a departure from anxieties, worries, and loneliness.

I decided to buy a property there—to have my own place there, to feel at home. The same agent who helped me rent the condominium took it upon himself to take me around the island showing me the homes for sale. I didn't like any of them. They had small yards, and the houses were right next to one another on the canals, which led to the gulf. The prices were very high.

"I'd like something on a bit of a hill, set up higher, with a larger yard."

"Okay," he agreed after a moment of thought. "I think I have something that would be right for you!"

He drove me to the southern part of the island—the whole island measures ten miles wide and twelve long, most of which is taken up by canals and bays—to an area where villas stood a good distance from one another on a hilly terrain surrounded by a vast bay, Caxambas Bay. On the very top of the tallest hill stood a house that was hidden among bushes and palms. We drove up a steep side street to the yard at the back of the house. I looked around. The view was very promising—an orchid tree covered in purple flowers; a bougainvillea bush that was dark purple with an abundance of flowers; huge, golden goblets of hibiscus near the white steps; an orange tree full of fruit further on, as well as a grapefruit tree and some other kind that was unknown to me.

There was a thick jungle full of trees, vines, prickly agaves all around—it was impassable. The house reminded me of a large wooden barrack surrounded by a large yard with a good-sized swimming pool. The inside of the house was vast, and there was a view to the horizon from almost every window thanks to its having the highest location, not only on the island but in all of southern Florida. I found out that that hill was the site of an old Indian burial ground. Thus, the house stood on old holy ground. I liked the view from the windows and the swimming pool. I could redo the inside, and I already had my sights set on recreating Moorish architecture, a result of my excursion to Spain.

The price turned out to be manageable. The previous owners, an older retired couple, were moving to a condominium community where they would be given meals and medical and nursing care. Not thinking too much about it, I gave a down payment.

Four hours later, the agent informed me that my offer, which had been $20,000 lower than the asking price, had been accepted. I came to the conclusion on the basis of this quick outcome that I had done something foolish and overpaid. I went to see my agent in the morning. He welcomed me warmly and asked if I really wanted to buy that house. The question surprised me. Why was he asking this, especially as I had already given a down payment?

"We have another candidate for the house. He's offering $20,000 extra. The other agent and I will each take $6,000 of this sum, and you can have the other $8,000.

The proposition was very promising, not because of the $8,000, but because the value of the property was clearly rising. I asked him to present the property plan to me. It was much larger than I thought when I looked at it at first because it was covered with jungle on the outer edges. I looked at the house again. It seemed more solid and spacious than at my first impression. After this inspection, I told the agent:

"I'm not backing out of the agreement. I'm buying the house."

After making the first payment, I went back to Detroit. I was seeing patients when the phone rang.

"It's Pat Wilkins (my agent). I have a beautiful house for you. You won't have to put any money into it, because what you get from resigning from the house you are buying will be enough. My client is giving $50,000 extra. I'll give you $46,000, and I'll take $4,000."

It's easy to understand my surprise at these words. I didn't resign from the house. I told a younger colleague of mine about these incidents.

"Janusz!" he said with a grave expression on his face. "There has to be somebody buried there or something. They're scared! Be careful!"

IN FRONT OF MY HOME ON MARCO ISLAND, FLORIDA

I went back to Florida. It was my first night in my new home. The lights on the street shone only at the front part of the property. There was only impenetrable darkness on my hill. Tropical nights can sometimes be very dark. I had ended up with such a night. In an empty unfamiliar house, feeling uneasy with thoughts of the unknown Indian bodies buried there and with the dead silence of the night broken only by the cry of some nighttime bird, I went to bed.

A horrible noise woke me up! Someone was banging on the back door of the house. I went numb. My colleague's warning popped into my head. Someone wants to kill me, I thought. The noise didn't cease and lasted a good half an hour. Then, it was silent. When I carefully left the house in the morning, I saw the trash can overturned with all its contents spilled all over the place. The nighttime visit had been made by a raccoon—he was my closest neighbor!

I soon learned that I had a lot more of such "neighbors." I ran into a large black snake in the yard. He quickly slipped away at the sight of me. Many small lizards that were busy catching bugs crawled on the screen of the lanai. A colorful bird banged on the window in the morning. A white egret was walking around on the grass by the driveway—it looked dignified on its long legs and much larger than a stork. A squadron of mosquitoes attacked me along with small biting flies that were barely visible, some local insects called "no-seeums." The huge ball of the sun quickly rose from the green horizon of the Everglades—marshes drenched in salt water—and started burning down with strong rays.

I got my spirit back and went into town to do some shopping to get basic things and to find a painter to renovate the inside of the house and put up wallpaper. The man I was referred to was a former policeman from New York. After talking for a few minutes, we figured out that we both knew the same places in Manhattan. His particular enthusiasm reminded me of a certain bar, where those having drinks sat in a dim room around a piano on which an older black man played the melancholy blues.

I left him to do his work, hanging up the keys to the house, and returned to Grosse Pointe. It was already February. The cold was bone chilling, and the glazed frost that was lightly powdered with snow forced you to be careful. My housekeeper, Regina, and I packed up the car. I had already sent some of my things through a moving company.

Early in the morning, my friend, Adam Sygulinski, came over, and we got on our way through the continent from the north to the south. The weather was good for driving, cloudy but no rain. We drove through the plains of Ohio, the huge bridge dividing this state from Kentucky, and then we found ourselves among beautiful wooded mountains. Every minute there was a new view to behold. Adam, who was going to switch driving with me, occupied himself with filming this wild beauty. We switched every few hours.

Atlanta was already behind us—it had been burned during the Civil War but beautifully rebuilt—and we reached the Florida border in the late evening. We stopped at a small motel for the night. My dog slept with me in the same bed. The air was already different than Georgia, warmer and milder, and young grass was emerging everywhere.

We were back in the car in the early morning, without having had breakfast. After a few hours, I started to look around for some place to stop. I saw an exit and a building with a colorful restaurant sign at the end of it. I left the highway and parked the car. I noticed some strikingly colorful placards on the building. We got out of the car. We agreed that Regina and Adam would go eat something first, then I would wait with Chitah in the car and go afterwards. They came back after a moment. Regina had a confounded look on her face, while Adam was amused. It was a restaurant alright, but the waitresses were naked with only a garter on their thighs for dollar bills. You can imagine the shock of a religious woman when she came in contact with such a sight. We got on our way, still hungry. Finally, we found a restaurant along the way without such attractions.

The landscape changed with every moment. Pine forests emerged with thick undergrowth, undersized palms, trees braided with vines, and increasingly more intense sunlight. After seventeen hours of driving at an average speed of seventy-five miles an hour, we finally reached my house.

I started a new life, the life of a calm retiree—far from my responsibilities, far from work, and far from everything that had made up the essence of my life until that point.

Sunny Florida, painted with exotic flowers, presented a radical contrast to the dreary cold and damp day of our departure from Michigan. The warm rays of the sun pierced with thousands of flashes, plundering birds called out as they flew majestically through the sky, and the thicket was filled with the songs of others—it was spiritually calming and reviving.

We had to get to work. We were in a house in which the yard had been neglected—it was a wild jungle. I had read so much during my boyhood years about the adventures of travelers in tropical jungles. The first confrontation with its realities was a far cry from my impressions from those adventure novels. The first experience and disappointment was the grayness of this tangled plant life. The trees were partially dried out, braided with budding vines. Beneath the green far reaching tops of the palms hung a gray skirt of wilted huge fingerlike leaves, interspersed with dried out budded branches. There were also a countless number of agaves with sharp stiletto-like ends and hard gray-green leaves. You could smell the strong scent of laurel trees, at the base of which was a ton of small plants that were interspersed with flowers and prickly and thorny vines—it was a thickness not to be broken through, pulsing with the piercing tone of cicadas mixed with the whiny buzzing of thousands of mosquitoes, attacking every intruder with no mercy. A sandy dune covered in age-old calcified shells stretched out in a further enclave of this tangled plant life—thousands of years ago, this was the base of the ocean. Now, there were spiky cacti with large yellow flowers on it.

I was nearly overcome with horror—how would I live here, how would I cope with all of this? I wanted a surveyor to outline the borders of my property, but he refused. He just didn't think it would be possible to get through the thick vegetation. Fortunately, a Mexican man showed up who spoke broken English. His name was Jesus Padilla. He turned out to be a saving grace for me. We communicated rather easily, mixing words from English and Spanish. It came time to negotiate. We settled things with a handshake, and the next day, Mexicans whom he had brought with him suddenly appeared. Short, small, with dark skin and black hair, they distinguished themselves with an easygoing manner, good spirits, and most importantly, a hardworking attitude. They cut through the vegetation around the edges of the property with razor-sharp machetes and then got to work removing the decomposing plants, gradually clearing the yard. They placed it all neatly on a trailer truck and drove it off to an unknown place. After the initial clearing of the yard, leaving the larger trees and the whole island of agaves, we could begin landscaping the property. Still, the weeds grew back almost immediately. The battle with them was pretty much hopeless. The Florida oak trees, which had nothing to do with oak trees as I knew them in Poland, were decorated with bunches of parasitic plants that had to be removed; their crowns were tangled in vines that were hard and impossible to break apart by hand, defending themselves with sharp thorns.

The house was located on the top of a hill, or rather on a huge dune that had been formed over a million years by the receding ocean. Its foundation was made up of light, almost white sand interspersed with limestone rocks and a countless number of ancient shells. From the side of the street, the slope was over-grown with plants that looked like asparagus, though they were much harder and prickly. You couldn't walk into this thicket of plants without the risk of scratching your bare legs or ripping your pants.

The house was reminiscent in its appearance of a military barrack—long, covered with brownish paint, and a gray gloomy-looking roof. The interior, however, was bathed in sunlight that penetrated the huge windows. And the view went on forever—to the ends of the earth.

I had a vision in my head of columns and arches like those I had seen in Alhambra, the terraces of Andalusia that had been similarly drenched in sunlight. It became my near obsession to transform this property into my Moorish vision. I sketched plans for the changes and reconstruction. At the same time, we cleaned up the slopes of the hill. It was really exhausting work, for those asparagus-like plants were rooted very deeply. The Mexicans rolled it like a blanket and then cut it into smaller pieces. Then they brought in huge trucks filled with soil (to this day I don't know where it came from), and created three grass terraces on the hill, each held in place by a wall of white limestone rocks. Such reinforcements were not necessary on the side of the street, because the hill there was held in place by a five foot high wall. We planted the edges of each terrace with ixora and bougainvillea. The terraces were laid out with St. Augustine grass—thick, rough, and the only one capable of surviving the dryness of Floridian winters.

I found a young architect and presented my thoughts on rebuilding the house. He understood what I wanted. Soon, I had formal blueprints in my hand. Now, I had to find someone to carry out the plans. Construction firms were overloaded with contracts in this part of southern Florida and practically speaking there was no way to find anyone who would undertake such a task. My architect had a great idea.

"You know, you should contact Eddie. He would be perfect for this job."

He gave me his phone number. The next day, Eddie came to see me. He had light blue eyes and a full face, with tousled blond hair and a meaty body that revealed his love of the culinary arts. I learned that Eddie was a master engineer, but despite the fact that he had such a diploma, he preferred to work alone, with his own hands. He looked at the plans and said that they were possible. He asked to come with his father, with whom he worked. Soon, they came to work. His father spoke Polish well—he had built homes in New Jersey for many years.

We settled the conditions of the contract and signed it in the presence of a lawyer. With all his advantages, Eddie distinguished himself with one particular fault in carrying out this task. If, for example, he said that he would begin work on Monday, it wasn't certain which Monday he meant. And this wasn't intended as a lie—he just didn't confirm which Monday it would be! I waited more and more impatiently for the arrival of the building team. After a week went by, Eddie brought over a pile of used boards, some tools, and finally, he arrived with his father. It became clear that he and his father made up the whole "building team!"

They got to work covering the house with netting for the plaster. They started in the back so that no one would see them doing this work. I asked why they were conspiring like this. Another surprise—Eddie had "neglected" to purchase a work permit. Such a permit was required for every step of the work; after doing a certain amount of the construction, a district inspector has to come to confirm it and then agree for the next level of work. I got the address for the permit office from Eddie. My task, which I had not agreed to in the contract, became to go to the office, stand in lines, and take care of the successive permits. It's no wonder

Eddie didn't like it! In the end, I became almost a permanent fixture there. Taking care of the following rungs of building bureaucracy became easier and quicker for me.

With all his eccentricities and faults, Eddie really loved his work and did it reliably. Every once in a while, he would bring in a few people to help, but most of the time he did the work himself. He nailed the netting beneath the plaster to the house, dug the area for the foundation of the addition on the northern side. He also dug, shaped, and prepared a cascade of steps and terraces under the windows in cement.

They got huge steel poles that were supposed to go into the construction of the addition as well as the upper level, on which a colonnade with Moorish arches would hold up the roof. In the front of the house, he built a large terrace surrounded by the same kind of colonnade with Moorish arches. By the addition, they constructed a "lanai," a patio laid out in colorful cement blocks with steps and huge planters for shrubs and flowers. The whole thing was wrapped in a light, white aluminum construction that was isolated from mosquitoes by a nylon screen.

The whole thing turned out to be a miniature reproduction of one of the Alhambra courtyards! Steps led up from the patio to the upper part of the construction, to a widespread terrace under a roof with light pink roof tiles surrounded by a colonnade. The view from there was fascinating—surrounded on three sides by Caxambas Bay, the skyscrapers standing in the distance on the Gulf of Mexico, and further on, its blue waters in the sunlight. On the other side a never ending sea of the greenery of the Everglades.

The roof was covered with the same roof tiles, the eaves encircled by white gutters. Despite the rather painful delays, the work progressed rather quickly. Finally, a Cuban man, Carlos, showed up with his wife, and they got to work painting the fresh plaster that had been put up by some Haitians. During the course of their work, the Haitians spoke to each other cheerily, teasing and joking. I couldn't understand them. They spoke in a French dialect, but so different that it wasn't comprehensible to an outsider. I chose a pale yellow, slightly green paint for the walls and white for the columns. The steps and the whole area of the pool were laid out in tiles, as was the terrace at the main entrance. Light wallpaper and fresh light floor lining were the crowning moments of the renovations. All of it emerged like a truly Moorish villa surrounded by palms and old trees.

One of them looks into my room as I am writing this. This "gold tree"—indeed it really radiates bright yellow-gold flowers in the early spring.

The years during which I worked had passed by. I found myself in another world—a world free of obligations, deadlines, and nervous glances at my watch. An oasis, in which the telephonic ring of a "beeper" that is always worn by a doctor in the hospital didn't disrupt the quiet moment—nothing disrupts the quiet here except the taking care of everyday matters. I wasn't yet completely adjusted from that "quick pace" to this arid one. I will never again walk into an operating room as a surgeon—maybe I would find myself there as a patient in a horizontal position. All that had made up the essence of my life, my goals, my ambitions, my wishes and aspirations—all this had passed irrevocably.

This sudden and unending torpor did, however, have its attractive plusses. No one had to wake me up in the middle of the night. I wasn't startled by the ring of the telephone. I could also now take care of the things I had otherwise neglected because of the high pressure environment in which I had worked.

I was woken up by a clanging knock at my window. Not even looking there, I knew that it was a small bird with a colorful cap on his head, knocking because he saw his reflection in the glass. The voices of many kinds of birds reached me from outside, so different from those to which I was accustomed. The sharp, slanted rays of the rising tropical sun lit up the room and raised my spirits with their own natural goodness and innate optimism. I widely opened the doors to the patio; lizards lurk for bugs in strategic positions ready for attack on the screen of the lanai. From time to time, a purple balloon puffs up under their little throats—supposedly a mating call. Nearby, there are hibiscus bushes with large, light-green leaves interspersed with goblets of huge flowers. Two small rabbits go by, not really concerned with my presence. Somewhat further, a dignified white egret, moving around in ostentatious pride, walks around the lanai—perhaps lost in eschatological contemplation of the futility of this world.

Every once in a while, through the sunlit greenery of the grass, the ominous shadow of a plundering bird crawls through—a falcon or vulture, osprey, or the native swallow—unfortunately not having anything in common in its appearance or lifestyle with the Polish swallow. They move without even fluttering their wings, taking advantage of terminal velocity, making wide circles, raising themselves up and then falling like an arrow into the thicket with a decided purpose. Their chirping cuts through the various singing of smaller birds, competing only with the cries of black rooks. The music of huge crickets arises from the thick greenery and grass—penetrating and far-reaching, varying in tone, repeating frequently. Sandy dunes stand perpendicular to the narrow roadway and cut through the gray strip of asphalt where a large turtle walks slowly. He doesn't quicken his pace, as the rules of the road don't interest him—his goal is the sandy dunes set out in the scorching heat of the sun. It is there that the female lays the almost clear—similar to cherries—eggs in a hole. It digs into the sand with its belly and leaves the eggs there without further care for them. The hot sand serves as an incubator and also as a layer of protection from overheating.

I go outside in the company of my dog, Nikki (a long-haired miniature dachshund). I am immediately blinded by the brightness of the sun. I look all around. Far off on the horizon, through the skyscrapers of hotels and condominiums, the smog of the Gulf of Mexico hangs silvery in the air. Closer, the wide waters of Caxambas Bay encircle a rather small peninsula, framed in a green band of tropical plants. From my Moorish tower, the view extends even further, to the horizon and beyond the line of the horizon, to the endless masses of green in the Everglades, above which a mass of immobile clouds cuts into the clear light sky.

I run into a now familiar large black snake in the yard. He immediately disappears into the thicket at the sight of me. I was sure that he was a "good" neighbor. His main occupation was hunting for rats that were nesting in the palms. Despite a certain level of familiarity, running into him wasn't pleasant. Then, I ran into other such snakes in the yard, and even in the garage under the house. One time a small brown snake was found in the kitchen. I don't know how he squeezed in there.

You can see light gray-green frogs with large brown eyes among the blades of grass. They can climb up a wall, even moving along glass, without difficulty. Their croaking in the evenings completed the chorus of nature consisting of the voices of retiring small birds, cicadas and cranes.

Apart from the rather small number of people living on that part of Marco Island, a lot of other "inhabitants" lived there. I ran across a peccary several times. Large vultures with red necks, similar to turkeys, sat on the branches of old dried out trees. Huge pelicans majestically flew by along the bay.

One day, I saw an orange cat in the yard. He seemed emaciated to me, though somewhat larger than cats I had seen before. He looked at me very still from the shadow of the thick mambo-limbo tree. I noticed that he had ears that were somewhat different from a cat's ears—they were not sharp and pointed at the top but rounded. I went closer; in a few steps he had disappeared into the thicket. I found out afterwards that I had met with a local Floridian lynx. He lived close by. Later, we ran into each other several times, but he never allowed for any sort of familiarity—he always kept his distance.

I went for a walk with my dog. By one of the streets, in a widespread yard covered with dry grass and weeds, two small gray brown birds sat in the full sunlight on a perch with some measuring equipment that had been put there by a surveyor. When I went closer, they didn't flee. I looked at them closely. They were small owls dozing off in the full Florida sun with no shade whatsoever. You could clearly see the opening of a hole under the perch where the female had laid her eggs. During the next weeks and months, I walked by that way many times—it was hotter and hotter, and the sun burned down like fire. Two young owls were added to the parents. Soon, seven of them dozed in the tropical sun. When I returned to Florida after the summer break, I saw that same pair on the perch. The children had left the comforts of home and were living somewhere on their own. The parents were busy caring for their upcoming group of descendants.

The sun sets faster here than up north thanks to the proximity of the equator—with the earth's orbit, a larger distance has to follow this path in the same time. In the evenings, the western side of the sky is drenched with shades of red pouring over the darkening sky, and the unnaturally large sphere of the sun slips quickly down into the water of the ocean. Dusk falls, and moments later, the darkness of night. Stars shining in the black velvet sky seem closer; the sickle of the moon is turned with its "back" down—so different from up north! The first bird of the night penetratingly and rhythmically calls forth his monotonous song. It is accompanied by the croaking of frogs under the windows. Nikki, my "bodyguard," sometimes bristles and barks obstinately, but she stays on my bed. Then, I know that in the morning I will see the footsteps of a raccoon that had been feeding in the night on the gray tiles of the stairs.

In the yard, apart from the mambo-limbo, palms, and citrus trees, I also have a beautiful orchid tree and a cacao tree. Slender coconut palms with bunches of fruit under vast leaves lurk in the next-door neighbor's yard—and further dignified straight columns of royal palm with widely spread leaves. The dunes are scattered with prickly cacti with incredibly small thorns: they easily pierce the skin and are unbelievably difficult to extract. And finally, there are also agaves with their long, fruit-bearing trunks. Mexican natives produce their famous alcohol, Tequila, from these plants.

A MEXICAN WOMAN WITH A PARROT;
PAINTING BY THE AUTHOR

20

New Age–A New Tyranny

ISN'T THE QUESTION of who we are and how we function fascinating? How is it that we see and hear, that we have a whole array of feelings and emotional states, and that we have a creative streak in us? How is it that each of us is himself, that we have awareness, and that we also possess feelings of good and evil?

Answers to these questions have been given for thousands of years in various ways. There was never a philosopher in the history of humanity who was not obsessed with the riddle of the essence of human nature. Answers offered by various religions are a priori. They require you to accept as truth that which is given to faith. The Bible teaches us that we are created in the image of God. What does this really mean, in the image of God? It has been said that this knowledge is a revelation, so again it requires us to accept "as truth" a claim that we do not understand and that we cannot get our minds around. Where did we come from? Where are we going?

When you analyze the human brain from an anatomical and functional point of view, it reminds you of a big house to which countless additions have been added. The part of the brain called the limbic system, which is responsible for basic instincts, like satisfying hunger, sexual needs, self-preservation, and the instinct to preserve the species, distinguishes us to a very small degree from lower biological forms. The hypothalamus, the part of the brain responsible for basic emotional reactions, is almost identical in a cat as in a human. And indeed, we have much the same instincts—we can react with anger or fear, we can be passive or aggressive, and there is no significant difference on this level. For years, I mapped this "emotional brain" of cats—I was in awe of the similarity between the structure of this part of the brain in a cat to our own.

What distinguishes us as humans? After all, we have come so far as a result of millions of years of evolutionary development. Biologically we are very similar to the other primates. Our genetic pattern differs from a chimpanzee only in 2%. The 98% is for all practical reasons the same. What differs in us is our creative streak, an unsatisfied desire to know, hidden in that 2% difference.

Mapping the function of the brain with the help of electrophysiological methods—by stimulating particular areas and recording the resulting potentials—revealed that, in terms of climbing the philogenetic ladder, the newer brain structures somehow take over the leading role from the inferior ones. A lizard can stick out its tongue and catch a fly with incredible speed—the extension is immediate, direct, and precise. It doesn't use calculus to figure out the flight speed of the fly, and it doesn't choose the precise moment to stick out its tongue. It has an innate mechanism—an immediate and precise reflex that allows the lizard to sustain itself. No one of us could do such a thing. Why? Because, our actions depend upon the control by the higher centers of the brain, which allow for endless possibilities in variations of movement and choices. Thanks to this, or rather because of this, we lose the ability to react immediately like the lizard does. In exchange, we get the ability to choose and modify our actions. You might say that in exchange for the loss of this reflex, we get an ability to react in an incomparably more sophisticated way.

In spite of our tremendous development of the brain, specifically the brain cortex, some old basic reflexes remain, necessary for our functioning. A classic example would be our righting reflex, stabilizing us when falling down. We have an ability to perform an incredibly precise action with such speed that might be considered almost "unnatural." When three pianists perform Bach's concerto in C major on three pianos they are synchronized with unbelievable precision by a quite primitive old reflex, which has nothing to do with the higher levels of the brain. They have managed to suppress their higher brain functions and release the lower functions, more automatic and driven by the rhythm of the music. Playing a Bach concerto is a uniquely human achievement, which cannot be rationalized but requires the ability to achieve a unique stage of consciousness in which more basic reflexes can be utilized. On the other hand we only achieve this suppression of the basic instincts through utilizing that 2% of genetic difference.

We are able to control our aggression, our sexual urges, and to a large degree, our emotional reactions. The more our control mechanisms over basic instincts are developed, the more we are "humanized." In a specific situation, like in combat, suppression of basic instincts can be released. The reasonable young man starts acting like a dangerous predator.

Suppressing instincts gives us the ability to use them as stimulating forces, motivating us to higher purposes, to creative work and the development of personality. The sexual drive is an example of this. When it is rechanneled to cultural development such as the sciences, arts, and sports during adolescence it can be a very forceful factor in human development. Similar relationships can be drawn from other basic instincts.

Upbringing, parental influence, teacher influence, environment—all of these factors shape the ability of selectively controlling these basic urges. When a small child wants a toy, he reaches out his hand, and when he can't reach it, he cries and yells. An adult, who has a developed ability to control his reactions, behaves differently. He can convince himself that the object he desires doesn't belong to him and, thus, that he doesn't have the right to have it.

Unfortunately, the presentation of crimes and porno pouring from television screens and radio stations, reflecting only the worst margins of society, feeds into the most primitive instincts. This resorts in the uncontrolled release of most primitive drives leading to dysfunctional behavior. This is particularly true in the period of human development when basic psychological structure is not well established. The normal youths can be led down the path to sociopathic behavior. A sociopath doesn't distinguish between good and evil. He is motivated only by desire. One example could be the behavior of drivers after an accident. Both parties get out from behind the wheel and evaluate the damages. But a sociopath, if armed, might kill the other party in the accident without hesitation and then calmly drive away. It is an aberration of development that is undoubtedly extreme but still understandable in its mechanism.

What horrifies me is the possibility of "dehumanizing" a human being. Psychological tests carried out by U.S. military centers showed that over the course of about six weeks, you could transform a normal nineteen-year-old, using the appropriate techniques, into a cold-blooded murderer. That's how you train commandos, and that's how the infamous Russian *specnaz* were trained. This dehumanizing was skillfully used among the Hitlerjugend, in the Soviet "Komsomol," as well as in ancient Sparta over two thousand years ago. One of the most macabre examples of "dehumanization" is the Cambodian killing fields, where even children were taught to kill and torture.

The most horrifying part of this programmed "dehumanization" is when it takes on an ideological or even philosophical posture. After all, Nazism grew out of Nietzsche's concept of the "superhuman." Marx and Engels were the precursors of the theories which motivated future communist crimes. Sartre gave life to the "Khmer Rouge" with his nihilistic ideas (Pol Pot studied at the Sorbonne, was an admirer of Satre). All of these ideologies, always utopic, have their common sources—they come out of the void that remains after the denial of the transcendental origin of moral

norms. Bringing these ideologies to life ended in massacres, genocide, and total terror.

Nazism, communism, etc. were extreme forms of moral relativism in which the leading utopian ideology overpowered transcen-
dent morality. Present day moral relativism is the fundamental
ideology of New Age. Consequently the moral code is determined
individually and thus does not present—or accept—a uniform system of morality. It is worth considering what methods are used by
this movement of global coercion and what the mechanism of its
action is.

How often we hear hard rock blaring from radio speakers. The
recordings of these pseudo-musicians sell over millions of copies,
and rock concerts bring forth thousands of hysterical teenagers.
Why? Besides the fact that it is a product that is incredibly primitive and monotonous, with a melody that is lamentably poor, it
is also destructive to hearing, because its decibels surpass normal levels of tolerance. The pulsing of lights is then added to this
obsessive racket, which demolishes hearing and vision and dimin-
ishes moral self-control.

Why do young people fall into a trance at such events? I found
the answer in a neurophysiology lab at Walter Reed Institute—
the central institute of neurophysiological tests of the American
Army. I saw a monkey there with electrodes attached to its hypothalamus, the area of the "emotional brain" that is responsible for
feelings of delight and is close to if not identical to the center of
sexual orgasm. The monkey was immobilized in a chair and had a
large collar on so as not to touch her head. Her hands were free,
so she could move them around. She could stimulate her brain
with the help of the electrodes that had been placed there. The
picture was horrifying! Each movement of the handle caused a
feeling of delight; the monkey could pull that handle for thirty-six
hours, without a break, without eating or drinking, until extremely
exhausted. It was a kind of masturbation of the brain!

Rock music is none other than this kind of stimulus to the
hypothalamus. It is generally known that young people can orgasm
during such concerts. A black man once, in a German porno bar,

stood there naked, moving to an unending background rhythm. This rhythm led him to a state of erection and ejaculation.

Thus rock music seems to be an ideal method of "dehumanization." If satanic phrases full of nihilism and hatred are weaved into that music, then it is easy to understand the degradation of today's youth. Moral hindrances they may have had are totally suppressed. This happens because the brain cortex no longer functions, only the brain stem does—this part of the brain isn't that different from a frog's brain stem! Add on the influence of drugs, which unsettle the hormonal balance of the brain even more, especially the hypothalamus, and you have further degradation. In effect, it leads to the total destruction of personality and to the transformation of a young life into a sad, hopeless ruin.

I saw so many of these individual tragedies! And yet, this New Age poison spreads like wildfire over the whole world. A tormenting question arises—who or what forces are counting on this? And who opposes it? It's interesting that not only the Catholic Church and other Christian denominations for which faith in God is a compass for life, but also the believers of Judaism and Islam, condemn and separate themselves from the plague of the New Age. I recently read a book written by Tad Szulc called *To Kill the Pope*.[5] This somewhat sensational tale is nothing other than written support of New Age philosophy. I was struck by the way in which Mr. Szulc divided the world into two camps. The first was the progressive and advancing, while the second was fundamentalist, to which the conservative branch of the Catholic Church and Islam belong. It's interesting that Szulc didn't specify the diversities of Judaism. After all, it is "fundamentalist" Orthodox Judaism that leads the fights against New Age ideology!

The creators of the philosophy of New Age are predominantly so called "progressive" Jews who have abandoned traditional Judaism. They introduced the idea of "political correctness" which allows persecution of any form of faith in God. That's why Christians and other theistic faiths are under siege in present day

---

5. Tad Szulc is the author of the insidious antipapal biography of John Paul II, *Papiez Jan Pawel II, Biografia* (published by PRIMA, Warsaw, 1996)..

society. While there are many differences dividing them, a common factor of these denominations is recognition of God and the transcendental character of moral values.

That's why crosses are thrown out of American schools. It is why people of liberal mindsets are enraged by the thought that schools with religious affiliations can get financial support. It doesn't matter that many schools "produce" illiterate youth. It doesn't matter that "Sex Ed." leads to experimental orgies among teenagers. It doesn't matter that young people who grow up nowadays don't have a moral backbone or basic moral beliefs. It doesn't matter that the number of suicides among minors and the plague of drugs are both always growing. What's important is that the libertine philosophy of "social engineering" as propagated by the supporters of the utopia of that new and "better world" to be built on the ruins of the present one.

When I write this, the destructive activism of global liberalism and libertinism that has its basis on the famed French Revolution shines in triumph. But societies are starting to wake up from lethargy and indifference at the peak of this wave of destructiveness. Will they, however, be able to reverse New Age and fix the evil that has already been done?

* * *

When admiring the artistic acquisitions of many previous ages, the beauty, lightness, and spiritual nobility of gothic cathedrals, the dramatic expression of the Pièta, or listening to Gregorian music or the amazing majestic movements of Bach that approach the spirit of God, I wonder how far this process of "dehumanization" has gotten. Will there really be a "new era" after decades of decline, an era of rebirth and spiritual blossoming after this current medieval age of the soul?

I hope so. I would like to live to see at least the beginning of such a conversion.

A person, this "unknown being," is a creator from the beginning of history. The creators of paintings in the caves were already blessed with the creative streak of art, and more importantly, the desire to outwardly express their spiritual needs. When we experience the achievement of a work of art, whether a painting, a story, a poem, or a piece of music, we have aesthetic and intellectual impressions. These impressions contain some emotional weight. We do not accept or reserve the thoughts, feelings, and experiences weaved into them—we simply succumb to the aesthetic experience, confronting what is being proposed in these achievements with our system of aesthetic and cultural value. They resonate with us like the plucking of unclaimed strings, striking our sensibilities.

The endless array of feelings, atmospheres, experiences, and events hard to express in words are the instruments of these experiences. And again, the question arises—what is the mechanism of these resonances, these intimate relations? Upon what does their character and scale depend?

On former experiences? Undoubtedly yes. Or on individual psychological structures? Certainly. But, how do you really experience this? What are the psycho-physiological mechanisms that influence a work? What elements are responsible for given opinions and impressions?

I was never really fond of the artwork of battle-focused Matejko,[6] and though I know I might be speaking blasphemously, that's how it was and is. Still, regardless of this particular style of painting, it was and still is beautiful—the figures, the features, the play of feelings and emotions, the precision of the movements, the configuration of the hands, and the general situation of the positions—they are simply excellent! So, why do his paintings not speak to me? The answer might be rather banal—simply that my system of perception of his achievement is somewhat primitive to understand the full threat of the *Battle of Grunwald* or the excellence of *The Prussian Tribute*. Maybe in this case my perception is as primitive as a Guinean man looking at the same paintings.

Some time ago, I read that primitive Guineans, who were can-

6. Famous portraitist and battalistic artist at the turn of the 20th century. One of his famous paintings decorates a wall of the Vatican.

nibals until recently and some say even to this day, couldn't recognize the object that was shown to them in a photograph—they
couldn't even recognize familiar tribesmen! Photographs didn't
speak to them. Maybe it's similar with me, though I don't think
I am as primitive as they were. Still, why can I be thrilled with
impressionists, whose style of painting is a quite loose and subjective representation of reality so much different from the battle-
focused work of Matejko? Why are Goya and El Greco's paintings so close for me, and why does Egyptian art, that kind of two-
dimensional work, speak so easily to my aesthetic "screens?"

I looked for an answer to this question. I concluded that
Matejko, who was nearsighted, painted the whole composition
not in relation to a central point, a central figure, on which the
gaze would rest, but rather centered his vision on each detail sep-
arately—so each fragment of his painting is in itself the central
point. But we don't see in this manner; our vision is only central—the further you move to the side the more blurred it became.
Thus, my problem with Matejko isn't a lack of possible aesthetic
understanding of his creation, but rather the chaos resulting from
non-physiological presentation of reality. The battle-focused
paintings (I'm not talking about his portraits—these are terrific)
overwhelm with their details; they distract, forcing you to move
your glance from place to place, from detail to detail.

How excellently impressionists understood these visual perception traits!

We get to know the world through the senses of sight, sound,
touch, smell, and taste. These sensory experiences are not directly
transmitted to the associative centers of the brain where they are
recognized, but instead they undergo modification and integration
into fuller patterns on the way. How does this process occur?

Individual impulses and electric potentials are built in a more
complex system; this integration happens selectively by way of
eliminating the "unnecessary" elements of information while the
"essential" become the complete product, appropriately made in
the form of a rather complicated electrical pattern that eventu-

ally reaches the appropriate associative field (cognitive). In accordance with the resonance theory of Lorente de No', there are a billion neuron systems functioning in the brain on which electrical impulses run. The real wonder of nature is the fact that each such impulse stays there continuously, so the record is permanent.

This doesn't mean that a person can recreate this information whenever he wants. Essentially, our ability to remember is really limited. It makes up a minute percentage of the information that is actually encoded in the brain. We gather new information through our senses, and if a similar one is already running through our brain, then there is a resonance, and we recognize the character of the information. Here's an example—if I see an apple, a very familiar object to me, I recognize it on the basis of, "yes, that's an apple," as the sight of the apple supplied an impulse that resonated with a pattern of this object that already existed in my brain.

It is fascinating how the nervous system has the ability to eliminate the unnecessary elements of an observed pattern. When we hear, "it is nice out today," then we really don't get the whole of this statement, only the most essential elements from it, those necessary points of the pattern determining its character. That's why a person who knows a foreign language only from a textbook will not understand it when it is spoken. One simply is not able to constantly single out the appropriate idiomatic patterns because the spoken language is too fast—one can no longer capture the gist by way of analysis. I know this very well from personal experience! My first experience in an environment of only English-speaking people was a nightmare! I understood very little even though I had "mastered" the language rather well.

The better the brain's ability to capture the most essential elements of information, thus eliminating the more trivial elements and details, the better we receive the whole of the information. A landscape created by a good painter, regardless of his artistic convention, speaks incomparably more to us than a photograph does. The artist completely and subconsciously eliminates everything that is less important to him while keeping his impression, keeping what is essential. What's more, by presenting the essential elements and enlarging them, even overvaluing them, through this purposeful deformation, they become even more intensely received by viewers.

Let's expand on this. We may be familiar with figures like Zagloba (a well-known character from the classics of Polish literature) in the *Trilogy*,[7] like Pickwick in Dickens's unforgettable tale, or like Count Krzeszowski in *Lalka*,[8] a figure that was sketched almost like a caricature. And thanks to such redrawing, these figures become so very lifelike, with enough plasticity to be able to speak to us. A writer would never achieve this same speakability with detail-ridden realism. The impression given off by the author also depends upon the experiences, personality, and emotional state of the reader. Each of us "sees" Zagloba differently—everyone has a different impression of him—and you can notice this most clearly if you encounter a previously established impression of the story, as in a film production. Because I understood this mechanism, I never wanted to see *Pan Wolodyjowski* on the big screen. When I was finally forced to watch this movie, I was disillusioned—the film ruined the novel's images of the heroes that had been established in my imagination in my youth.

You can reveal the most essential features of a personality in a portrait painting in thousands of different ways, using the most unexpected compositions of colors or even caricature-like deformities in which the most characteristic features are purposefully enlarged. The painting technique might be rather primitive, out of scale, full of colorful stains, thick, or sketched, but the goal is still achieved. I admire Stanislaw Wyspianski's[9] portraits; he was a genial person who had truly versatile talents. His artistic technique is rather simple, but it is a refined simplicity—decided contours, faint shadows, and a rather meager palette of colors set the backdrop for figures that live and have expressions, personality, and spirit.

---

7. Written by Nobel Prize winner, Henryk Sienkiewicz.

8. Famous novel by Boleslaw Prus, written at the turn of the 20th century..

9. A famous writer and painter from the impressionist period.

I once met a Chinese doctor who came from a long Mandarin line. He was an average doctor, but his forte was in his excellent knowledge of Chinese cuisine and literature. Being curious by nature, I wanted to understand the composition of Chinese poetry. It wasn't easy for him to explain the knowledge of these subjects, poetry and cuisine, to me. Finally, he was able to explain the sum of his knowledge of these two seemingly distant arts. The field of poetry is one of pictorial writing—the reality of objects, such as a house, rivers, sunlight, etc. Then, it became necessary to explain actions and characters. The latter are indicated through a compilation of signs that represent real objects as a whole while at the same time giving them new meaning. The possibility of creating is unlimited. The higher the degree of education and culture of the writer, the more refined the expression of his thoughts and feelings might be. My teacher claimed that by examining the poetic writing style, you could easily recognize the author's knowledge of literature. What's more, the poem would have a somewhat different meaning depending on the audience's level of education. It might also have a rather different meaning and reception for people with the same education, for the poet's interpretation is to a large degree subjective. Thus, you can compare such a poem to a crystal that reflects the colors of the rainbow—it will be a different picture for everyone. The example of the Chinese poem relates to all of us in a way—everyone is different, each one of us has his own encoded system of information, and finally, each one of us is given individual patterns of emotional reactions.

The perception of the same piece of artwork is different in each individual case. So, you might say that one painting hangs on the wall, but in reality, there are as many paintings as there are viewers.

It is certain that expression, in painting as well as in music, reaches our most basic feelings and also stimulates intellectually, transmitting compilation of emotional and rational messages. Abstract art operates only on the placement of colors and abstract forms, trying to bypass the brain cortex and reach the "emotional brain."

Just like beating out a monotonous rhythm inspires a reaction in the subcortical level, even having an influence on an EEG reading, so the exposition of surreal splotches of color and linear designs that cannot be verbalized can stimulate the same way.

With the current "disco" music, this method of abuse is geared towards young people, with a crazy but monotonous rhythm, a monotonous perception of a few tones, and flashing laser lights. The synchronization of these elements creates a feeling that is difficult to describe. It has nothing to do with aesthetic experience like those you have when listening for example to pieces of classical music, admiring a painting's interplay of shadows and light, or standing before gilded altars where reflections of light from an ancient lamp dance across the sculpted faces of saints.

Thus, a work can "humanize" us, but it can also move us backward, destroying our individuality and making our feelings more primitive. A real work of art will speak to all that is good in us—all that is wonderful and reaches the spirit. A false one takes away all hope and leads to despair, nihilism, and self-destruction as a supposed "outlet." As with nihilism, the realization of Satanist philosophy leads to tragedy for millions of people; similarly, a work, or rather a pseudowork, used for the same purposes can similarly destroy entire nations.

I have nothing against progress in artistic creativity. But no one will ever convince me that placing cutouts of newspapers or a few geometric figures on a pink background is a work of art or that it possesses meaningful expression. No one will convince me either that beating a simple rhythm played at a deafening decibel with pornographic movements is music. Nikita Khrushchev, the former leader of "Satan's Empire," once visited an exhibit of abstract art. He walked from painting to painting surrounded by servants, and his face looked more and more consumed with anger. Finally, he yelled out, "Any donkey could do this with his tail!" and walked towards the exit. I agree with Khrushchev—for the first and only time!

I once heard this anecdote: "Bach's music, with all its might and dignity, is obligatory in Heaven. The angels, however, secretly listen to Mozart's music, while God, knowing about all this, eaves-drops with a smile."

Now we have an idea of how a work reaches us and what the mechanisms are of its reception and experience. We understand the danger of this potential weapon—it can be wielded for good or bad purposes. Unlike "rock" and "uninhibited" artistic production, I prefer the silence of temples fragrant with incense, Gregorian chant, and the beauty of nature untouched by a human hand. Then and only then, I feel that I am a small part of something unknown, wonderful, and grand.

In one of her mystery novels, Agatha Christie admitted, "I think poorly of people, and the truth is even worse." I don't share her opinion. I have always been convinced that people on the whole are not endemically bad. They are often weak, wavering, sometimes morally and ethically deformed, usually because of the environment in which they grew up. So, why are there still such macabre atrocities, to the scale of genocide, in this world? Where does such cruelty—stepping on human dignity on a scale beyond comprehension—come from? These evil actions are ironically usually dressed up with slogans like "peace" "friendship," "broth-erhood," "freedom," and "respect for citizens' rights."

These questions have been with me all my life, from the early years of my youth since that memorable September of 1939, when literally, during the course of one day, everything that made up my good life, my house, my school, the simple pleasures of child-hood, going to the movies on Sunday, and most of all, that feeling of safety and stability—all of it was suddenly shattered. When I looked at the German military creeping into Lublin, at their gray-green uniforms, at the black crosses on the tanks, I also looked at the faces. They were the same people, just like my father, like our closest friends. True, they did speak another language and were distinct in those uniforms—but other than those two things, I didn't see any difference.

When the black smoke from the rubble of Warsaw somewhat cleared up in the beginning of 1945, when Soviet tanks were rolling in, I again saw soldiers and also women soldiers on them wearing different gray-olive green uniforms and fur hats with red stars on them. These were different people—with prominent cheekbones, slanted eyes, and darker skin that betrayed their Mongolian descent. But even these soldiers from the victorious Red Army were simply people, even more ordinary than the German soldiers or the Polish before them, because they were simpler and less advanced in terms of civilization.

I have come across people of every race and ethnicity in the United States. They were my patients, ready to put their health and life over to my hands with trust. Many of them became close to me—Italians, Germans, Anglo-Saxons, blacks. I didn't see any difference between them and myself apart from the secondary traits that arose from the environment in which they grew up, with different customs and means of expressing themselves. The same universal human with all his hopes, fears, and reactions lived under the shell of customs or race.

Everyone's blood is red; everyone's anatomical structure is virtually identical with minimal variants from person to person—so then why discrimination and even genocide.

I repeat the question—what leads to such macabre cruelties? No one has given a convincing answer to this question other than to say that cruelty and egoism are rooted in human nature.[10] For ages, there has been talk of an endless battle between Good and Evil, about Ahriman and Ohrmazd, when really we are speaking about human nature. Still, the structure of personality in the human species doesn't explain all these barbarisms, the systematic mutual destruction of whole nations or ethnic groups. The epoch has long since passed when the caveman defended his family and cave with a club. When you look, even superficially, at the drama of the twentieth century, you might be filled with fear and doubt. No other age bore witness to such mass carnage while at the same time achieving such a high degree of culture, technology, and communication.

The common denominator of the tragedies of the twentieth

---

10. All of those who attain great profit in wars could give a simple and direct answer to this question.

century was the domination of ideology which rejected God and promoted utopian ideals. The key to understanding this might be a statement made by Mrs. Jean Kirkpatrick, a well-known American conservative and a professor of political science at Georgetown University: "I'm not afraid of agnostics, but God save us from those who know!"

That's it! When you look through the history pages of human civilization, it became obvious that the tyrant was never a skeptic. It wasn't those who didn't know who were the tyrants but rather those who "improved" the world in the name of one ideology or idea. In the name of preserving religious tradition, Christians were murdered in arenas of the Roman Empire. In turn, Christians, in the name of spreading Christianity, massacred pagans in the bloody Crusades. In the name of protecting dogma, fires were set at the feet of heretics.

Is there some kind of common regularity in these explosions of hatred and carnage? Is there someone or some group of people pulling the strings in this macabre theater of puppets whose paranoid goals and ideologies always lead to hell on earth?

I can almost hear the voices saying that I have a paranoid view of human reality; that the manipulation of masses does not exist; that one social movement or another, or this or that leader, are products of disconnected and unintended coincidences.

The road of my life, full of bumps and traps, required me to look at reality with my eyes wide open, at its concrete situations. As if in a lens, this approach also comes into focus in the neuro-surgical profession. First, you have to recognize and understand the course of the illness, and then predict the results and consequences of surgical intervention. These methods carried over into my view of reality outside the hospital.

I am sure that I'm right in seeing common elements and traits among all the main ideologies that so tragically determined the fate of the world in the twentieth century.

The first illusion in undertaking the movement towards a criminal utopia is the assumption that it's possible and should be done, and that the creation of a new world, a new system of human relations, will of course transpire on the rubble of the present one. The devoted "idealists" are really strange in their fiery speeches and their proclamations exciting the masses. They say that a man is capable of creating paradise on earth, and of full justice for all. And yet, they strangely exclude themselves, treating themselves as the "anointed" and all-knowing saviors of a mob that doesn't understand their supposedly wonderful ideas. They have to then direct these masses, using a variety of means including, terrorism or genocidal methods, if necessary.

The common trait of all these supposedly various ideologies is the elimination of a transcendental concept of morality and the replacement of it with the "morality" of Nazism, communism, or some other nonsense like "a fight for one's faith." As you know, Lucifer had once been an archangel of God, but instead of being himself as the "Bearer of Light," he transcended moral codes and became Lucifer, the Prince of Darkness. This type of *non serviam* is the sinister black thread that spins twistingly through thousands of years of human events and is so apparent in the present day.

A natural consequence of the utopia of an ideal society in the human model is the dogma about there being a "chosen" or "holy" people—that only they should and could decide about the direction of change and the shape of future history. And that's how we inevitably come to the evident and genocidally realized concept of the "chosen nation." Each ancient empire recognized its own right to conquer, murder, and violate those who were weaker. They thought of themselves as "better," and thus justified in doing this. We were given an example of this racial genocide in Hitler's agenda.

The global Jewish community claim that they are not usurpers in their unique discrimination, calling themselves "chosen people." According to them they are the only race with whom God established a covenant thousands of years ago. Yahweh, was a tribal god coexisting with other "gods," as for example with Baal. Obviously Judaism came out of a polytheism so common at that time. The only difference between Judaism and their contemporary polytheistic religions was consideration of Yahweh as the most powerful god. And then, by their own nomination, they recognized themselves as a nation destined to lead, and at the same time created a nation to act as a collective Messiah, because somehow the coming of their biblical Messiah was dangerously late. After the Mongols defeated China, a Mandarin caste was created to whom the subordinated society was subject. The Mandarins were a class that made up the highest caste. They were subject to different rules and likewise different privileges.

During the reign of Queen Victoria, the Anglo-Saxons nominated themselves "chosen people." The sun never set on the British Empire—while it did on Australia or India, it shone still on England. They plundered India, destroying its timeless culture and treating the native people there like subhumans—a precursor of Nazism. It's enough to read Nehru's memoirs to see the macabre suppression by British occupiers of India. The opium wars in China that were sparked by Great Britain with the goal of extorting submission of China through the import of lethal drugs, were the same kind of genocidal crime as the concentration camps and the Soviet labor camps. The methods vary, but the goals are always the same.

Then the Germans announced themselves as the "chosen nation." They considered themselves to be superior racially to the obvious conclusion that other races should be subservient to them. When millions of those ostensible "superhumans" died fighting in the same way the "subhumans" did, Hitler and his followers devised a solution. They planned for SS troopers to inseminate the English women (after killing all English males) so that the master race could flourish again. A minor shortcoming in that plan was that England did not surrender but fought on to victory.

Communism, the bastard of the same satanic cult also put forth social equality and justice as their principal tenets—the old deceit of the macabre French Revolution. The communist variant of Satanism has somewhat different traits. Communism was not the goal in itself but rather an even more effective tool in the hands of one revolutionary sector of the Jewish community.

I would like to clearly and precisely state that in speaking about the "Jewish people," I do not mean the religious Jews who try to live in accordance with God following the Ten Commandments (Decalogue). I am speaking about those who, in accordance with many prominent rabbis, became "worshippers of the golden calf."

This is a significant distinction. For those who may not remember biblical events that well, it's worth noting that when Moses came down from Mt. Sinai with the Decalogue, he found the Jews worshipping a golden calf. In despair and anger, he broke the stone tablet of the Ten Commandments, lamenting the fact that his people had abandoned God.

To this day, that event in the Bible, deep in its symbolism, is a subject of lengthy consideration in Judaism. It concerns a rather simple matter. Those worshippers of the "golden calf" had cast aside a transcendental concept of moral codes, cast aside the Decalogue, and aimed to create their own Jewish world of happiness through moral relativism, unbridled license, and a ruthless pursuit to calm their desires *per fas et nefas* (using just and unjust methods), not accountable to anyone or anything. They simply placed themselves beyond God, beyond His Revelation.

Marxism-Leninism is just another modernized tool in the hands of worshippers of the golden calf—the same "chosen" people who are descendants of those other "chosen." For them, genocide and barbaric terror were a natural and accessible means to use in realizing their goal—world domination. Humanity paid for this with roughly 250 million casualties; we will never get a precise figure of this hecatomb. They were victims of Russia, China, Eastern and Middle Europe, the countries of South America, Africa, and Asia—everywhere that the "golden calf" of communism established its bloody clutches.

Is it over? Are Nazism, communism, and other "isms" of mistaken utopias now nonexistent, no longer lurking? What if they exist but have only taken other forms?

But of course! They exist and are doing wonderfully! Their general tool is New Age ideology, pouring over the world in various forms of the same plundering globalism. I came across a book written by Melinda Ribner. The title is, *New Age Judaism—Ancient*

Wisdom for the Modern World. It was very interesting and very significant work! The author's goal was to protect the purity of Judaism in the sea of New Age propaganda, to preserve the value of this religion by raising young children to accept the transcendental nature of moral codes. It is a book that is in a sense the antithesis of the New Age movement, because it casts aside moral relativism, basing the need for such a casting aside on the thousands of years of knowledge of Judaic philosophers.

I also came across a book by an orthodox rabbi who also fought against the New Age movement. The rabbi went so far as to say openly that the destruction of Christianity in the United States by the followers of the "golden calf" would also lead to the destruction of Judaism. What did the rabbi conclude? That we should protect Christianity and its rules, because its extermination would also mean the end for Judaism!

Is New Age philosophy so mighty, so tempting, that it might be a tool used to subordinate the world to the class (or caste) of "chosen people?"

For now, it has had horrifying success. It's enough to look at the popularity of pornography, the licentiousness of minors, the increase in drug addicts and alcoholics, and the breakdown of the family unit in the United States and all over the world.

So, is there no way out of this macabre situation? Does the world have to reach the lowest level of degeneration, to succumb to "social engineering?"

Like any utopia, the New Age one also has to step down from the stage of history. It won't last, because no one is able to change the fundamental and inherent traits of human nature. Implanting ideology of the "general good," such as communism in all its various guises, didn't triumph in the Soviet Union, nor will it last today or into the future. The young people in Russia had the same wishes as their contemporaries in other countries, cultures, and social and economic systems—the same, though somewhat impoverished, as they had been shaped by the poverty of that society that had been determined from above.

Are there symptoms of renewal, of rebuilding? I think so. It's enough to look at the opinions of young Americans in universities. Another telling sign that people are casting aside the ideology of evil, globalism, and the "New Age," was the result of the 2000 presidential election in the United States. Those who supported Al Gore nearly sparked a coup d'etat, which I wrote about in several political commentaries during the dramatic turning point in the presidential election.

But, the attempt didn't work. The pendulum of history swung in another direction.

21

Philosophy of Life

I T IS AMAZING how differently people can perceive the world—and how different it looks depending on the eyes of the beholder! We usually don't contemplate the obvious fact that our feelings are triggered by an interaction of objective reality with the subjective possibilities of perception. Thus, for everyone, all that surrounds us is his own, broken apart from the rest of the world. A dog sees the world in poor colors, but his vision is much sharper than a human's, not to mention a plundering bird's, which can spot a fish from a great height and then fall onto it, dive into the water, and emerge with the catch in their beaks. How differently an alligator sees the world, which only sees sideways and really doesn't see anything in front of his nose. How different it is in the eyes of ants, in the eyes of flying insects, and in the eyes of all the creatures that walk, swim, and crawl.

People are also varied in their visual abilities. They can react differently to stimuli. There are those like Wyczolkowski, for example, who could find elements of beauty even in a Krakow courtyard with a trash can in the corner in his unrepeatable watercolors that are bathed in sunlight, soaked with intangible beauty and attraction. I feel pity for those who don't have the capacity for deeper feeling and experience of the unique wonder that is the world. I feel pity for those who, looking at the navy blue sky full of the gold sequins of stars, cannot pause to reflect that they are standing before something infinite, that they are seeing something incomprehensible in its excellence—and cannot appreciate their own minuteness in relation to the secrecy of this grandeur. And I feel pity for those who, lying on their stomachs in the grass, cannot see all the miniature treasures of life rolling along, enduring, and pulsing around them—the hurry of marching ants to a designated purpose, the beauty of a butterfly hovering on a blade of grass or grain, the hardworking march of a black beetle.

I recently found out that insects have a system of communication. Supposedly, people have recorded their conversations! Now, with the help of computers, they are trying to decode them. Isn't this fascinating? And isn't the intelligence of dolphins and whales who were given hefty brains with developed brain cortices awe-inspiring? Their brains differ to a great degree from other animals in the philogenetic line and even from us.

Philosophers of various epochs and times tried to create a concept of "clarifying" the world and our role and place within it. They explained this "logically" and "objectively." Some of them came to the paradoxical conclusion that only our subjective reality exists and nothing apart from it. Others found that a person is the navel of the world while everything else that exists is beneath him and there to serve him.

But, I cannot convince myself that the mosquito biting me is doing it for my own good. I don't believe that my fate concerns an ant carrying a mighty piece of a stick on its back. It would be better if we were able to understand that all of this amazing world living its own life, is something much larger and more wonderful than what our reason and our thoughts can comprehend. If all of us would be so humble as to recognize our smallness, our minuteness, we could enrich our lives with the ability to see and appreciate our surroundings and especially so that we would respect our defenseless neighbors, to whom the Creator also gave this earth for common use.

There was a lot of untouched jungle around my Floridian property. Now, the noise of car engines starts to interrupt the voices of the birds. Fewer and fewer ibises walk along the canal. New homes are appearing surrounded by freshly cut St. Augustine grass. Civilization attacks and destroys that which for hundreds of thousands of years existed and lived in harmony—truthfully a plundering harmony but one in accordance with the rhythm and needs of nature.

Is the question, *"quo vadis Homo sapiens,"* really a question only for philosophers?

The feeling of guilt and knowledge of sin is not only in the domain of people. It's enough to look carefully at a dog in a moment when he clearly feels guilty—he has lowered ears, a sorry look, and a visible desire to be forgiven. In this nook of common existence, a human and an animal do not differ greatly. What thus makes a human a human? This is a question to which until now there has never been a clear answer.

The curve of evolution of Homo sapiens is curious. He has existed on this earth, as has been confirmed, continuously for millions of years. He coexists with a hard-to-survive environment, and through this huge expanse of time, he hasn't moved even one iota forward! But, in the past several thousand years, our evolution has taken a geometrical curve with huge acceleration. Today's possibilities of a man are really unimaginable—limitless. And yet, I don't think any of the former ages, back to ancient times, were as distinguished with such cruelty, such mass genocide, as the minions of the twentieth century. There is a horrifying dichotomy between people's current technological possibilities and the moral state of human society. After reading my article on this subject, one reader sent me a letter in which he claimed that the whole problem leads up to a brutal truth—man is a carnivorous beast, as is also apparent in his anatomical build.

You might also look at the dilemma this way. I think, however, that this is a rather far-fetched simplification of the matter.

The most primitive form of life, the virus, is already very complex. It's enough to look at the first molecular biology textbook to confirm the incredible logic at this most primitive level of life—at its capacity to adapt to the environment, at the possibility of multiplying itself at the cost of other creations. The invasion of the virus in the body of another cell may result in a strange symbiosis—leading eventually to formation of even more complex and adaptive forms of life. When we move up the phylogenetic ladder what is striking is the appearance of all the more complicated and specialized organisms, which are better adapted to their surroundings and have greater functional plasticity. A crocodile—a remnant of creatures living before dinosaurs—doesn't distinguish itself with particular intellect, but it can move excellently in water and get on land very quickly, though for a short distance. His possibilities for adaptation to environmental changes are incomparably better and more varied than the possibilities of coral that can only exist in ocean water and feed on plankton.

The expansion of adaptive possibilities pulled another significant area behind it—specialization. For example, the arm of a chimpanzee or an orangutan is adapted to move through the trees and vines quickly. It is very different from the arm of a man, not to mention the specific ability that a man possesses of opposable thumbs, giving people completely different possibilities. It's interesting to compare the front paw of an iguana with the arm of a human. In this respect we are more similar to the iguana than to the chimpanzee. The chimpanzee thus made himself better, specializing himself to his designated treetop lifestyle.

A man, like an animal, is driven by instincts—the preservation of the species, self-defense, fleeing from danger, the ability to gather food and to have emotional reactions, such as fear and anger, and an attachment to the sexual partner and the progeny. Apart from these basic reactions that condition existence, more values also exist that are not specific only to humans. One such value is friendship. I once saw a naturalist film in which the author showed that he could even befriend an octopus, a very primitive biological entity, not to mention the close bonds that can grow between a dog and his owner.

Everything that exists is genetically "programmed" much like a computer. The higher on the philogenetic ladder, is the less automatic are your responses. The variability of those responses is almost unlimited. A turtle stubbornly wanders in the direction of the ocean immediately after laying her eggs. She is directed by instinct, not by some decision of her own, not by choice. When we look at representatives of the animal world that are more advanced in evolution, we can see two interesting parallel areas. They possess a range of conscious activity that isn't solely determined by instinct. By the same token more complicated creatures require much longer periods of care and training within their families after coming into the world. I once saw a goat in the Tatry Mountains teaching her little ones how to slide down the snow! A chimpanzee needs at least two years of motherly care before he can make his own decisions. It is a similar case among gorillas and orangutans.

Animals are capable of feelings that are not completely explainable by instincts, those programmed reactions. One British naturalist raised a lion from the moment it was born. The lion was attached to her as if she were his mother and walked behind her like a loyal dog. It was decided, however, that this huge animal should return to nature. The lion was taken where other lions lived in freedom. After some time, the naturalist went back to that terrain. The lion found her again and showed its joy. What's interesting is that it showed up in the company of a wild, untamed female which treated her also with friendliness. This feeling of friendship and attachment remained strong enough that it suppressed the natural instinct of aggression even in a situation in which they were feeding on a fresh kill.

A friendship between another naturalist and a chimpanzee is well-known. She got the trust of all the members of the group and could move safely with them. A bond grew that could not be explained by programmed instincts.

I was very moved by a film in which a small monkey, a Capucin, was taking care of a quadriplegic man who could only make minimal movements in his fingers. The monkey showed full understanding of the patient's situation. It gave him water, wiped his mouth, and fixed the pillow and sheets, demonstrating almost motherly care. I don't think that even the best nurse would give so much of herself. The small Capucin monkeys were specially prepared for such care. The most curious thing is that this monkey did not only understand and do her tasks very well, but also clearly showed the patient sympathy and kindness. This also crossed over the boundary of programmed instinct. Furthermore, what kind of instinct could explain a dog wandering over half a continent to find his caretakers? How can you explain the despair of a dog that starved himself at the grave after the death of his master? I know of an example in which the master died and his dachshund went to his master's grave and starved herself to death.

I am horrified—and I'm not the only one—by the defenselessness of the animal world against the merciless destructive force of humanity. Claws, quills, and quick legs are a rather poor defense in comparison to firearms. Millions of years of adaptation of insects to their environment became useless against the poison poured on the sides of the road, lawns of houses, and cultivated fields.

It is amazing that human arrogance can lead to the annihilation of the wealth of flora and fauna—the wonder of creation—and onto a straight road to the self-annihilation of the human race. The question thus arises—how does a man differ from animals, though differences undoubtedly exist and are huge with respect to the level of evolution. In any case, he is not very different in the same level of instinct—these are still basic motives for his activity. The sameness of these instincts with animals is made milder only by our greater ability to suppress instincts. He doesn't differ to a meaningful degree in his emotional reactions—just as a dog can be faithful, just like that monkey was capable to feel, care, and be a hero to others—he can also die from grief after losing a beloved being. He can also, like a cat playing with a mouse, perform horrifying acts of cruelty against other people and whole groups of people. In the name of "higher ideals," he is capable of murder, torture, and destruction.

A man can also be jealous, and again, he is not privileged in this feeling. I once brought home a female puppy schnauzer. We had a grown female cocker spaniel in the house. In my naiveté, I counted on the fact that the older dog would act with motherly feelings towards the little one. After seeing the intruder, she left and went upstairs to her bed. She didn't want to go downstairs and refused food! She acted in a neurotic way, totally irrationally. There was nothing else to do but take the schnauzer back to its owner the next day. The spaniel greeted my lonely return to the house without the little intruder very enthusiastically!

When I follow the ambitious schemes of people, even those with high levels of intellect, their pull towards domination, their small-mindedness and envy, I do not share the opinion that these are traits belonging only to people. The same thing happens in the animal world. A candidate for the presidency or a senatorial position doesn't differ emotionally from my dog. After all the candidate is controlled by the same instincts, the only difference being that he has an ability to some degree to suppress them. But unfortunately not always!

So, when we ask ourselves the question about the difference between people and the animal world, many claim that a true essential difference doesn't exist. And yet, it does exist and rather obviously. In terms of basic instincts, the differences are minimal. We can have feelings like animals, and these reactions can't be interpreted as instinctual reactions. And so, even in this field, it is difficult to find some greater differentiation.

Thus, what decidedly and irrevocably distinguishes a human from the animal world, what makes him noble in the ranks of the highest being, is the ability to create. The higher forms of monkeys can break off a branch and use it as a tool to break apart a beehive so as to get honey. But that is where their creative inventiveness ends. And a chimpanzee can easily learn sign language. He can learn about six hundred words and visual symbols with no problem. But, the ability to create remains only in the domain of the man, beginning with the discovery of the wheel and ending in the creation of complicated electronic structures. These creative possibilities do not end with the production of increasingly more complicated mechanisms. A man is also in possession of another essential "spark of God"—a desire to learn about and understand everything in which he lives. In the present day, science creeps up on the tracks where simple "rational" thought is not sufficient. How can we imagine the fifth or sixth dimension; and as a result, how are we in a position to understand the abstracts of metalogic, which is so incredibly efficacious, so helpful?

Finally, the third attribute of a person is the ability to create works of art and to experience their beauty. Only a human created and creates monumental buildings, only he can carve the beauty of the human and animal form, the beauty of nature, in stone or on an artist's canvas. Only a person composes polyphonic music, counterpoint, and the unending spectrum of musical creations. He is also capable of perceiving the beauty created by others, can pass on his experiences to others. It was recently discovered that a giraffe prefers Mozart's music to other forms of musical creations. Cows that are exposed to Mozart's music become calmer and even give more milk! But that's all—they cannot compose the music.

The creative predisposition of a man, however, has two edges. He can create beautiful uplifting forms, but he is also ready to use his creative talents to bring forth evil, crime, and various wicked acts. As a caveman, he was a threat only to the inhabitants of neighboring caves. Now, when he has mighty destructive tools at his disposal but still remains in primitive emotional states and yields to primitive instincts, he becomes a threat not only to his neighbors, not only to his tribe, but to the whole population of Homo sapiens.

And that's what the dismal naked truth looks like.

* * *

What does this mean, to be a creator? Does it mean that you have to be in possession of unusual talent at the level of Michelangelo, Leonardo da Vinci, Mozart, or Beethoven? Or rather that a person given average capabilities, average in the general sense of the word, can't be a creative person? And being of average status, should he resign from his ambitions?

Mozart was a phenomenal musical talent. He played concerts as a child, composed in his teenage years, died young, yet left a huge creative legacy. At the same time, he was struggling with poverty and human ignorance.

This Mozart, apart from his talent that was his gift from God, distinguished himself in being incredibly hardworking and having inner discipline. Similar traits distinguished Michelangelo, the creator of the frescoes on the ceiling of the Sistine Chapel. The level of his self-denial, the total resignation from the pleasures of life for the goal of his craft, is evident in the fact that he became crippled after painting for several years on a scaffold with his head tilted backwards. To become familiar with human anatomy, to create the beauty of the human form, he risked a lot secretly performing autopsies on corpses. He wanted to understand more, to become familiar with the human body and to use this knowledge in his artwork.

People described as geniuses, apart from having talent, possess traits in their personality that distinguish them from average or even above-average people. These traits are unbendable will, iron inner discipline, and a readiness to give up anything that might not promote their main goals.

But not everyone is given talent by God. So, can you expect extraordinary things from average people?

Years ago, when I was working under the direction of Dr. Cooper in New York doing stereotactic surgeries, I came to the conclusion that with a certain minimal change in localizing purposeful damage, performed during surgery in the nuclei of the basal ganglia in those suffering from Parkinson's disease, you could get better results. Of course, such a surgical change had to be proven theoretically. In other words, I had to neatly work out and write up this whole problem. The idea itself was suggested to me by one of the patients in whom a somewhat deeper localized lesion gave much better therapeutic results. I mentioned this to my chief as an intriguing piece of information. His reaction was surprising to me, so different from the world of communism, full of empty words and professional torpor.

"If you think that really happens, then get to work! I will give you the necessary working conditions to resolve this problem."

Ordinarily, simply, informally, concretely—the result of our brief conversation was my publication based on clinical and experimental material that gave a better understanding of the functioning of the brain and the treatment of illness.

How could you define creativity? My definition would be the following: to use one's own energy, ability, talent, and endurance, regardless of material means, to create something positive that expresses one's aspirations, desires, and personality. This doesn't have to be the unrepeatable beauty of the Pietà or Raphael's *Madonna*. This doesn't have to be Chopin's Revolutionary Etude. It can be something completely simple and prosaic, but something that is the fruit of passion, work, and aspiration towards self-realization. Creativity embodies the movement to constantly better ourselves by living everyday with satisfaction for the things already achieved, the wish to go further and further. That is the essence of creativity to me.

And it's not important if the effects are beautifully tended flowers, nicely made shoes, well-sown suits, a well-done surgery, a gorgeous bridge connecting two distant shores. No, that is not essential. What is important is that aspiration to achieve a goal that is not ultimate and never perfect but one to which we try to get as close as possible with our own energy, own self-denial.

You can really discern two approaches to life in the mass of humanity—consuming and creative. The goal of the first is the garnering of as much as possible for oneself, without sharing one's wealth, whether material or spiritual, with others. The second, so much less numerous, group lives and works not only for themselves. Their inner imperative is to give something of themselves to the outside, to others. The first ones might be connoisseurs of artworks, striking in their knowledge, penetratingly analyzing political situations, traveling all over the world and inspiring others with their knowledge of that which humanity created over the ages. There is nothing wrong with this. Most of these people, however, won't do anything that will influence the course of history even minimally, throwing their own simple useful brick there, a product of their talent, hard work, and knowledge.

To create, you have to possess still another essential attribute—a love of what you do, faith in your own possibilities, and the capacity to calm down your own desires with your achievements. Creators as a rule do not aspire to satisfy their "consumer" desires. There is a famous anecdote about one writer. He was asked if he read this or that, and he responded with a note of impatience, "I don't have time to read. I write!" He was right. His work, his vision of the goal, was for him more important than the fruits of a well polished dilettante.

An iron truth also strikes the eyes—creators do not rule the world! What's more, they don't even care to. A carpenter who produces beautiful furniture, an operating surgeon, a cultivator of flowers, a farmer trying to get the greatest crops—they do not have the desire or the need to rule over others. On the other hand unproductive people are, however, motivated to rule over others, become dictators, become the elite of the ruling party and nomenclature, become also billionaires. And it is they who rule over the world, for a creative person doesn't have either the time or the desire to fight for power and money.

Most people have a rather awful opinion of themselves. They are convinced that they weren't blessed with talent and aren't capable of achieving anything. They thus live from day to day because that's how their lives happen to "fall into place." It's horrifying how many people are convinced that their work isn't at all interesting, not giving satisfaction, only a heavy daily exertion and monotony of thrashing rewarded with rather low pay. How unhappy these people are! How difficult it is for these people to go through life with this feeling of such imprisonment!

A creative man believes in his own possibilities. I remember an anecdote about an older Scottish man who was asked if he played the piano. "I don't know," he said. "I never tried."

Such a response inspires a smile, a chuckle, but it's an appropriate reaction. He who doesn't try to measure himself against his own possibilities will never know what those possibilities are. The first attempts will be unsuccessful and awkward. Some stop at the very beginning mired in constant betterment of his own mistakes and grappling with his own unhappiness. Others do the opposite—they stand up to battle and they push further.

As in an old tale that my grandmother told me, there were once two boys sent out to work with a blacksmith. One was from a poor family and had to earn money by working to pay for his education. The other, from a rich family, was placed in a leather sack hanging from the ceiling of the forge from where he could observe all the work comfortably and not dirty his hands learning the trade. A few years went by. The poor boy put horseshoes on horses, fixed plows. The other one had time to get fat, but he still didn't know how to do anything and didn't become a blacksmith.

Recently, a young girl was visiting me—I observed her serious face while sitting on a small stool by the children's table with pleasure as she created. Of course I had to recognize her hard work and praise her. As a result, we both had a good time. On the other hand, the effect of watching television and not developing either thought or character is really upsetting to me. This passive, thoughtless watching of idiocy, this deceitful indoctrination, destroys creative predisposition in its embryo.

The scale of achievements isn't important in the end. It's not important how far we get. It's important that we stick to this road and always sense motivation to develop. Then, we won't be bothered by complexes and pretenses of "fate" that treated us poorly. We will be in a state of satisfaction, appreciating that the magnificient gift of each coming day.

* * *

A mosquito bit me on the shin—in the full sunlight, not beneath the bushes where they usually lurk. I mechanically hit my palm in that spot. My smeared blood and its remains on my skin, the committed atrocity didn't affect me at all. Actually, the opposite, I was totally satisfied with the committed murder as I scratched the itchy bump caused by the toxin of the mosquito's bite.

I started thinking about this. After all, I'm supposed to be a "man of creation"—supposedly this world was given to me in faith—but such a tiny thing like a mosquito doesn't take this fact into account and bites me, in accordance with his instincts and needs. How strong they must be for him to expose himself even to death so as to suck some blood from his victim. The mosquito clearly doesn't care about the fact that I am a "man of creation" and that he is subservient to me. He simply lives his own life that nature bestowed upon him. It is an incredibly precise organism, perfected over millions of years, possessing the instruments that allow him to preserve his species and survive in various ecological conditions. If you look at one under magnification it is obviously built with incredible precision, possessing the ability to move on the ground and in the air. When he walks, the pattern of his legs is the best possible. When he flies, his sense of direction and precision of movement in a three-dimensional space is worthy of admiration in its precision. The build of its organs, muscles, and mechanism of orientation, of distance is also incredibly precise and to this day hasn't been identified anatomically. We know that the whole "plan" of its development and life is encoded in his genes, where the appropriate links of DNA determine one or another element of his structure and existence. If you go further in these inquiries, to the level of molecular biology, you can extract not only single genomes but also identify their meanings in the development and function of this living thing.

I read somewhere rather recently that the analysis of spider webs showed that spider thread, in proportion to its diameter, is stronger than the most advanced artificial threads. They were able to identify the gene responsible for the ability to produce a spider web. This gene was then injected into the genetic makeup of a goat. In its milk, a substance appeared from which you could produce such a thread! Now, there is already talk of producing new varieties of ropes that are more enduring than everything that has been produced up until now.

Billions of various forms of life living on our globe, beginning with the most primitive viruses to the human being, possess a common element that no one yet has been able to understand and recreate. This element is life. Yes, we speak about "growing" crystals, and there are people synthesizing long chains of pseudo-proteins—and yet the mystery of life remains inscrutable. One truth is worth considering: even the simplest biological structures function very precisely. The most advanced new computers and chemical factories are nothing in comparison to the functioning of one cell. From where does this precision come? From where did the knowledge come? How did it all happen? These are questions to which people still have not found out the answers.

One thing remains certain—a mosquito, whose life ended on my leg, was not living "for me" but for himself. His aggression comes from his instinct for survival and preservation of the species. These two properties permeate the whole natural world. That's why a mosquito had the right to bite, and I had the right to kill him, though I did it involuntarily under the influence of the initial pain and then didn't regret my crime under the influence of the growing itch. Destroying this perfectly miniaturized creature, I protected my own right to survive. A tree sucking essential moisture by its roots doesn't care about the grass and shrubs growing under it. Every living thing, to live and survive, has to kill! That is the law of nature, and the mosquito and I are only links in this chain of life fighting for survival. Is that how it has to be in the world of people?

In my rather long life, I have seen virgin forests full of huge fir trees and ferns—forests in the Rocky Mountains, tropical jungle, the desert of the American steppe on which the wind rolls the tumbleweeds along.

It is only there where the human being has not intervened that life rolls along in its original rhythm. The crumbling trunk of an old tree ripped apart by a hit of lightning is a home for birds and bees. Little birds hide from plunderers in the tangled vines. The always lurking black rabbit sneaks around under their protection.

An almighty ecological balance exists according to which the weaker die so as to become food for the stronger, and these stronger ones, in turn, become food for the even stronger. The most prepared, youngest, and strongest members of a species survive. The weak have to yield to the stronger. Even painful disasters, like a forest fire or flood, fulfill a goal that was established thousands of millions of years ago. From the ashes of the forest, from the enriched soil, grows a new forest and everything that coexists with it in a symbiosis of various types of flora and fauna. A flood similarly destroys and overwhelms but also enriches.

It's hard to fathom the source of a human arrogance that usurped the position of the highest rank even above a cockroach or fly. Did this arrogance arise from the fact that people are the most destructive forces on earth? It is true that humans can surpass all living creatures on this globe in destroying the environment. The comparison of human bad behavior to that of animals, which is so often overused to describe many of our barbaric acts, is insulting for animals. Animals never kill for the sake of killing; they don't torment or torture victims. They kill to survive and kill in such a way as to take their victim's life as quickly as possible. A marten or skunk can kill half a chicken coop, not for the satisfaction of killing, but only as a reflex of gathering supplies.

My anatomy professor once said that people can be compared to a malignant tumor that destroys, kills, and in killing, hurts itself. Do our intellectual possibilities cause us to be a type that is "better" or "the best?" Or maybe worse, the worst? Why do we regard ourselves as the navel of the world?

I was once interested in the contemplative nature and teachings derived from cabbala knowledge. In accordance with it, you should carry yourself through your thoughts into eternity. Supposedly, you should proceed by going forward into space in all three dimensions. As a result of this, each such journey leads to eternity, then each person giving himself to such meditation finds himself in an ideal center of time and distance, because each point in eternity is a central point. Are we really this central point, which leads us to feel egocentric? Or maybe, it's the other way around—maybe we are only a tiny fragment of something unfathomable, so big that it is not even imaginable?

Admiring the scattered gold of nightly stars, we don't recognize their distance from us. Beyond them, beyond the reach of our vision, there exists another enormous universe with billions of other stars, planets, and whole galaxies. We thus don't have the least bit of reason to think that only our planet was able to establish conditions to create life. There exists a large probability that life existed or does exist on other planets in one form or another. They don't necessarily have to be green people with antennas on their heads like in Disney movies. They might be different, hard to understand forms of living material.

I saw some special worms in the Museum of Science in Boston. They are over one foot long, ten inches in diameter, white because they live in total darkness. They do not have any organs, because they get their food and oxygen through their skin and eliminate waste the same way. They are possibly the largest currently known primitive form of life, accustomed to the awfully high pressure at the bottom of the depths of the ocean. And after all, they don't live down there alone—they have to feed on something, so there have to be other forms of life that become its food.

On Ash Wednesday, the first day of Lent, we hear the ominous words, "From dust you arose and to dust you shall return." Isn't this true? And does this truth require some kind of proof? We know this, yet it is difficult for us to agree that we are subject to the same laws of ceasing and dying to which other creatures are subject. So, then apart from the battle for existence and ultimate annihilation, does nothing else exist?

The judgment doesn't belong to us. With our limited possibilities of recognition we were able to understand one thing—that the reality that surrounds us is much more intricate and complicated than we can possibly conceive. We also cannot ignore the unshakable conclusion that everything that surrounds us and to which we belong, as a piece of "all this," is like a reflection of unfathomable intelligence of its own making beyond our recognition.

Apart from the battle for existence, or rather a mutual devouring, we also see a place that in a certain way calls this rule into question. How can you explain the attachment of a dog to his master, how can you explain or motivate heroism, examples of sacrificing even one's own life for others? Such positions are not only attributes of people—how can you explain the heroism of a dog carrying a human baby from a blazing house? And again our unfortunate arrogance! We shouldn't usurp the heroic positions and actions for ourselves as they are also present in the animal world. St. Francis of Assisi understood this. He could harmoniously coexist with nature and in nature, loving and understanding it.

Years ago, I watched a Canadian film entitled, *I Heard The Owl Call My Name* based on the book of the same name by Margaret Craven. In accordance with the beliefs of Indians in the northern part of the Rocky Mountains, a person who was nearing death would hear his name being called out by an owl.

A young Catholic priest, before whom career possibilities were opening up and who was supposed to go for further studies to Rome, had minimal, though progressing, symptoms of a disease. The test results revealed that he was actually in the final stages of cancer with metastasis and that he would soon die. He didn't know this. The bishop called him in and told him that he wasn't going for further studies until the following year, and that for now, he would have to take on a position as pastor in a distant Indian village in the Rocky Mountains. Deeply hurt in his hopes and ambitions, the young priest journeyed to this far-off place. He was in awe of the majestic nature there, in awe of the Indians full of a dignity that can only be achieved through long contact with nature. The rebellion with which he came faded away. In the evenings, he looked at the colors of the setting sun, listened to the birds. He calmed down. He began to understand the bishop's decision. One day, he heard his name being called out monotonously by an owl. He already knew what this meant from the Indians. He wasn't afraid of this sentence. He could now accept the fact that his life would cease.

I've never met the author. I only know that she understood the sense of human life.

Hans Fallada, a writer drenched in pessimism, is the author of a story with the title, "Everyone dies alone." The truth of this title needs no confirmation.

Living in full force, are we not alone? Most grow up in a family, then marry, raise children, live in a specified society, speak the same language as others, go to the same church. So, how can you talk about their loneliness?

And yet, our conscious lives are only ours and no one can access them. No one is in a state to experience that which we experienced, which shaped our awareness; no one can experience the enormous emotions, the feelings determining our personalities and perspectives of the world.

Our pasts are only ours to know. We cannot share them with others, despite the various forms of such attempts—memoirs, daily papers, storytelling creations. How many biographies, memoirs, how much emotional baggage fills the tales of Hemingway, Steinbeck, Zeromski, and Tolstoy! Are the adventures of Tom Sawyer at the pen of Twain the most obvious denial of the theme of our individual loneliness, of life inaccessible to others, even to those closest to us?

We can find solidarity in our feelings and experiences with others and empathize with them, understand them, completely sympathize with them, and yet, we cannot step into the soul of another person and experience exactly that which he is experiencing.

My secretary, who was Sicilian and raised in Brooklyn, New York, was able to simply illustrate her childhood to me. I was in this neighborhood no more than two or three times. And yet, I can see clearly that building, one of many, creating a long line with small yards in the back, overgrown with weeds. I can see the open window, her grandmother reigning over the large group of young children, because the older ones were already at school, while the parents' days were spent working outside the house. I see her alone, how she plays in the street with others, mixing Sicilian slang words with English. I see the old stores open on the street, full of vegetables and fruit, in which dark-eyed women did their shopping. I see a fish store, before it a long table with the gifts of the sea, with manta rays and octopuses. I even sense the irrevocable smell emanating from that place. On the basis of her description, I can see a small, young girl nicely sitting at her lessons, and her father, a small, restless, and impatient man returning home after a long day at work. The plasticity of these expressions is awe-inspiring. And yet, the world of her personal experiences, the spiritual coloring of her past experiences, is not accessible to me.

From my grandmother's stories, I can recreate fragments of her young Vilno childhood, when Polish culture was subject to merciless Russianization. I can see her, in a long line of students, as she has to go to the Russian Orthodox Church on Sunday, even though she is Catholic. I can see her in class, where raw discipline and brutal denationalization was to make these children into an obedient herd of human automatons. But, I also see their inner resistance—reading Polish books at home, learning the history of the Piast and the Jagiellons families attesting to the greatness of their nation. I see and understand the growing resistance in my grandmother and her peers, their hatred of the occupier. I also see Vilno in those days. A crowd spread out before the Ostra Brama, packed into the narrow medieval street, the amazing statue of Jesus of Antokol. I see ladies in big dresses and huge hats decorated with feathers, carriages and wagons delivering goods every morning, the scent of freshly baked breads. I see this whole, no longer existing world, that was so different from the one in which I grew up.

I similarly see the world of my mother's childhood. I see Warsaw under the "May coup d'etat," in which Polish blood was shed by other Poles. I see a high school class of teenage girls passionately talking about this coup d'etat by Pilsudski. And, another picture I see—a young girl in the countryside of Vilno amidst fires, with Kozaks on horseback carrying torches from one haystack and wheat field to the next initiating the fires—like bloody flames in a dark sky. This young girl is my mother, horrified and at the same time overcome with curiosity.

Recently, my loneliness was visited by two young people with two children. The boy was eight years old, the girl four years old. The children understand Polish, though they prefer to speak in English. They are exactly the same children as the world has seen a millions times over. They want to know and play, they want to enter into their lives by imitating adults. I looked at these children and thought, "The new generation." They live in different conditions, in a different world than the other one that I experienced—different also from the world of their young parents. They are tied to their mother with thousands of invisible threads, but they are beings of an already different world. Not even their parents will have access to their world, much less some old outsider like me.

There is no past. It has already gone by. There is also no future. It has not occurred yet, is yet to come. Everyone lives in the present moment, in that tight crevice between two worlds of time. Everyone lives in that particular tightness of the current moment, but is not aware of the fleeting nature of that "now." The memory of the past becomes a very personal, integral part of our personality. Without this anchor, we would be nothing, a phantom devoid of history.

Not too long ago, the following experiment was done—a young healthy man who was blindfolded was submerged in water in a watertight diving suit. In this way, he no longer had information from his hearing, sight, or even proprioception, because he found himself in a situation of near weightlessness. What did he do? Very quickly, he lost all orientation of distance. He didn't know which way was up and which was down. Then, his thoughts yielded to confusion. In the end, he fell into a state of complete unawareness. The cause was the loss of actual working stimuli. Without them, our life is almost impossible.

Just as these stimuli condition our lives and functioning, so also do we need our memories of the past. Everything that coded our experiences through the years is in this most perfect computer that is the human brain. The recording of millions of those emotionally colored events is, of course, different in every person, unique and unrepeatable. For this very reason, we are not in a state to give to others that which makes up the most essential element of our personality. How often people who live long next to one another and are attached by mutual knots sometimes barely know each other. How often this is the cause of various tragedies, divorces, unwillingness, and even hatred. If by some "miracle" they could creep into the soul of the other person, of course, they would be in a state to understand his reactions, behavior, and decisions—and to accept them. Unfortunately, this inner world of others is closed and only through mutual love and attachment can we understand and tolerate each other.

Those who have long ago passed on still live in our thoughts. We see them in various situations of that past life, can sometimes fleetingly feel their presence; they sometimes come to us in dreams of our once shared lives. Sometimes we look for rescue in them when we are standing before a difficult dilemma. They are somewhere far away, and the time distancing them casts their figures in a gray fog of forgetting, erases the contours of the figure, the face.

When that eternal separation comes, when someone close leaves us forever, then after the period of pain and shock, we begin to see as if with different eyes—somehow more acutely though from a greater distance. We can then see in this person what we were not able to see while living next to them—their personality, motivation of behavior, and the problems they had to face—their very character. And then, we wish so deeply to be able to talk with him or her, one more time, even if briefly, to express our feelings. And to say that now we understand everything and we are sorry for our past behavior.

In moments of loneliness, we can only return to the old world. We can again be with them, experiencing this with the film of our lives "rewound." Moving at full force, we are not likely to engage in such retrospection, for it seems a paradox, a loss of time and emotion. Our self-preservation instinct lies like one hired to do the job, deceiving us with the conviction that we will live forever—others might and will die, but not me. We look only to the future, before us, eager to achieve, climbing up, thirsty for experiences, impressions, and above all else successes. Sexual instinct erases the sharpness of our judgment and creates an illusion of possibility of achieving full happiness and calming our other instincts.

At a certain phase of our lives, however, we are able to see that we are subject to the same laws of nature to which the other living creatures of the world are subject. And it is from this very moment that we are more and more open to the past. The blueish transparent cloud of time separates those who passed more and more, making them more distant. Yet without the anchors of memory and sentiment we would not be able to exist, to be who we are—we would be like that person underwater with blindfolded eyes. The world of our past imperceptibly becomes one of our most valuable treasures to which no one has access, which no one is in a state to steal from us, to claim for their own or destroy.

One day, that blue fog will surround us all around. And we will go where there is no more pain, no more suffering—and from which there is no return, because it is our final departure, or may be rather the ultimate return.

In one of his novels, Rudyard Kipling described the following scene: two young, British second lieutenants, cocky and self-assured, find themselves in India. They curiously mingle with the exotic crowds at the Hindu bazaar. At a certain moment, they stop near a gray-bearded older man with a turban. The old man doesn't seem to be selling anything. He just has a huge vat before him filled with water.

The young Englishman asks insultingly, "What are you selling, man?"

"You want to know what I'm selling? Then dunk your head into this vat, and you'll soon find out," the older man replied.

The young man didn't need to be asked twice. He dunked his head, but he very quickly pulled it out. His companion looked at him and was horrified. In the eyes of his colleague was the sheer terror of a person who had suddenly seen something awful.

"What happened? Tell me, for God's sake! What did you see?"

After a moment, from the white lip of the colleague fell the following response, "Listen! I experienced another long life in that moment! And even my death!"

The old Hindu said nothing, lost in his meditations.

I believe deeply that this story is based on a real experience—an example of masterful hypnosis that revealed only the relativity of time. Truthfully, our lives roll along in time, seconds make up hours, hours into days, months into years, the threads of Holy Mary on the rosary of our life. The ticking of the clock doesn't stop even for a moment; each experienced moment, even the last one, the most actual—already belongs to the past.

Is that really how it is? Perhaps so because the awareness of time is a conventional category—after all, God was not nor will be, only is. Present knowledge confirms unbreakably that time is a relative concept. If you were to put up a sky-reaching tower and install a chronograph at its base and another at its top, then after a while—assuming that they function absolutely exactly—both would show a difference in time. If someone could go through the "black hole"—that part in the cosmos with an incredible concentration of matter—then he would probably find himself in another system of time.

We debate a lot about eternity. We imagine it as a never-ending chain of days, as a lengthening of our earthly experiences felt in an earthly span of time. We speak about infinity, and, of course, infinity is immeasurable, and more so, it can be an immeasurable moment!

We are able to understand very little. We are three-dimensional creatures, and yet we are sure of the fact that there exist further, unfathomed measurements that already have practical applications in present-day astronomy. Objective reality on a macro scale is not really known to us. Long ago, one philosopher used the following comparison: if there existed a two-dimensional being and it was placed on a smooth surface of a sphere, then it would be convinced that it found itself on a never-ending large terrain. It's similar with us—we don't have the capacity to directly verify that which is not completely obvious to us but that really exists.

Christ said to Pilate, "My kingdom is not of the world" (John). What was he talking about? What kingdom? Where is it found? "God is not a God of the dead, but of the living" (Matthew). We will all die, "from dust you arose and to dust you shall return." So looks our daily experience. That's how we see our reality! Christ taught that there would be no more death in His Kingdom. "Because you can no longer die, you will be both angels and sons of God, being sons of the resurrection" (Luke).

Truthfully, these words are not fathomed, and yet—how convincing! Christ presents one condition to enter into the "kingdom of heaven." That condition is the passion for doing good. That condition is also the admission of mistakes and faults. That condition is also love of fellow man and compassion. These are keys to something that we cannot fathom with our intellect.

Each one of us walks down a road of life. Better or worse, but he goes. Each of us falls down and gets up along this journey. Some are able to get very far—as did Holy Father Kolbe—offering his life and suffering for the good of another man. Others do not get that far. The most essential in this marathon is that everyone is going in the same direction. And those who don't do this knowingly, spreading murder and hatred, are lost in a hell of despair and doubt.

I do not know where I will wander when I pass over into that light-blue fog of my last moments. I wish, I really wish, that I could see all my loved ones again who departed so long ago. To be able to tell them what I never told them in our mutual lives, and what is now for me the most important. That painful feeling, love and understanding, and regret, that I couldn't do it at the proper time when we were together, when it would have been so easy to express.

I wish, I really wish, to experience the past even for a moment— and those joyous moments of our lives together!

I hope that I will meet everyone there with whom my life came into contact. Melinda in a white dress, heroic, caring only for her mother to the last moment of her life. And that patient with lung cancer, whose last dream was to find himself on a still lake, in the full sunlight, among reed-filled rushes in the wetlands, somewhere in upper Michigan (I'm sure that that's where he is). That I will meet everyone with whom I shared suffering and torment in my long life.

I wish to be able to see my dogs again who were not an eccentricity of an older man but became an integral part of my life. Black dachshund Bary, with whom I experienced so many dramatic moments. In the first part of my memoirs, in the book *In the Shadow of Satan*, I allowed myself to place his full-sized photograph among dozens of other photographs—presenting my parents and me during my childhood and early teenage years, photographs from my surgeries in Poland—and I ask the readers of that book, just as with this one, to see that photograph of Bary, who wasn't very different from Chitah, to not take the size as an indication of value, simply as the relationship between a man and his favorite four-legged creature. They are with me, with us, and were members of our family.

I wish to also meet with the feisty dachshund Baj, full of unlimited attachment to my mother, who I had to put to sleep, though I didn't want to give him over to the veterinarian. And Dar, and the black-haired spaniel, Lili. And the companion of my lonely days, Chitah. They all live in my heart and memory. I think that the good Lord will allow me to see them again.

I wish to find myself again on that little meadow on the Wilia River, fragrant with the scent of herbs in the rays of the July sun, set against a backdrop of dark forest. Moving through it are the lazy ribbons of the river sparkling in the sun's rays, here and there hiding in the shadows of shore-side alder trees.

I hope to find myself there where pain and suffering do not exist, where torment does not touch not only people but also any living feeling creature.

I hope to find myself there where the clouds of doubt do not darken the blueness of the sky. Where there is no room for inner turmoil, breakdown, and where there is no more dissension.

Will this be only a moment, or will it be eternal? That's not essential. I know one thing—I am only a minute particle in this huge work of creation. And when my final moment comes, I wish to join myself with what is great, unfathomable, and perfect—with God.

For my soul is restless until it rests in the Lord.

◈

Also by Janusz Subczynski:

IN THE SHADOW OF SATAN

*The author's eyewitness account of growing up amidst the
horrors of Nazism and communism—and his brave escape*

ISBN 0-9674128-5-4
336 pages · Hardcover · $24.95

Keller Publishing
www.KellerPublishing.com

1-800-631-1952

"I just finished reading *In the Shadow of Satan*. As an English major I
used to hope that I would read literature that was descriptive enough to
make me feel I was in the middle of the book! Your biography delivered!"
—Judy Benefiel

"Your story is an inspiration and necessary reading for others.
Your book begins to elicit an understanding of the real-life
struggles in foreign countries, societies, and individuals."
—Maureen M. Coller

"I loved it! Now I need to know what happened . . . I
need the next book. I feel like the little kids must feel
when they are waiting for the *Harry Potter* books."
—Maureen H. Rudel

About the Author

JANUSZ A. SUBCZYNSKI was born in Poland on the fifth of September, 1928. He completed his primary and secondary education partially in the underground during the Second World War. From 1946 to 1951, he attended medical school in Poznan, and in 1951, he received his diploma of physician (M.D.). Independently, he also completed the study of psychology at the University of Poznan and obtained a Masters in Psychology. In 1957, he became a Specialist of the Polish Board of Neurosurgery.

In 1961, he arrived in the United States to be trained in stereotactic surgery of the brain. In 1963, after establishing this type of surgery in Warsaw, Poland, he returned to the United States. He obtained the title of the Diplomat of American Board of Neurological Surgery. He also became a Fellow of the American College of Surgeons.

For over twenty-five years, he worked first as an independent neurosurgeon, then as a chief of the section of neurosurgery at St. John Hospital and Medical Center in Detroit.

After retirement, he wrote three books, published first in Polish. Dr. Subczynski was involved in anticommunist action as a member and then coordinator of the Polish-American organization POMOST.

He is currently retired in the warm climate of Florida, devoting his time to writing and providing political commentary on American/Polish radio.